Reflexive Ethno

Reflexive Ethnography is a unique guide to ethnographic research for students of anthropology and related disciplines. It provides practical and comprehensive guidance to ethnographic research methods, but also encourages students to develop a critical understanding of the philosophical basis of ethnographic authority.

Charlotte Aull Davies examines why reflexivity, at both personal and broader cultural levels, should be integrated into ethnographic research and discusses how this can be accomplished for a variety of research methods. She introduces students to data collection methods including participant observation, interviewing, visual methods, narrative and auto-ethnography along with analysis of findings and writing up. This revised and updated second edition includes:

- A new chapter on internet-based research and 'interethnography'
- Chapters on selection of topics and methods, data collection and analysis, and ethics and politics of research
- Practical advice on writing up ethnographic study
- New and updated research examples.

Postmodernist relativism can lead to an over-emphasis on reflexivity that denies the possibility of social research. *Reflexive Ethnography* utilizes postmodernist insights – incorporation of different standpoints, exposure of the intellectual tyranny of meta-narratives – but proposes that reflexive ethnographic research be undertaken from a realist perspective. *Reflexive Ethnography* will help students to use and understand ethnographic research practices that fully incorporate reflexivity without abandoning claims to develop valid knowledge of social reality.

Charlotte Aull Davies is a Senior Lecturer in Sociology and Anthropology at the University of Wales, Swansea. She is author of *Welsh Nationalism in the Twentieth Century* (1989) and co-editor of *Welsh Communities: New Ethnographic Perspectives* (2003).

Reflexive Ethnography

A guide to researching selves and others

Second edition

Charlotte Aull Davies

LONDON AND NEW YORK

First edition published in 1998
by Routledge

This edition first published 2008
by Routledge
2 Park Square, Milton Park, Abingdon, Oxon OX14 4RN

Simultaneously published in the USA and Canada
by Routledge
711 Third Avenue, New York, NY 10017

Routledge is an imprint of the Taylor & Francis Group, an informa business

Typeset in Sabon by
HWA Text and Data Management, Tunbridge Wells

British Library Cataloguing in Publication Data
A catalogue record for this book is available from the British Library

Library of Congress Cataloging-in-Publication Data
Davies, Charlotte Aull.
Reflexive ethnography : a guide to researching selves and others / Charlotte Aull Davies. – 2nd ed.
p. cm.
Includes bibliographical references and index.
1. Ethnology–Research. I. Title.
GN345.D37 2007
305.8007'23–dc22 2007012598

ISBN 10: 0–415–40902–0 (hbk)
ISBN 10: 0–415–40901–2 (pbk)

ISBN 13: 978–0–415–40902–5 (hbk)
ISBN 13: 978–0–415–40901–8 (pbk)

Contents

Preface to the first edition

Anthropology, as an academic discipline, has been slow to develop an explicit concern with either research methods or the provision of research training. Thus, as someone whose postgraduate training took place in the 1970s, I was fortunate to have been required to prepare an annotated bibliography of anthropological sources on research methods before undertaking my first major fieldwork. This task at least made me think not only about *what* I wanted to find out but *how* I might do so, and I am grateful to my supervisor, Richard Fox, for suggesting it to me, as well as for his guidance and encouragement subsequently.

I have learned most about research methods from the people whose social circumstances and cultural understandings I have studied. Some of them, and the research in which they cooperated, are referred to in this book. But all of them, whether explicitly mentioned or not, have helped to develop my ideas about ethnographic research, and I sincerely acknowledge their cooperation over many years.

Various members of the publications committee of the Association of Social Anthropologists have played a part in the development of this book: Felicia Hughes-Freeland originally suggested that I consider such a project. Cris Shore and Harvey Whitehouse provided helpful advice and constructive criticism of the original proposal. The assistance of the editorial staff at Routledge has also been invaluable; I would particularly like to thank Heather Gibson, who originally commissioned the book, and Victoria Peters, who has seen it through the production process.

Although I found to my chagrin that lecture notes are not readily transformed into a manuscript, I am grateful nevertheless to several generations of students in my Social Research Methods course at the University of Wales, Swansea, for their responses to some of the ideas and examples that I was working on for the book.

Finally, I would like to thank my family for their support and encouragement. In particular, my husband, Hywel Davies, has provided both intellectual support and a safeguard against some of my occasional excesses in the use of academic jargon. And our daughter, Elen Gwenllian, has been invaluable in helping me to keep the entire project in perspective.

I gratefully acknowledge the contribution of all of these individuals and groups to this book, while taking responsibility for its failings.

Preface to the second edition

It is to be welcomed that ethnography and ethnographic writing have come to be accepted, as research and reporting strategies, in a wide range of subject areas from cultural and literary studies to applied social sciences. Unfortunately, in some instances, ethnography has become scarcely more than a legitimizing label for activities that bear little relation to the evolving tradition of ethnographic research and writing as it is understood in the discipline in which it was first developed and for which it continues to be a core strategy. In this volume, I discuss the philosophy and practice of ethnography from the perspective of anthropology, the discipline which originated this distinctive methodology for learning about human societies and cultures and which has developed, modified and refined it, by means of example and critique, over most of the past century. I hope that this book will prove useful to professional anthropologists, as well as providing a resource for those in other disciplines who choose to use this complex but rewarding strategy in their research.

Sadly, I currently feel a great sense of irony in writing about the centrality of anthropology to the practice of ethnography in that the administration of my own university has recently taken a decision to 'disinvest' in anthropology and in our sister discipline of sociology. The consequence of this action is the gradual disappearance of these two disciplines both from the university and from the area of southwest Wales that we principally serve. I sincerely hope we may see their eventual return in a future less driven by the accounting culture that currently controls higher education.

I am grateful to Routledge for providing the opportunity to prepare this new edition, which has given me the opportunity to include an entirely new chapter on internet ethnography and a new section on the increasing importance of applied anthropology, as well as to update examples of good ethnographic practice. I would also like to thank the Anthropology and Religion editorial staff at Routledge for their assistance – and particularly Gemma Dunn for her constant encouragement. The suggestions and advice of the reviewers of the proposal for this revised edition have been very helpful, and I would like to acknowledge their contributions to its final form.

As always, the advice and encouragement of family and friends has been invaluable.

I sincerely acknowledge my indebtedness to all of these while accepting full responsibility for any shortcomings to be found in this revised edition.

Cover photograph: *Llawr Fforestfach/Returned Parquet* – an image of an installation prepared by the Welsh artist Tim Davies for a site-specific exhibition in Belize in 1999. On discovering a 150-year-old mohagany parquet floor in a reclamation yard in Swansea, south Wales, and researching the history of the extraction of hardwood from Belize in the 19th century, Tim Davies conceived the idea of returning the floor to the rain forest. The image shows the flooring some time after it was installed as the jungle began to reclaim its own. The work is particularly appropriate because of its basis in a reflexivity not limited to the artist's personal experience but encompassing a much broader social and cultural 'turning back on oneself'. *Llawr Fforestfach/Returned Parquet* © Tim Davies.

Part I
Preparations

Chapter 1

Reflexivity and ethnographic research

In doing research of any kind, there is an implicit assumption that we are investigating something 'outside' ourselves, that the knowledge we seek cannot be gained solely or simply through introspection. This is true for both the social and natural sciences, although in the latter the separation of researcher and research object may appear both more self-evident and more readily attainable. On the other hand, we cannot research something with which we have no contact, from which we are completely isolated. All researchers are to some degree connected to, or part of, the object of their research. And, depending on the extent and nature of these connections, questions arise as to whether the results of research are artefacts of the researcher's presence and inevitable influence on the research process. For these reasons, considerations of reflexivity are important for all forms of research. Although the connection between an astronomer and distant stellar events may seem very tenuous indeed, no more than an ability to observe secondary indications of such events by means of sophisticated extensions of human sensory equipment, even astronomers take account of their relationship to these occurrences, for example in discarding assumptions about simultaneity of observation and event. And in the realm of particle physics, questions about the effects of observers on their observations are of fundamental importance. If reflexivity is an issue for these most objective of sciences, then clearly it is of central importance for social research, where the connection between researcher and research setting – the social world – is clearly much closer and where the nature of research objects – as conscious and self-aware beings – make influences by the researcher and the research process on its outcome both more likely and less predictable. These issues are particularly central to the practice of ethnographic research where the relationship between researcher and researched is typically even more intimate, long-term and multi-stranded, and the complexities introduced by the self-consciousness of the objects of research have even greater scope.

Debates about reflexivity overlap with concerns about subjectivity versus objectivity in social research, although they are not coterminous. Nevertheless, responses to the difficulties apparently raised by reflexivity frequently involve attempts to ensure objectivity through reducing or controlling the effects of the researcher on the research situation. Such attempts include maintaining distance through using observation and other methods in which interaction is kept to a minimum or is highly controlled. Alternatively, claims to objectivity – or at least to reduce the effect of researchers on their results – are also made on the basis of a very high level of interaction, based on complete participation, in extreme cases even concealing the identity of the researcher. These approaches have been identified with positivist and naturalist methodologies, respectively (Hammersley and Atkinson 1995: 16–17). However, even the most objective of social research methods is clearly reflexive. Survey research based on structured interviewing, for example, can ensure a form of objectivity through training of interviewers to reduce the effects of their individual attributes on respondents and employing technical tests of reliability. But survey researchers cannot remove another, and more fundamental, form of reflexivity that inheres in their construction of a highly artificial research situation, which is dependent upon a set of cultural understandings as to the nature of interviews, their conduct and appropriate forms of responses to them. At the other extreme, covert participation may eliminate the researcher's influence *qua* researcher but it does not eliminate effects of their presence on their results and may render such effects less visible.

Reflexivity, broadly defined, means a turning back on oneself, a process of self-reference. In the context of social research, reflexivity at its most immediately obvious level refers to the ways in which the products of research are affected by the personnel and process of doing research. These effects are to be found in all phases of the research process from initial selection of topic to final reporting of results. While relevant for social research in general, issues of reflexivity are particularly salient for ethnographic research in which the involvement of the researcher in the society and culture of those being studied is particularly close. The term ethnography is used to refer both to a particular form of research and to its eventual written product. I adopt a broad interpretation of ethnography as a research process based on fieldwork using a variety of mainly (but not exclusively) qualitative research techniques but including engagement in the lives of those being studied over an extended period of time. The eventual written product – an ethnography – draws its data primarily from this fieldwork experience and usually emphasizes descriptive detail as a result (cf. Davies 2002; Ellen 1984: 7–8; Hammersley and Atkinson 1995: 1–3).

Not only the personal history of ethnographers but also the disciplinary and broader sociocultural circumstances under which they work have a profound effect on which topics and peoples are selected for study. Furthermore, the relationships between ethnographer and informants in the field, which form the bases of subsequent theorizing and conclusions, are expressed through social interaction in which the ethnographer participates; thus ethnographers help to construct the observations that become their data. In an early recognition of the need systematically to incorporate reflexivity into ethnographic research methods, Powdermaker argued that participant observation requires both involvement and detachment achieved by developing the ethnographer's 'role of stepping in and out of society' (1966:19). In order to incorporate such insights into research practice, individual ethnographers in the field – and out of it – must seek to develop forms of research that fully acknowledge and utilize subjective experience and reflection on it as an intrinsic part of research. Furthermore, given the contribution of the ethnographer's sociocultural context to the research, these contexts too must be considered. They become a part of the research, a turning back in the form of cultural critique that has moral and political implications as well.

On the other hand, this turning back, or self-examination, both individual and collective, clearly can lead to a form of self-absorption that is also part of the definition of reflexivity in which boundaries between subject and object disappear, the one becomes the other, a process that effectively denies the possibility of social research. This outcome is closely related to various postmodernist and poststructuralist critiques which, in their most extreme forms, are essentially destructive of the enterprise of social research. Nevertheless ethnographers must seek to utilize creatively the insights of these postmodernist perspectives – insights that encourage incorporation of different standpoints, exposure of the intellectual tyranny of meta-narratives and recognition of the authority that inheres in the authorial voice – while at the same time rejecting the extreme pessimism of their epistemological critiques. In this book I develop epistemological and methodological foundations that encourage and incorporate genuinely reflexive ethnographic research while maintaining that such research can be based on a realist ontology, which assumes a social reality independent of our knowledge of it. In developing this perspective, I draw heavily on the work of Roy Bhaskar and other critical realists (cf. Archer *et al.* 1998) and also on pragmatism, particularly the insights of G. H. Mead.

From this perspective, the purpose of research is to increase our understanding of social reality by developing explanations of social forms and events, as well as critically examining the conceptualizations used in these explanations. However, critical realism also accepts that social research is inextricably tied to questions of meaning and interpretation due to the self-conscious nature of its subject matter. Unlike the natural sciences it is involved in a 'double hermeneutic', that is, it is answerable both to the scientific community and to those being studied (Sayer 2000: 17–18). This implies that social research is a conduit that allows interpretations and influences to pass in both directions, and final products thus may take a variety of forms and be addressed to different audiences. Nevertheless, I will argue that the results of anthropological research based on ethnographic fieldwork, informed by reflexivity and assessed by a critical scholarly community, are expressive of a reality that is neither accessible directly through the actions and texts of those being studied nor simply a reflection of the individual anthropologist's psyche. This means that both good and bad research are possible, and the development of criteria to recognize the difference should provide the basis of anthropological authority. My principal aim is thus to consider critically the actual activities of research in the context of an epistemological basis for anthropological knowledge that fully incorporates reflexivity while being rooted in a realist ontology.

Before looking in detail at various ethnographic research processes and methods, therefore, several other topics need be addressed. First, a more careful consideration will be given to the forms reflexivity assumes and its relationship to questions about ways of knowing and the nature of knowledge. Second, I briefly discuss the ways in which anthropologists have viewed reflexivity and its changing relationship to actual research practice and consider the implications of various postmodernist critiques for the practice of ethnographic research.

Finally, I develop more fully a critical realist perspective that allows for the continuing practice of meaningful social research, while also benefiting from sensitivity to issues of reflexivity and responding to postmodernist and poststructuralist critiques.

Reflexivity and knowledge

Reflexivity in social research is not a single phenomenon but assumes a variety of forms and affects the research process through all its stages (Roberts and Sanders 2005). Babcock (1980) enumerates a series of dichotomies to describe varieties of reflexivity: private/public; individual/collective; implicit/explicit; partial/total. Some of these various dimensions can be placed along a spectrum: at one extreme is the relatively private, individualist and hence partially reflexive activity of the fieldworker keeping a journal – what has been termed 'benign introspection' (Woolgar 1988b: 22); further along is the public, collective activity of traditional rituals which display a form of 'social reflexivity' (Turner 1981; also cf. Rappaport 1980). But even examples of this level of social reflexivity must still be judged far from total in their implicitness (lack of self-awareness of their reflexive nature), in contrast to the journal writer. Total reflexivity requires full and uncompromising self-reference. Thus, it is argued, no process of knowing is fully reflexive until it is explicitly turned on the knower, who becomes self-conscious even of the reflexive process of knowing – what has been termed 'radical constitutive reflexivity' (Woolgar 1988b: 22). In this fullest form, reflexivity, in spite of its unavoidable and essentially desirable presence in social research, becomes destructive of the process of doing such research; as researchers we are led 'to reflect on our own subjectivities, and then to reflect upon the reflection in an infinitude of self-reflexive iterations' (Gergen and Gergen 1991: 77). It will be helpful to follow this process through by reviewing briefly the various levels of reflexivity and the ways in which they influence social research.

In its most transparent guise, reflexivity expresses researchers' awareness of their necessary connection to the research situation and hence their effects upon it, what is sometimes called reactivity. This has often been conceived in terms of the subjectivity of the researcher, with attempts being made, especially from a positivist orientation, to ensure objectivity. For example, in conducting interviews, techniques are promoted (such as standardized wording of questions and controlling interviewer responses) so as to limit the effect of the interviewer on this particular social encounter. In ethnographic research, fieldworkers have adopted various strategies to make themselves inconspicuous and hence reduce the dangers of reactivity. They may rely on literally being an inconspicuous bystander; or they may take the opposite approach and reduce reactivity by participating as fully as possible, trying to become invisible in their role as researcher if not as human participant. Nevertheless, the impossibility of controlling the social encounters that provide the ethnographer's data during fieldwork based on long-term participant observation has long been implicitly recognized in that claims to objectivity in fact came to be based less on the nature of the research encounter than on the objectifying rhetoric of reporting forms (Crick 1982a; Grimshaw and Hart 1995). Fuller recognition of the role of reflexivity eventually moved researchers beyond naive attempts to objectify the research encounter and towards an acceptance that in social research, 'the specificity and individuality of the observer are ever present and must therefore be acknowledged, explored and put to creative use' (Okely 1996b: 28). A developing critique of objectifying forms of ethnographic writing has accompanied this recognition (Marcus and Cushman 1982; Rosaldo 1993 [1989]).

Reflexivity in this form, while clearly calling attention to the nature of research as a social process, is still very much focused on the individual researcher. Yet even at this individualist level, considerations of reflexivity are compelled to move beyond the notion of the researcher's effect on the data and begin to acknowledge the more active role of the researcher in the actual production of those data. Thus, 'the ethnographic enterprise is not a matter of what one person does in a situation but how two sides of an encounter arrive at a delicate workable definition of their meeting' (Crick 1982a: 25). Steier (1991b) goes further in viewing the research process as one in which researcher and reciprocators (not respondents) are engaged in co-constructing a world.

Ethnographers first came to consider the collective social dimension of reflexivity through identifying reflexive processes among the peoples that they studied. This perspective has been particularly useful and prominent in studies of ritual and performance. Perhaps the most frequently cited example is Geertz's interpretation of the Balinese cockfight as 'a Balinese reading of Balinese experience, a story they tell themselves about themselves' (1973: 448). Such social reflexivity may be explicit, a deliberate and conscious reflection of a people upon themselves, but it is more commonly presented as fully revealed only through the interpretative insights of the ethnographer. However, social reflexivity, especially in this latter form, preserves a privileged, and essentially non-reflexive, position for the ethnographer (cf. Watson 1987).

When the insights of this sort of social reflexivity, especially those that are grounded in a relativist and/or interpretivist perspective, are combined with the reflexivity of the individual researcher in recognizing that data are very much a cooperative product, then they tend to stimulate reflexivity of a more searching and critical form which encompasses the knowledge claims of social researchers themselves. Why should this be so? If we argue that the activities and texts of our informants are really expressing not their obvious surface message but an underlying one about the nature of their society, then, in a reflexive displacement of this analysis, we may question the researcher's (our own) activities in producing a text about these others. Are researchers' activities and results also really carrying a deeper message, not about those they study, but about themselves and the nature of their own society? Gudeman and Penn (1982) argue, for example, that the so-called local models developed by ethnographers are no more local than is the interpretative model through which their analyses are constructed. This latter model (which they call a Euclidean model) is simply another local model, one based in the Western cultures of the ethnographer, but one with universal pretensions. The question of how proponents of a local model develop and sustain such pretensions to universality is clearly a political one, having to do with differential access to power. In this light, the research process is more clearly perceived as an encounter in which knowledge is constituted in ways which reflect and maintain various power relations, a process with ethical implications to which I return in Chapter 3.

This more radical reflexivity thus contends that the activities and results of social research are constructed from and reflect both the broader sociohistorical context of researchers and the disciplinary culture to which they belong. It must be accepted that 'anthropology is a part of itself. Any statement about culture is also a statement about anthropology' (Crick 1982b: 307). However, the fullest expression of reflexivity in research is realized when the 'also' in the above statement is dropped, and it is argued that social research is essentially about itself. At this point, it ceases to be research or to promote the fieldwork activities usually taken as constituting ethnographic research. We do not undertake to travel great distances, to situate ourselves among other social groupings, to talk to other individuals simply to learn about ourselves and our own cultures. Such activities might be pursued haphazardly in a search for personal enrichment in order to increase introspective insight; however, the more systematic directed activities of even the most open-ended forms of ethnographic research would not be undertaken without some belief that we are learning about something 'other' than, 'outside' of ourselves.

It is useful to consider briefly the consequences of this full incorporation of reflexivity in an area of research that has moved further than most in this direction, namely, research into the sociology of scientific knowledge. Researchers in this area, inspired primarily by ethnomethodology and following Kuhn's (1962) work on normal and revolutionary science, have developed a thoroughgoing analysis of scientific knowledge as being socially constructed by a community of scientists. However, the challenge they face is to see the knowledge they themselves produce about the production of scientific knowledge as equally socially constructed. Furthermore, so must their reflexive knowledge about their knowledge be socially constructed, leading to an unending inward spiral, what has been referred to as the '*tu quoque*' argument (Ashmore 1989: 87–111). Such theorists face two related difficulties: how to do research which recognizes the radically reflexive nature of their activities (cf. Steier 1991c; Woolgar 1988a); and how to write about such research in a suitably reflexive manner. Such considerations have not led to much substantive research; instead most of the collections that discuss the potential for research based in this perspective have concentrated on ways of reporting on research, for example, incorporating conversations about the research both between researchers and with research subjects, as well as other 'new' literary forms. This preoccupation leads to a certain defensiveness in presentation – 'We must remind ourselves that we tell our stories through others. Further, our self-reflexive stories need not be trivial' (Steier 1991a: 3) – as well as to a somewhat sterile and precious self-consciousness – 'Do you think we could ever have an adequate introduction to a project which attempts to engage in the kind of reflexivity it endorses?' (Woolgar and Ashmore 1988: 10; cf. Pinch and Pinch 1988 for a critique).

Thus the question arises as to whether this inward spiral can be broken without losing the insights into the reflexive nature of knowledge. Is knowledge of anything other than knowledge of reflexivity possible? And if so, how is it achieved? The answer may lie in consideration of the dual nature of social research: that it depends both on some connection with that being researched and on some degree of separation from it. I turn to this question in the final section. But first it will be helpful to consider how and why questions of reflexivity have become so prominent in anthropology and to examine more carefully some of the 'post-' critiques, of which this reflexive spiral is one manifestation, and how they may affect the conduct of social research.

Reflexivity and anthropology

Interest in reflexivity as a positive aspect of ethnography has been growing among anthropologists since the early 1970s. Prior to that it was primarily regarded as a problem to be overcome in keeping with the positivist orientation of those who originated and promoted the method of participant observation (cf. Urry 1984). Thus from this earlier perspective the influence of the ethnographer was to be eliminated insofar as possible from the research findings. Since this was clearly impossible under conditions of long-term participant observation, the alternative that was adopted in practice was to minimize the ethnographer's influence in reported observations, primarily a matter of rhetorical style. What developed in classic ethnographic texts was the inclusion of some sort of arrival story to give authenticity to the findings (Geertz 1988; Pratt 1986); subsequently personal references were diligently avoided or carefully circumscribed. Such a practice has a clear irony in that the point of arrival is precisely when interaction is likely to be most superficial and open to misinterpretation. 'The anthropologists' opening descriptions focus predictably on the superficial, visible contrasts and first encounters. The account cannot by definition convey the responses and insights from the hosts' (Okely 1992: 14).

However, in the late 1960s anthropology began to undergo a process of self-criticism initiated by a recognition of the ways in which the discipline had been a product and beneficiary of colonial expansion and furthered by considerations of whether and how it may have inadvertently aided the designs of the colonizers (Asad 1973a; Hymes 1969). For example, the concentration of anthropologists on precontact social forms of native peoples meant that they ignored, or attempted to weed out of their descriptions and analyses, any effects that were the result of contact. Thus questions of racism and economic exploitation were ignored, as they would have required study of both the colonizing and colonized societies. Both the structural functionalism of British anthropology, following Malinowski and Radcliffe-Brown, and the emphasis on cultural complexes of American anthropology, following Boas, ignored the contemporary reality of the lives of the people they studied in their attempts to reconstruct 'pure' social structures and cultural forms without regard to the influence of colonial contact, of which the anthropologists were themselves a part. Kuper (1988) has suggested that for a century much of the theorizing of anthropologists was based on an idea of the nature of primitive society that had been developed at the end of the nineteenth century, the source of which was in evolutionary ideas about the progressive development of modern society.

First reactions to the recognition that anthropologists were ignoring the contemporary lived realities of the peoples they studied tended to concentrate on the ethical dimensions of this blinkered vision. An early set of essays (Hymes 1969) that developed this self-critique in anthropology was stimulated in part by the then recent uncovering of the use of anthropologists and ethnographic fieldwork more generally as a cover and a source of intelligence gathering in certain parts of the world, in particular in South America and southeast Asia[1] (Horowitz 1967; Salemink 1991). Berreman (1969), in this same collection, questioned what he perceived as the lack of any human purpose in a discipline that engages in the study of humankind and argued that anthropologists must discard the positivist idea of value freedom for an acknowledged commitment to act ethically on the basis of the knowledge they accumulate and to seek knowledge that is relevant to the problems of the peoples among whom they work.

> This is the substance of the searching questions of the peoples of the third world and others: namely, 'What has been the effect of your work among us? Have you contributed to the solution of the problems you have witnessed? Have you even mentioned those problems? If not, then you are part of those problems and hence must be changed, excluded, or eradicated.'
>
> (Ibid.: 90)

However, once the distortions in anthropological knowledge introduced through ignoring the effects of colonialism were widely recognized, this led inevitably and very quickly to a recognition that ethnographers could not effectively study simply the effects of colonialism among colonized peoples, but that ethnographic attention must be turned as well to a study of the colonial forms, their interrelationships with native peoples and, finally, to a study of the colonizers themselves. Thus ethnographic research was criticized for being both unethical and false in its attempts to concentrate on native peoples. The critique of its complicity in colonialism led to a call for reflexivity in the sense that studies of others must also be studies of ourselves in our relationships with those others. Thus Scholte called for a reflexive and critical anthropology based on the recognition that 'fieldwork and subsequent analysis constitute a unified praxis, the first results of which are mediated by the "in here" as much as by the "out there"' (1969: 438).

Recognition of the distortions that had been a part of anthropological perceptions due to ethnographers' determination to ignore the nature and impact of colonial societies among the peoples they chose to study led to a critical questioning of the products of this research. Thus it was suggested that classical ethnographic research was not simply presenting a distorted view of native societies and cultures, but that it was not seeing them at all, that in fact these ethnographies were primarily reflections of the preconceptions of ethnographers, based on their own disciplinary and Western cultural expectations. Anthropologists were perceived as having themselves constructed their objects of study (Fabian 1983; Kuper 1988). This view was given a very powerful impetus in the critique of orientalism by Said (1978), directed not specifically at anthropologists, but arguing that the intellectual and academic discourse about the nature of non-Western societies was really a projection by the West of its own preconceptions and imaginings.

This critique of the nature of anthropological knowledge and its deficiencies based on its own unreflexive perspective is a part of a much broader epistemological critique with important implications for social research that is generally included under the terms poststructuralism and postmodernism. Postmodernism is a broad and diffuse set of ideas about what are perceived to be fundamental changes taking place in society globally, changes that constitute a general transformation affecting all areas of life from aesthetics to economics to science. There is disagreement as to whether such changes are actually transformative in the sense of constituting a move into radically and qualitatively different social forms (e.g. Crook, Pakulski and Waters 1992) or whether they are better understood as extensions, a radicalization and universalization, of existing characteristics of modernity (Giddens 1990). Clearly such disparate views on the significance of contemporary social processes produce quite distinctive definitions of modernity and its alleged successor and, in fact, the range of meanings proposed for postmodernism is very broad. I want to concentrate on the significance of the postmodernist debate for social research and will thus consider one of the general characteristics that has been suggested as distinguishing between modernity and postmodernity. Lash (1990), while not a postmodernist, proposes a distinguishing characteristic of modernity and postmodernity which is also accepted by those who consider themselves postmodernists (Crook, Pakulski and Waters 1992). Lash argues that the major hallmark of modernization was a process of cultural differentiation particularly embodied in the Kantian distinction between theoretical, ethical and aesthetic realms, which became relatively autonomous. This differentiation and ensuing autonomy made possible the growth of realism in a variety of fields, in particular for our interests here, a form of epistemological realism. This position holds that ideas can give a true picture of reality; it depends on the differentiation of such ideas from the reality that they are held to represent, hence scientific ideas are separate from but truly represent nature. In the same vein, ideas (theories) about society represent the autonomous, separate and objective realm of the social. The autonomy of the social was particularly stressed by the Durkheimian position that explanations of social facts must be sought in the social, not in terms of the individual. This was a major theoretical impetus behind Radcliffe-Brown's development of structural-functionalism focusing attention on the ways in which social structures were interrelated, so that societies were to be analysed in terms of the functioning of their various social structures, without reference to any external influences. Another manifestation of this differentiation may be found in the structuralism of Lévi-Strauss with its explanation of a great variety of surface social and cultural phenomena from kinship systems to myths in terms of underlying analytical categories of a universal nature. Similarly, classical Marxist analysis may be interpreted as differentiating infrastructure from surface appearances and explaining the latter in terms of the former. As these comments suggest, poststructuralism, which criticizes the range of such structuralist epistemologies, is an integral part of the postmodernist critique in anthropology.

In contrast to this, postmodernism is a process of de-differentiation, of breaking down boundaries and rejecting the autonomy of different realms. One of the first major consequences of this process for social research is epistemological – that is, it challenges the knowledge basis of such research by problematizing the relationship between ideas (theories) and reality. In anthropology this has been glossed as a crisis of representation – that is, a denial that the products of ethnographic research may be legitimately perceived as in any way representing the separate reality of another society. Clearly such an epistemological critique was fundamentally subversive for any and all structuralist accounts, in that the structures they proposed, of whatever ilk – social, economic, or universal binary oppositions – were no longer to be interpreted as representing anything beyond themselves; they were images, no longer representations, that were collapsed on to themselves. This turning back of the representation on to itself, the denial that it is anything beyond itself, also makes clear the fundamental radical reflexivity of postmodernist critiques.

Another aspect of the breaking down of boundaries is to be found in the process of producing ethnographies based on fieldwork, even if these ethnographies are in an interpretivist rather than structuralist tradition. Such ethnographies are open to the general epistemological critique that denies their being seen as reporting on a separate reality. This involves a breaking down of the distinction between ethnographers and the peoples they study, leading to the contention that ethnographers create their objects of study, they do not discover them. This kind of 'defeatist postmodernism' implies 'a complete repudiation of the distinction between fictional and nonfictional accounts of the world' (Stones 1996: 20). Furthermore, the process of de-differentiation encourages a breaking down of the distinction between author and ethnography; ethnographers are not viewed as pronouncing on something that lies outside themselves but rather are intimately connected to their particular ethnographies. This breaking down of the boundaries between author and text has two implications: the first, and most obvious, is the inherent individual reflexivity of the ethnographies that are produced; carried to its logical conclusion, it could be argued that they are about the ethnographer, not the people ostensibly studied. The second implication is the denial of authority, of a privileged voice, to ethnographers in their presentation of their ethnographies. This denial is part of the postmodern rejection of meta-narratives – that is, explanations of broad historical processes and grand theory. In this view there is no privileged explanation, no basis on which to judge one perspective more correct or truer than another; there are only perspectives.

This critique had a particularly profound effect on the ways in which ethnographies are produced – that is, in the general self-consciousness about the process of writing ethnography – and there developed an extensive postmodern critique about the production of ethnographic texts (Clifford and Marcus 1986; Marcus and Cushman 1982). In its most radical manifestations, this argument contends that writing ethnography is an individual creative act more akin to fictional writing than to any vision of ethnographic research as a basis for a social science. Thus such products are not really accessible to the critical evaluation of an informed collectivity, nor are they to be understood in terms of a realist ontology. One response to this perspective has been the production of highly individually reflexive works – subjective accounts of how fieldwork affected the ethnographer rather than accounts of understanding or perspectives gained about the nature of other peoples (cf. Jacobson 1991: 119–22). As this makes clear, although postmodern ethnographers are uncomfortably aware of the authorial voice and are at pains to minimize it, they do not necessarily take the classical ethnographic approach of expunging it from the text. Instead of making the ethnographer disappear, they make themselves more visible, even central in the production with the idea that in so doing, in presenting their gropings towards understanding, they undermine their own authority so that their interpretations become simply one perspective with no superior claim to validity. Another favoured approach is to hand the presentation over to the 'other' by employing extensive use of transcripts of recordings with little or no commentary or overt analysis. Such an emphasis on dialogue rather than text still privileges the ethnographer's vision in the selection of such dialogue and in other ways to be considered in subsequent chapters. Other postmodern techniques are efforts to allow the variety of perspectives to appear through attempts to be both multitextual – in their use of less standard, often non-verbal materials such as photographs and films, commodities, the body, poetry – and multivocal – in their presentation of varying perspectives without attempting to order or evaluate them (cf. Fontana 1994: 211–18).

Another major area in which postmodern perspectives have challenged and affected social research is in questions of ethics and the politics inherent in such activity. In the breaking down of boundaries between different realms, postmodernists deny the separation of political and ethical considerations from the analytical considerations of social theories. In this view all perspectives are political perspectives. This particular view accords with the criticisms developed by feminists and Marxist-inspired critical theorists of much social theorizing. They argue that the positivist goal of value freedom was really a disguised political position, one that supported existing power relationships, in particular patriarchal and class-based forms of oppression. Thus these perspectives maintain that social research must be politically committed. However, the postmodern critique, with its according of equal validity to all perspectives and voices, its denial of any privileged ethical perspective, poses a problem for these other positions in that they aspire to action, whether in research or theorizing, which advances the political programme of a given collectivity and, hence, which does privilege a particular political view. I return to these debates in Chapter 3.

When we take postmodernism as a process of de-differentiation, the breaking down of boundaries that this entails operates on several levels in its effects on ethnographic research. At the same time, all of these levels respond to this process through a greatly increased reflexivity in some form. At the level of the individual ethnographer, the breaking down of boundaries is most evident in reporting styles in which ethnographers try in various ways to show how they are implicated or included in their discussions of other peoples. This often leads to ethnographies that seem to be more about the ethnographer than the people being studied. At a collective disciplinary level, the recognition of the role of the discipline in constructing its objects of study has tended to turn social theorizing back on to itself with the eventual development of a critique of the possibility of theory or causal explanation. Similarly, boundaries between author and audience are erased with attempts to make subjects into authors through use of extensive 'unedited' transcripts as well as seeking input from research subjects into the texts written about them. Many of the critiques developed by postmodernists provide very valuable insights – such as the exposure of the particular perspectives based in power relationships hidden in meta-narratives and the related authority built into the construction of texts; others, equally valuable, seem almost truisms – in particular the multivocality and polysemic nature of all social activity. At the same time, the logic of these critiques leads us inexorably to the forms of reflexivity that continually spiral inward, a process that is ultimately destructive of one of the two pillars of social research, a belief that we are able through these activities to learn about things outside ourselves, not knowable through introspection. The question that I address at a general philosophical level in the next section, and in terms of research practice throughout the remainder of this book, is how we can incorporate these postmodern insights and utilize reflexivity fully in ethnographic research without falling into this ultimately pessimistic, unproductive and completely inward-directed perspective.

Researching reflexively: a realist alternative

The search for a philosophically sound basis for ethnographic research which fully accepts its inherent reflexivity while still maintaining that its products are explanations of an external social reality requires both an ontology that asserts that there is a social world independent of our knowledge of it and an epistemology that argues that it is knowable. Such an enterprise also involves overcoming the dichotomy between a positivist understanding of social science and various hermeneutical perspectives, especially the interpretivist position in the ethnographic tradition. The critical realism of Bhaskar (1997, 1998; also cf. Outhwaite 1987; Sayer 2000) offers a philosophical basis for such an integrative position. Some see Bhaskar's realist philosophy as an attempt to develop and transform positivism (e.g. Hughes 1990: 85–6), whereas others regard it as linking the positivist and interpretivist positions (e.g. Silverman 1985: 33–5). However, I would suggest that Bhaskar develops an integrative perspective out of his critiques of both these positions and provides a philosophical grounding for social science in general that is compatible with the practice of many social researchers. Those working from this perspective aspire to provide explanations, not simply descriptions, which have applicability beyond the confines of their specific research subjects and sites, without sacrificing the hermeneutic insights into the pre-interpreted nature of their subject matter and the reflexive implications of their research practice. While a comprehensive account of this philosophical position is beyond the scope of this book (for this see Archer 1995; Archer *et al.* 1998; Bhaskar 1997, 1998), I want to consider its utility for ethnographic research, in particular the contribution it can make to developing a fully reflexive yet realist basis for research practice that can be expected to yield explanations which are open to informed debate and criticism and which provide qualitatively better understandings of human societies and cultures.

Bhaskar argues that the debate between positivist and hermeneutic perspectives has tended to concentrate on epistemology, on ways of knowing, in that it has been centred on the distinction between the objects of natural science and human subjects. Thus both sides have accepted the self-conscious nature of human subjects as providing the main difficulty in the study of human society, with positivists attempting to reduce the resulting reflexive effects while interpretivists (phenomenologists and, especially, ethnomethodologists) have argued that the understandings of their human subjects are their proper, and only, subject matter. Bhaskar's realism in contrast concentrates 'first on the ontological question of the properties that societies possess, before shifting to the epistemological question of how these properties make them possible objects of knowledge for us' (1998: 25). He argues that both perspectives have over-simplified and misunderstood the nature of the social, with positivists taking it to be 'merely empirically real' – that is only existing in observable behavioural responses of humans – and interpretivists treating it as 'transcendentally ideal' in their insistence that society exists only in the ideas that social actors hold about it. These perspectives give us 'either a conceptually impoverished and deconceptualizing empiricism, or a hermeneutics drained of causal import and impervious to empirical controls' (ibid.: 12). In their place Bhaskar proposes a much more subtle and complex view of society in which human agents are neither passive products of social structures nor entirely their creators but are placed in an iterative and naturally reflexive feedback relationship to them. Society exists independently of our conceptions of it, in its causal properties, its ability to exert deterministic force on individuals; yet it is dependent on our actions, human activity, for its reproduction and can be transformed by this activity. It is both real and transcendent. In this sense Bhaskar likens it to the objects of study of the natural sciences which, he argues, have been misrepresented by the empirical realism of the positivist position. For example, magnetic fields are not perceptually real, in the sense of being directly observable: they are human concepts, yet they exist independently of these concepts (as expressed in their effects on iron filings, for example). This is the transcendental reality that the natural and social sciences share.

This concept of transcendental reality is also at the root of Bhaskar's contention that what he calls naturalism,[2] an essential unity between natural and social sciences, is possible without postulating either an identity of subject matter or a uniformity of appropriate methods. Thus society and human individuals represent distinct but inextricably interconnected ontological levels, with each dependent on the other for their existence, yet capable of exerting deterministic force on, or of transforming, the other (ibid.: 36–7). It is this ontological status that then allows us to move beyond the epistemological dilemma discussed above. It suggests that we can neither take behavioural observations as simply representative of some given social world nor fully reveal or reconstruct the social through our understanding of actors' meanings and beliefs. 'Society is not given in, but presupposed by, experience. However, it is precisely its peculiar ontological status, its transcendentally real character, that makes it a possible object of knowledge for us' (ibid.: 53).

Thus a fundamental premise of critical realism is that social reality is stratified. This can be seen in the two distinct but interrelated levels of society and human individuals, or structure and agency.[3] It is also apparent in the critical realist premise regarding different domains of reality: the real, the actual and the empirical. This ontological depth underpins the rejection of a social science based only on observable sensory data. 'Thus empirical realism assumes that what we can observe is all that exists, while "actualism" assumes that what actually happens at the level of events exhausts the world, leaving no domain of the real, of powers which can be either activated or remain dormant' (Sayer 2000: 12). Explaining observable events thus requires a consideration of the conditions that enabled these events – 'observing a cherry tree in England depends on its prior importation from China, just as experiencing educational discrimination is posterior to a given definition of achievement being institutionalised' (Archer 1998: 196) – and this introduces a necessary historicity into explanation along with an acceptance of the contingency of social explanation. This distinction between the real and the actual also implies that explanations may legitimately be sought for why events do not occur as well as for actualized events.

Another facet of the peculiar ontological status of society as perceived by Bhaskar is the fundamental reflexivity involved in our knowledge of it. He fully accepts the hermeneutical (and postmodernist) position that the production of knowledge about society is a part of the entire process of social production, that it is part of its own subject matter and may transform that subject matter. Yet he argues that such causal interdependency needs to be distinguished from existential intransitivity – that is, the existence of society as a knowable object and hence a genuine practical object of research. The existence and properties of this object are independent of the process of investigation. 'For if it is the characteristic error of positivism to ignore (or play down) interdependency, it is the characteristic error of hermeneutics to dissolve intransitivity. As will be seen, both errors function to the same effect, foreclosing the possibility of scientific critique, upon which the project of human self-emancipation depends' (1998: 47–8). I will return to this concern with the 'project of human emancipation' in Chapter 3.

Before considering briefly one example of a small-scale study that was undertaken from an explicitly critical realist perspective, it will be useful to clarify the implications of such an ontological and epistemological position for the practice of ethnographic research. In the first place, such a position does allow for the possibility of a social science – that is, studies of human society can produce law-like statements – and further there is an essential unity between the natural and social sciences in the sense that they do not represent totally different ways of knowing. Such unity is based in part on the recognition that the natural sciences themselves are not the paragons of positivism that they are taken to be by interpretivist critics. Neither natural nor social sciences assume theory-neutral observation (Popper 1963) and both are socially organized forms of knowledge (Kuhn 1962). The differences between them are based in two main areas: the more profound reflexivity of the social sciences which recognizes that they cannot legitimately objectify what they study; and the nature of the social as manifest only in open systems where experiments are not possible, which means that social theories cannot have decisive test situations constructed for them and must always be explanatory rather than strictly causal or predictive. Measurement in social theory is thus of limited theoretical utility, often substituting mere generalization for genuinely explanatory abstraction (Collier 1994: 252–6); qualitative forms of research practice are favoured, with a recognition of the importance of understanding based in language and dialogue (Bhaskar 1998: 45–6). Thus we can ask of ethnographic research that it provide explanations, but not strictly causal statements such as those based in constant conjunction or statistical regularity. Furthermore, social sciences must recognize that they are rooted in the specific, in time and place. 'The law-like statements of the social sciences will thus typically designate historically restricted tendencies operating at a single level of the social structure only ... they designate tendencies ... which may never be manifested, but which are nevertheless essential to the understanding (and the changing) of the different forms of social life, just because they are really productive of them' (ibid.: 53–4). Thus critical realism provides a philosophical basis for ethnographic research to provide explanatory (law-like) abstractions while also emphasizing its rootedness in the concrete, in what real people on the ground are doing and saying. Critical realism promotes a creative tension between the empirical, the actual and the real to produce explanation without encouraging flights of theoretical fancy. Such a position is ideally suited to ethnographic practice, which in its knowledge-seeking activities is continually forced to evaluate and rework theoretical abstraction in the face of concrete experience.

Another aspect of critical realism that is particularly well suited to ethnographic practice is its recognition of different ontological levels. Both human actors and social structure are accorded ontological reality. Neither is fully determined by or produced by the other; rather they are interrelated in that each level may affect the other. Hence ethnographers are encouraged to explore the phenomenological reality of actors' understandings and interpretations and their effects on social structure, but not to take these interpretations as fully constitutive of social structure. The level of social structure may not be studied directly but only observed in its effects on human actors, yet this is not to deny its reality or to suggest that it cannot be a legitimate object of study and theoretical attention.

In a similar manner, critical realism accepts the reflexivity of the social sciences in the fullest sense, recognizing that they are 'part of their own field of enquiry' (Bhaskar 1998: 47), that in other words 'there is a relational tie between the development of knowledge and the development of the object of knowledge' (ibid.: 48). On the other hand, Bhaskar argues that such 'causal interdependency' – which he distinguishes from 'existential intransitivity' – still allows us to know and study something as an object so long as we are sensitive to and take account of our own implication in and effects on that object. Thus critical realism requires a continuing reflexive awareness as part of the condition of ethnographic practice, without allowing such awareness to blind us to the existence of a reality beyond ourselves which provides a legitimate basis for the production and critique of theoretical abstractions.

Whereas much social research seems to be undertaken from a perspective that is fairly close to this critical realist position, it is not generally acknowledged as such. However, one small-scale ethnographic study (Porter 1993) has attempted explicitly to base itself on such a philosophical argument. This study looks at the ways in which racism and professionalism interact, concentrating on relations between white nurses and black and Asian doctors in an Irish hospital. The study, which is based on three months of participant observation while its author was employed as a staff nurse, develops an explanation that individual doctors are able to use professional advantage, in varying ways (display of superior clinical knowledge, insistence on formal occupational deference), to overcome the disempowering effects of racism, which was only expressed 'backstage' in some of the nurses' comments on doctors' actions.

In what ways does the methodology of this ethnographic study represent critical realism? First, in its concentration on the bidirectional flow of influences between structure (in the form of racism and professionalism) and human agency (in doctors' use, and nurses' acceptance, of professional resources to subvert racist undermining of their positions). Secondly, this concentration on particular pre-identified structural factors means that the empirical enquiry is focused on them and the eventual reporting form makes no claim to 'reproduce the social situation studied' (Porter 1993: 607). Ethnographic evidence is provided in the form of brief dialogic sections, with additional contextualizing comment taken from field notes. Thirdly, the study is contrasted with another similar study (Hughes 1988) in which the findings differ in that overt racism was expressed in the relationship between doctors and nurses. Porter suggests that this difference, which he argues can be dealt with in terms of the variable manifestations of theoretical tendencies, shows the inadequacy of positivist concepts of causal explanation based on constant conjunctions and the importance of a stratified view of social reality that permits investigation of the non-occurrence of events (e.g. overt racism). Porter also shows reflexive awareness in his use of contextualized dialogue, rather than isolated quotations, in his presentation of the ethnographic evidence for his arguments. However, he fails to develop possible reflexive insights fully. Although he does examine his own position within the research situation in one brief passage, he does not pursue other reflexive issues, such as gender difference and its possible effect on the interactions he observed and of which he was a part.

To conclude this section, I want to look briefly at a theoretical argument on the nature of the self which is both highly reflexive and at the same time intrinsically social, and which I would argue thus fits well and complements the critical realist ontology and epistemology I have been discussing. Questions about the self seem to go to the heart of the postmodernist ethnographic dilemma regarding the knowability of other cultures and peoples, and the dangers of projecting our own cultural assumptions on them in our analyses. Marcus and Fischer (1986: 45–76) have taken this area of the self and the expression of emotions as one of the areas in which experimental ethnographies – what they call ethnographies of experience (ibid.: 43) – have been most active and effective in developing ways of writing that go beyond conventional reporting techniques. They suggest that 'focussing on the person, the self, and the emotions – all topics difficult to probe in traditional ethnographic frameworks – is a way of getting to the level at which cultural differences are most deeply rooted: in feelings and in complex indigenous reflections about the nature of persons and social relationships' (ibid.: 46).

However, such concerns beg the question of how we can know individual persons in other cultures any more readily than we can know the cultures themselves without projecting on to them our own selves and cultural understandings. One theory of the formation of the self and its relationship to society which seems both to be consistent with a critical realist perspective and to provide a way out of this dilemma of reflexivity is that developed by G. H. Mead (1934). As with critical realism, Mead is both critical of positivism and yet sees the possibility of a science of society based on pragmatic philosophy which recognizes the contingency of all knowledge (Baldwin 1986). He argues that the formation of the self is dependent upon symbolic social interaction. The self is distinguished from individual subjectivity in that the latter is based in experience to which individuals alone have access. The self, in contrast, depends upon the existence of symbolic forms of interaction, of which the most important is language, and the self emerges and develops in reflective experience – that is, through an ongoing inner conversation.[4] 'The internalization and inner dramatization, by the individual, of the external conversation of significant gestures which constitutes his chief mode of interaction with other individuals belonging to the same society – is the earliest experiential phase in the genesis and development of the self' (Mead 1934: 173). There are two important features of Mead's description of the self: first, it is social in origin and hence recognizes the causal powers of social structure in the development of, indeed the very existence of, the individual self; and, second, it is continually in process, never complete, and in this respect provides both for individual freedom and creativity and for the possibility of causal effects moving in the opposite direction – that is, for human agents to affect and transform social structure.

Mead develops these two aspects in his description of the two parts of the process of creating a self as the 'I' and the 'me'. The 'me' is that part of the process that is easier to comprehend, in that it is constituted of the individual's social experiences and reflections on these experiences. It is the most clearly socially based of the two parts: an individual's 'own experience as a self is one which he takes over from his action upon others. He becomes a self in so far as he can take the attitude of another and act toward himself as others act' (ibid.: 171). This is the 'me', the set of attitudes interpreted and taken over as a result of reflecting on social interaction. But social interaction and reflection upon it is ongoing, so that the 'me' is never complete but always in process; and the outcome of this process is never fully determined by what went before. The creative part of this process, that which is indeterminate until it has occurred, is the 'I'; thus the 'I' can only be glimpsed as its responses become a part of the 'me'. 'We distinguish that individual who is doing something from the "me" who puts the problem up to him. The response enters into his experience only when it takes place ... That movement into the future is the step, so to speak, of the ego, of the "I". It is something that is not given in the "me"' (ibid.: 177).

This twofold depiction of the self provides a basis and a rationale for ethnographic studies that seek to understand the nature of selves in other societies. Because the development of one aspect of the self, the 'me', is through symbolic social interaction, understanding other selves is inextricably bound up with understanding other societies. At the same time, because the other aspect of the self, the 'I', provides for creative variation no matter what the social and cultural determiners, we avoid the overly mechanistic and deterministic presentations of other selves as fully predictable and representative of other societies. Furthermore, Mead's conception helps ethnographers to overcome the objection that they cannot possibly have access to the selves of people from other radically different cultural backgrounds. If the self is continually under construction, then ethnographers' experiences when they participate in social interaction in another society clearly alter their own selves in accordance with the cultural expectations of others. Attention to this process of transforming the ethnographer's 'me' can provide genuine knowledge of the nature of others' selves and societies. So the reflexive bent of such experimental ethnographies seems justified on good realist and pragmatic grounds, so long as they do not lose sight of their responsibility to seek explanatory abstraction and not primarily to report on individual experience. The utility of this concept of Mead's further suggests that theoretical entities not directly observable may be both ontologically real and explanatorily useful, and this utility can survive movement to other societies without predetermining understanding or erasing their genuine cultural difference.

Summary

This chapter seeks to establish a philosophical foundation for doing ethnographic research which embraces its intrinsic multi-layered reflexivity without turning inward to a complete self-absorption that undermines our capacity to explore other societies and cultures. It also suggests that such research incorporate insights from postmodernist perspectives, such as their attention to multiple perspectives and their critique of meta-narratives, while avoiding the extreme relativism and antipathy to generalized explanation that is essentially destructive of the research enterprise. Such a philosophical foundation, I argue, is to be found in Bhaskar's critical realism, which accepts the existence of a separate social reality whose transcendentally real nature makes it a possible object of knowledge for us. In its recognition of the separation, yet interdependence, of the two levels of social structure and individual action, critical realism encourages a form of explanation that builds on the creative tension between theoretical abstraction and descriptive detail. I consider two brief examples of the application of this philosophical perspective: one is a specific empirical study deliberately undertaken from a critical realist position. The second is an interpretation of G. H. Mead's theory of the development of the self from a critical realist position. In the chapters which follow I will consider the process of doing ethnographic research – selection of topics, a variety of methods, through analysis and writing up – using this philosophical foundation to address specific questions about the significance and utility of reflexivity and the bases of ethnographic authority.

Notes

1 That this remains an issue for anthropologists is made clear by the recent criticisms of a CIA programme (Pat Roberts Intelligence Scholars) to finance undergraduate and postgraduate social science students in exchange for their working for the CIA. For a critical discussion, see *Anthropology Today* 20(4): 20; 21(3): 25–6; 21(4): 19–21; 21(5): 21; 21(6): 1–2 and 22(6): 1–3.
2 This should not be confused with another common usage of the term naturalism to refer to research methods which eschew 'artificial' settings, such as experiments and interviews, and advocate studying the social world in its 'natural' state (cf. Hammersley and Atkinson 1995: 6–10).
3 For a critique of other philosophical perspectives (Giddens' structuration theory and to a lesser extent symbolic interactionism), which accept the inter-relationship of structure and agency but not their distinctiveness, see Archer (1995), Parker (2000).
4 Margaret Archer (2003) also develops an argument that proposes this 'internal conversation' as the mechanism that mediates between structure and agency. She is, however, critical of Mead's analysis, maintaining that he 'over-socialised the internal conversation' and, in the process, what she regards as its three fundamental features of 'interiority, subjectivity and causal efficacy were lost as attributes of the individual' (ibid.: 79). While I accept much of her argument regarding the nature of the internal conversation as mediator between these levels of social reality, I contend that Mead's concept of the self – with perhaps a cautionary approach to its possible over-socialisation – retains its utility for social researchers.

Chapter 2

Selecting topics and methods

This chapter discusses the rather more down-to-earth question of how researchers go about selecting research topics and deciding on the methods that they will use in their investigation. While such selections do have a very practical aspect, they also entail considerations of how researchers are located, geographically, socially and theoretically, as well as broader questions about the nature of ethnographic research as characterized by selves studying others. I begin with the practicalities of selecting a research topic and deciding on methods, looking at some of the sources for topics and the ways in which researchers' personal histories, as well as the intellectual climate within their discipline and more broadly, are implicated in their choices. This leads to a discussion of the way that changing employment patterns for anthropologists, in particular the increasing proportion of professional anthropologists working outside academic institutions, are affecting the practice of anthropology and altering the relationship between pure and applied research. I then consider the nature and significance of the field and fieldwork in anthropological practice and argue that anthropological research must be resituated both geographically and intellectually. In particular, I advocate abandoning the idea of a self-contained field site, placing more emphasis on anthropology at home and on non-traditional topics, and modifying the exclusive methodological emphasis on long-term participant observation to allow for a greater variety of methodological approaches to address contemporary realities, such as globalization. Finally, I consider the ways in which methodologies may affect choice of topic and methods and how they relate to the research process generally by drawing on two examples: feminist methodologies, and a comparison between symbolic interactionism and ethnomethodology.

Sources

The research process is often presented as evolving in a logical and unilinear fashion, with only a minimal degree of overlap between its various phases. This is particularly the case when judging it by its final (usually) written product, some form of research report or monograph, whose production clearly reconstructs the process as a whole towards a particular end leading to the findings of the research presented therein. These end products tend to present the process as one in which the first stage is the identification of a problem or problem area. In some cases this problem may be quite specific, as for example Porter's (1993) study of racism in a professional context discussed in Chapter 1; more commonly in ethnographic research the problem area is relatively broad – for example Whyte's (1955) interest in discovering how a slum community functions. The process then moves through various phases in which data are collected in the field, analysed subsequent to withdrawal from the field and finally written up in a manner that supports a set of conclusions relating to the original problem area. This idealized scheme is not completely unfaithful to the usual set of activities that constitute a research project, and indeed it has been adopted for presentation of aspects of the research process in this book. But it does tend to downplay the often chaotic and unplanned nature of social research (cf. Bell and Newby 1977; Berreman 1962), as well as the ongoing processes of analysis from problem inception through data collection and in writing up, that requires researchers to respond flexibly to situations arising in the field and out of it, and which may challenge their research plans both practically and intellectually. For example, although Passaro (1997) assumed that her research on homelessness would primarily look at the problems of homeless women, her deliberately unfocused approach to her topic in the early stages led her in the end to a project that concentrated primarily on homeless men; this change of emphasis resulted from experiences in the field that suggested both that the long-term homeless population was mainly composed of men and that the problems of homeless men were much more intractable than those of homeless women. Thus, in this consideration of sources for research questions, I will emphasize the contingent nature of these questions, suggesting how they might develop in the process of doing research and stressing the need for researchers to examine the reasons behind selection of a particular research topic in order to respond effectively when it needs to be modified.

Before considering some of the more widely recognized sources of research questions, based in theoretical or methodological concerns or in policy issues, it is worthwhile noting that the selection is nearly always a combination of personal factors, disciplinary culture, and external forces in the broader political, social and economic climate. Powdermaker (1966) was among the first to examine, explicitly and in published format, this complex of factors that led her to various field sites and research questions during her anthropological career (also cf. Wax 1971; Roberts and Sanders 2005). For example, she links her determination to do fieldwork among black people in the American South of the 1930s to her concern for social activism, formerly expressed through working as a union organizer; but she admits she did not fully understand her own motivations until she subsequently underwent psychoanalysis (Powdermaker 1966: 132–3). Similarly, Myerhoff (1978) notes the way in which her own background and anticipated future affected her decision to study old people in a Jewish day centre. The way that personal biography and selection of research sites and subjects interact can also be seen in Mathews' (2000) study of the impact of the global cultural supermarket on individual identity. Working from a general theoretical interest in how individuals accommodate tensions between national culture and other cultural options made available by processes of globalization, he selected groups to 'represent three central forms of choice within the cultural supermarket today, those of art and music, of religion, and of cultural identity itself' (ibid.: 26). However, the specific groups he worked with were all ones with which he had had some prior involvement – as a teenager in the United States attending Buddhist retreats, as a young man in Japan learning to play the Japanese bamboo flute and also playing saxophone and flute as a jazz musician, and as a white Western anthropologist teaching at the Chinese University of Hong Kong. Thus even apparently impersonal theoretical interests are often linked to personal biography, whether as the original stimulus behind their appeal or by providing the means for addressing them in empirical research.

Any research to be recognized and taken seriously within a discipline must also be relevant to some of the current intellectual concerns of the discipline. Social research thus links ordinary phenomena that may appear puzzling in daily life with the theoretical concerns of the disciplines that take social life as their subject matter. Thus, in searching for a topic, researchers work at the interstices of everyday life and an intellectual tradition of which they are a part. The effects of the research tradition in which ethnographers work on the kind of study they undertake can be clearly seen by comparing products of two quite distinctive theoretical perspectives that characterized anthropology into the early 1950s: Benedict's (1934) study of individual Zuni psychology as a reflection of Zuni cultural themes, and Evans-Pritchard's (1940) description of Nuer corporate groups interacting to provide stability to a society lacking a separate political structure. Since that time, theoretical orientations have become more numerous and less hegemonic but they nevertheless continue to influence research directions. My first major research project, on ethnic nationalism in Wales, was very much a product of these kinds of influences. It was undertaken in the mid-1970s, when the acculturation model of immigration into American society was being challenged by the continuing salience of identities based in place of origin among so-called white ethnics. Given this debate, which had both popular journalistic and theoretical aspects, the 'emergence' of ethnic movements in other Western countries also became of theoretical interest. As a postgraduate in an anthropology department that was committed to the study of what were then referred to as complex societies, I was readily attracted to the particular research topic. The choice of Wales as my field site, from among several possible candidates, probably owed more to the vagaries of funding than anything else.

While this particular progression appears almost inevitable in retrospect, it is only one of many possible research choices I might have made for my doctoral research. It is doubtless the case that the choice of research topics is a more open one for a person's first research experience than at any subsequent time. Once extensive and long-term research has been undertaken in a given location on a particular topic, there are definite pressures arising from it that shape future research options. The investment in time and effort in coming to understand a particular people, such as learning a language, may argue strongly for further research to build on this understanding (see discussion of longitudinal studies in Chapter 9), as may personal ties developed during the research. Furthermore, the insights coming from extensive work in a specific theoretical area may deepen with continued application. And there are expectations from within the disciplinary social group that an individual's subsequent research be related, in terms of some sort of intellectual career, to past research experience. In spite of such considerations, it is equally important for researchers periodically to make quite significant changes in some aspects of their research – whether location, topic or methods – in order to retain enthusiasm as well as to encourage the creativity that often comes with a fresh perspective. It is not really as difficult as it may sound to fulfil these apparently contradictory requirements. In the first place, theoretical interests within the discipline will shift over time, and researchers will respond to and hopefully be involved in these shifts, in the process moving their own ideas along. For example, one of the major broad theoretical influences on social research since the 1970s has been the feminist movement, which forces researchers to consider gender in virtually all aspects of research and to do so in ways that often fundamentally challenge established analytical perspectives. I will return to the influence of the feminist movement on the research process later in this chapter. Furthermore, unless one's research site is interpreted in a quite narrowly circumscribed manner, as for example a particular small village, a shift in topic may involve the researcher with a completely different population even within the linguistic and cultural group they had previously studied. Certainly when I undertook a study of young people with learning disabilities in south Wales, I found virtually no overlap in personnel from my earlier research in the area. On the other hand, in spite of this new topic's apparently very different theoretical focus on the transition to adulthood, there was a body of theoretical material, common to both topics, particularly relating to links between social and personal identities. Given the much more widely recognized importance of such phenomena as tourism and various forms of international migration in the contemporary world, concentration on a particular linguistic and cultural collectivity need not imply remaining in the same geographic location for research on it. I will discuss the significance of globalization for the selection of research sites later in this chapter.

The other major influence on the selection of research topics is the availability of funding, a consideration that is also clearly linked to current events and policy concerns. Responding to such topical considerations does not necessarily mean abandoning previous research entirely in a quest after the most recent journalistic fashion. For example, the appearance of animal rights or environmental activists might be linked to previous research on other kinds of social movements, such as language movements or feminism. However, such current events clearly do influence research, and their possible political effects on research, as well as other implications of pursuing policy-related research, are discussed more fully in this chapter and Chapter 3.

For the moment, I will consider some of the primarily internal disciplinary and intellectual sources for, and influences on, the selection of research topics. It has already been noted that working within a relatively well-defined theoretical perspective will affect the research questions pursued and the answers developed – hence the contrast mentioned above between the work of Evans-Pritchard from within a structural-functionalist perspective and that of Benedict working with a rather more loosely organized set of ideas about culture complexes. All social researchers should be broadly familiar with the body of theoretical writings from the founders of social theory in the nineteenth century, primarily Durkheim, Marx and Weber. Such so-called grand theory, including some of its successors in the twentieth century, from the functionalism of Parsons to the structuralism of Lévi-Strauss, may play some part in the generation of research questions, but it is seldom a straightforward one. In the first place, such massive theoretical constructs were not built on empirical research nor are they accessible to either proof or disproof by such research. Grand theory takes a particular theme (e.g. forms of social integration; relations of production; rationalization) and argues for its primary explanatory relevance over a vast range of social phenomena and peoples. Social researchers, in contrast, are more liable to having their theories challenged by empirical observation and must be more cautious regarding the scope of their generalizations. Thus, while grand theory may be mined as a source of concepts (e.g. the conscience collective, alienation, forms of legitimation) that suggest ways of perceiving and analysing the social world, the ideas developed by social research are better understood as middle-level theory, both based in and testable by empirical investigation (see Chapter 11 for a discussion of grounded theory), but drawing generalizations beyond immediate empirical description. This form of middle-level theory building is based on what C. Wright Mills called 'an idea with empirical content. If the idea is too large for the content, you are tending toward the trap of grand theory, if the content swallows the idea, you are tending toward the pitfalls of abstracted empiricism' (1959: 124).

As the above comments suggest, middle-level theory is clearly and closely linked to empirical research. The exact relationship, in terms of which inspires the other, is less stringent. The more usual model for ethnographic research is for the ethnographer to begin research with a specified set of questions and general area of enquiry that allows both a sharpening of the questions and a gradual development of a theoretical explanation as a part of the ongoing interplay between theorizing and collecting data that is characteristic of ethnographic research. However, a somewhat more formal model in which a more developed theory may be said to be tested, and nearly always subsequently modified, by research can also be compatible with ethnographic research. For example, Festinger *et al.* (1956) used covert participant observation in a religious cult to test theories about the disconfirmation of belief. There are numerous instances in which experiences in the field have much more fundamentally altered the theorizing in a research project, to the point of changing the focus entirely and actually altering the theoretical questions being investigated. Silverman (1985: 6–7) reports undertaking a study of the social interaction between physicians and parents of young children with cardiological problems during consultations to decide for or against various kinds of medical intervention. In the midst of this fieldwork, which consisted primarily of observation of interviews between parents and physicians, he became aware of two very distinctive sets of criteria being applied. In most cases the decision was based on clinical considerations, but occasionally it revolved instead around social considerations of the child's current quality of life. The children in this second category all had Down's Syndrome. This chance observation became the primary focus of a study (Silverman 1981) that introduced new theoretical implications such as the effect of disability on life expectations, claims on social resources and even the recognition of personhood. It is the flexibility of ethnographic methods, which clearly depends as well on the openness and alertness of the ethnographer, that makes such a close relationship between data collection and theory generation feasible.

Such flexibility must also extend to the kind of data collected. In interviewing young people with learning disabilities, I had in mind a number of areas to discuss, from work to ways of socializing. However, I found that a great deal of my conversation with them turned around food. Initially I carried on such conversations just to help develop rapport, but I gradually realized that in these discussions of eating and drinking they were telling me a great deal more about the level of control they experienced in their everyday lives, and their attempts at resistance, than I was getting from other topics. I soon began to encourage this topic and to pay it more attention and subsequently pursued some aspects of it in interviews with their parents as well (Davies 2007.

Another area that will affect the selection of topic is the level of funding required. Funding bodies, whether public or private, have their own research agendas and these affect research both in shaping the kinds of proposals that are submitted to them as well as in their explicit selection processes. Often such agendas are policy linked. For example, the development of community care as a policy initiative was related to the encouragement of a great deal of research in the areas of mental health and disability. More broadly, concern about the shifting demographic profile of advanced industrial societies has stimulated funding for much research on ageing. The broader political issues associated with policy research will be discussed more fully in Chapter 3. However, the nature of anthropological research is affected not just by sources of research funding but perhaps more fundamentally by employment prospects for anthropologists which have begun to alter the kind of work many anthropologists do and to influence academic research.

Applied versus pure research

One of the major challenges both to anthropological theorizing and to its research methods derives from the changes, especially from the 1980s onwards, in the working experiences of professional anthropologists. From being a discipline whose practitioners were almost all employed in academic institutions, anthropology has seen increasing numbers forced – or choosing – to find employment in other kinds of institutions. A recent estimate is that nearly one-third of professional anthropologists in the United States are employed outside academe (Fiske and Chambers 1997: 290). In Britain there has been a cyclical pattern of encouraging PhD students to pursue research topics that would be attractive to employers outside universities during periods when the availability of academic positions contracted, but losing interest in such research once supply and demand mechanisms adjusted the employment market (Shore and Wright 1997: 142–3). Nevertheless there is an overall movement of increasing numbers of anthropologists into nonacademic employment and as a result a shift of anthropological research towards applied topics. This trend is beginning to affect the balance of power within the profession and is bringing in its wake a more critical approach to questions about the nature of the field and expectations regarding fieldwork, as well as questions about appropriate research topics, which challenge long-dominant ideas about the distinction between pure and applied research.

Without elaborating overmuch on the history of the relationship between mainstream anthropology and its applied subfields, it is clear that these subfields have held a very ambivalent position within the discipline. They have been regarded as making an important and worthy contribution by bringing anthropological insights to bear on policy and influencing social action, while at the same time they have been criticized as both theoretically uninformed and methodologically (and sometimes ethically) suspect. The source of this ambivalence lies in part in the discipline's unexamined assumptions regarding appropriate subject matter and expected methodology. For example, mainstream academic anthropologists have severely criticized the applied subfield of development anthropology for inadvertently contributing to relations of dominance in part due to their uncritical acceptance of a modernization paradigm as the basis for development. But Ferguson (1997) has argued that much of contemporary anthropological practice implicitly reproduces precisely this modernist dichotomy of developed versus underdeveloped – with anthropological subject matter located among the underdeveloped – by changing its terminology so that the idea of the 'local' has come to replace that of the 'primitive' or 'traditional'. Nevertheless, anthropological focus on the local does not open the discipline to research on a broad range of social questions from all sections of society as fully as the universal applicability of the concept of the local might suggest. 'After all, even if it is true that all social processes are in some sense local, it is also clear that, in normal anthropological practice, some problems, some research settings, even some people, are more local than others' (ibid.: 168). So, for example, research on policy issues or on more affluent settings, while tolerated, is less likely to lead to advancement within the profession.

Another aspect of this disciplinary discomfiture with applied research is to be found in concerns about its methodological purity. In spite of the widespread recognition among anthropologists that the traditional model of the field (as a bounded, culturally distant site) and of fieldwork (as an heroic enterprise in which a lone anthropologist braves hardship to spend a year or more learning the life-ways of a 'people') is no longer relevant to the contemporary world, this model can arguably be said to continue to function as an archetype of anthropological research and a rite of passage into professional anthropology (Gupta and Ferguson 1997). As such it unduly influences professional evaluations of what is good anthropological research. It also restricts the potential of applied anthropologists – who have to adapt research methods to meet sometimes quite severe constraints of time and resources (Finan 1996), who often work as part of multidisciplinary teams, and whose research is designed explicitly to address social policy and practice – to contribute fully to the theoretical and substantive development of the discipline.

Clearly this dichotomy between pure and applied research in both subject matter and methodology is undesirable and restricts meaningful communication in both directions. Although its consequences have been noted and decried over several decades (e.g. Grillo and Rew 1985; Wright 1995), it seems likely that these barriers will finally be most effectively breached as a result of the growing numbers and increasing influence of anthropologists working outside academe (cf. Fox and Field 2007). This changing balance of power within the discipline has the potential to transform anthropological research – its subject matter and its methods – by injecting genuinely new ideas about the location of the field, the nature of its subject matter and the applicability of its methods. Nor does this imply that the concerns of pure anthropology will be jettisoned. In my own experience I have found a very productive interplay between pure and applied research. For me, applied research, with a strong advocative slant, provided my personal route back into anthropological research and indeed academic anthropology after a number of years of wandering in a non-anthropological wilderness of computing-related employment following completion of my PhD. The research that initially provided a way for me to return to practising anthropology was a project that looked at the transition to adulthood of young people with learning disabilities. This project was funded by the Joseph Rowntree Foundation whose mission and aims were then, and still remain aggressively on the side of applied research, and it was designed to evaluate some of the then new policy directions in community care based on a philosophy of normalization. The initial dissemination of findings from the research was directed toward policy makers, practitioners and user groups and included articles for a regional journal produced by an advocacy group for people with learning disabilities (Davies and Jenkins 1993a, 1993b, 1994a, 1994b), as well as presentations to these various audiences. However, the project's outputs also included some work that unquestionably falls on the pure side of anthropological theorizing, specifically a discussion of the ways in which ideas of personhood in Western society are implicated in relationships with people with learning disabilities (Davies 1998b). It also produced other work on both social networks (Davies 1998a) and identity (Davies and Jenkins 1997) that has both applied and pure aspects. These theoretical concerns were generated by contacts on the ground with research subjects; they were part and parcel of the applied project, not something added to compensate for the applied perspective of the original research design. The research methods employed on the project were also of necessity far from the traditional methods of fieldwork. The field comprised a number of different sites related to one another only in their function of providing daytime activities for the young people in our project. The fieldwork was long term, but did not entail continuous contact with either specific individuals or particular locations, and consisted of both formal interviewing and periods of informal participant observation. This example suggests the kinds of advantages that can accrue to anthropological research as a consequence of fully incorporating applied interests into the discipline, in terms of both substantive and theoretical gains. It also serves to support the altered visions of the field and fieldwork that some anthropologists have been advocating since the 1960s.

As noted above, this project may also be taken as an example of engaged, or advocative anthropology. Certainly this was the intention of the funding body, who are committed to supporting research aimed at improving the lives of socially marginalized groups. My experiences in the field, however, brought out some of the difficulties inherent in such an endeavour. In particular, as anthropologists are well aware, all social groups contain a variety of perspectives, some that conflict with one another, so the question of for whom one is advocating (or with whom one engages) is sometimes problematic. In this research, I encountered widely varying perspectives and many disagreements among the young people themselves, as well as between them and their parents and carers, not to mention professional practitioners, about such fundamental issues as the best form of day care provision, the acceptability of certain kinds of risks, and the desirability of more independent lifestyles. The issue of ensuring a fair hearing for such multiple perspectives is one that is particularly acute when participatory research methods are being used (Sillitoe 2007: 156). That these difficulties are not insurmountable is attested by examples of successfully executed projects with an advocative approach, often as their main aim (Lamphere 2003). Nevertheless such engaged research clearly involves the ethnographer in essentially political questions regarding for whom they are advocating, and, as a direct corollary, who (or what social structures) they are opposing (Sillitoe 2007: 159–61). Chapter 3 includes a fuller discussion of the role of politics in social research.

The field and fieldwork

For anthropologists the selection of research topic has been so intimately connected with the choice of research site as to be virtually the same. In fact, classically the anthropologist's topic was an ethnography, in the sense of a full description of an entire way of life of the people they were studying. Even as this holistic goal began to lose its hold, it was not uncommon for anthropologists first to select the people among whom they would do ethnographic fieldwork and then, often after being ensconced in a particular village, to begin to look around for a topic. In the decades in the first half of the twentieth century when anthropology was being established as an academic subject, it came to be defined in terms of a complex of interrelated factors: its subject matter was primitive peoples; the method of studying them was to go and live among them; and the product of the study was an ethnography – that is, a holistic description of their way of life (cf. Asad 1973b: 11). After World War II all the elements of this definition were challenged. In the first place, it came to be widely accepted that the so-called primitive world was fast disappearing, if indeed it had ever really existed except in the anthropologist's constructions (Fabian 1983). Furthermore, along with theoretical challenges to the functionalist basis of holistic analyses, came other doubts about the viability of the closed units of study – bands, villages, tribes – which ethnographies purported to describe. This recognition was of course part and parcel of the growing awareness of anthropology's implication in the colonial system and the ethical and political doubts that this raised. In response to the first part of this challenge, anthropologists to a great extent simply replaced the primitive with the exotic; that is, the proper object for anthropological study was determined by its cultural distance from the West. If it was also geographically distant so much the better, but even ethnographic studies undertaken in Western societies tended to retain the requirement of cultural distance. Thus the influential sociological ethnographies of the Chicago School emphasized the exotic at home, usually deviant groups, such as hobos (Anderson 1923), street gangs (Thrasher 1963 [1927]) or marijuana users (Becker 1963 [1953]). Anthropologists working in Western societies also tended to select populations that were both circumscribed and distinctive; thus there were studies of urban ghetto neighbourhoods (Gans 1962; Whyte 1955), of racially distinct and socially oppressed groups (Hannerz 1969; Liebow 1967), of asylums (Goffman 1961), and of peasant communities in industrial societies (Friedl 1962).

This tendency to seek out cultural peripheries for study and then to exoticize them increasingly came under attack from various directions (cf. Fabian 1983; Hymes 1969; Said 1978). One strand of this critique maintained that this process of exoticizing is really a projection of ourselves on to others and concluded that the construction of ethnographies is primarily a literary activity (Clifford and Marcus 1986). Others who oppose this perspective and continue to value ethnographic research as a means of learning about a real social world, not entirely determined by our own internal musings, assert that the traditional bases for selection of sites and methods must be fundamentally altered (Ahmed and Shore 1995; Coleman and Collins 2006; Fox 1991b). They maintain that anthropologists must abandon their fascination with the exotic and turn their attention as much on their own societies as on others. Furthermore, anthropology must give up attempts to find or create populations that are imagined to be circumscribed and isolated from other social forces. Instead they must embrace the complexity of interrelated peoples and search for topics outside their conventional concerns. This endeavour will involve studying up, incorporating forces of globalization and developing completely new topics. It does not require abandoning all the precepts and practices of anthropology, but instead encourages utilizing the strengths of ethnographic research 'especially the concern for everyday life, participant observation, cultural relativism, and, most recently self-reflection' (Fox 1991a: 95). I will now consider more fully each of these new directions and, specifically, implications of the advocacy of anthropology at home and of the movement into new topics, involving both studying up and a concern with non-local forces.

There are compelling theoretical and ethical grounds for anthropologists to reject a definition of their research as based on exotic others and apply their subject equally to their own societies, and these positions have been recognized and debated for decades (e.g. Ahmed and Shore 1995; Jackson 1987; Wolf 1969). Nevertheless, the fact that resistance to the practice of anthropology at home continues to be expressed (cf. Bloch 1988) and the difficulties that those who favour this orientation sometimes experience in having their work recognized as real anthropology (cf. Jones 1997) indicate that the position is far from accepted. Nevertheless, if anthropology is to live up to its theoretical scope and comparative vision as a study of the variety of forms of human social and cultural life, it must not exclude anthropologists' own cultures from this study. 'The avowed aim of anthropology to study all of humanity is spoiled if it excludes the Western "I" while relying mainly on the Western eye/gaze upon "others"' (Okely 1996a: 5). The consequences of turning an ethnographic eye to one's own society are to some extent revealing of the sources of resistance to such practice. Rosaldo (1993 [1989]: 46–54) has demonstrated how many of the reporting conventions, as well as the theoretical categories used to describe others in classical ethnographies, appear little short of absurd when applied to a familiar society and culture (also cf. Miner 1956). Thus while the anthropological gaze turned on the West can enlighten our understanding of our own cultures by defamiliarizing them so as to reveal aspects previously accepted without questioning, it can also occasionally expose some of our theorizing about others as an exercise in exoticizing. One implication of applying anthropological research equally to selves and others, therefore, is to expose and problematize the essentializing of both.

Such a shift in focus highlights other implications of doing anthropology at home, and simultaneously problematizes the concept of so-called native anthropology. For example, Strathern points out that it is not at all straightforward to decide who is at home or when one is at home, that in fact any such exercise can readily degenerate to 'impossible measurements of degrees of familiarity' (1987b: 16). This is the case in part because of the heterogeneity of any society and the multiplicity of social boundaries thereby created, as well as being a result of the variety of ways in which individuals are felt to belong or not to belong to different social categories and groups.

Even as a Welsh woman doing research on gender in a former mining village in South Wales, Jones acknowledges her claims to belonging are still mixed:

> I am Welsh, and from a working class background, but am from a different geographical area of Wales and have a vastly different life experience from most people in Blaengwyn, having lived in London and East Anglia as well as Wales, and having spent nearly seven years in higher education.
>
> (Jones 2003: 28)

It is furthermore not surprising that anthropologists of non-Western origins report similar dilemmas when they undertake to do so-called native ethnography. For example, when Mascarenhas-Keyes (1987) began ethnographic research in a village in Goa on the west coast of India, she did so as a Catholic Goan who was brought up in the Goan community in Kenya and settled as an adult in London, with membership in the Catholic Goan community there. Her direct experience with her field site consisted of two family visits there. On the other hand, she had both prior social ties, which located her in various ways other than as a professional anthropologist, and substantial cultural knowledge of her field site on arrival. In fact, she reports that she had to develop various persona, becoming in her term a 'multiple native', in order to carry out the research she envisioned across several sectors of Goan village society. Considerations such as these caution against a too easy assumption that simply because researchers share a cultural identity with their research subjects, their status as an insider in undertaking research among them is unproblematic (also cf. Kondo 1990; Lal 1996). In spite of Strathern's warning that we cannot assume that 'non-Western anthropologists will stand in the same relationship to their own society or culture as a Western anthropologist does to his/hers' (1987b: 30), a point to which I return below, it is nevertheless clear that both native and non-native anthropologists when researching at home must examine critically their relationships with their own societies and refrain from assuming that belonging is either uncontested or unproblematic.

Another concern in doing research at home is found in the complexity of ways of belonging and the factors that may create distance. Thus Abu-Lughod (1991) calls attention to the ambiguities experienced by 'halfies', people who for various reasons, such as migration or parentage, have mixed or multiple cultural identities; and Narayan (1993) considers not only how her own multiplex identity has variously affected her research among different groups to which she can trace some cultural affinity, but also calls attention to the distancing effects of a professional persona that researches and problematizes others' everyday lived reality. It is a dilemma based in the need to reconcile professional and personal identities that poses difficulties for Motzafi-Haller (1997) in her pursuit of native ethnography. As a member of the Mizrahim in Israel, one of the socially disadvantaged groups of Jewish peoples who came to Israel from Asia and Africa, she nevertheless had a privileged educational background due to a special scholarship for gifted children from such disadvantaged communities. Her initial attempts at native ethnography foundered on the difficulties of reconciling her personal concern for political injustices with the feeling that such concern expressed in academic discourse would undermine her intellectual credibility. She was only able to approach native ethnography after experiencing similar contradictory statuses and conflicting identities during fieldwork in Africa. There, she was alternately treated as a privileged white ethnographer in impoverished Botswana and a coloured woman denied admission to a swimming pool in apartheid South Africa. These experiences and others like them eventually allowed her to approach the complexities of ethnography at home without either overly objectifying her subjects, through the use of professionally sanctioned analytical categories that deny the reality of their oppression, or overly romanticizing and essentializing them as an oppressed people in a way that obscures the complexity of internal divisions of class and gender.

An additional implication of altering anthropology's traditional focus on exotic others is the development of new topics and theoretical concerns which are not defined in terms of spatially circumscribed field sites nor contained within territorial boundaries. This applies as much to sociological uses of ethnography as to anthropology. As already noted, the groups sought out by sociologists for ethnographic study tended to be perceived as bounded by their cultural distinctiveness and their marginal position, and, in fact, these boundaries were to a large extent the product of definitions imposed on them from above. Thus ethnography both in foreign lands and at home came to be primarily studies of the marginal and powerless by those who represented or were supported by the colonizer or the establishment. The earliest calls for a refocusing of the subjects of ethnographic study were concerned to turn the enquiry on to the powerful, to study up, and they suggested that such a shift in attention would have fundamental consequences for theoretical developments in the field.

> Studying 'up' as well as 'down' would lead us to ask many 'common sense' questions in reverse. Instead of asking why some people are poor, we would ask why other people are so affluent? ... How has it come to be, we might ask, that anthropologists are more interested in why peasants don't change than why the auto industry doesn't innovate, or why the Pentagon or universities cannot be more organizationally creative?
>
> (Nader 1969: 289)

Of course in addition to affecting theoretical focus, such a shift in subject area also has implications for fieldwork methods. People in positions of power are less accessible to the traditional ethnographic approach of simply going to a location and hanging out, and they have greater resources to restrict researchers' access to their lives. Thus new methods are required that retain insofar as possible the strength of ethnographic insights into what real people on the ground are doing, while allowing researchers 'to broach, in their own ethnographic right, such things as electronic media, "high" culture, the discourses of science, or the semantics of commodities' (Comaroff and Comaroff 1992: 31). In subsequent chapters dealing with specific research methods, therefore, I have avoided the approach of treating ethnographic research as essentially defined by long-term participant observation with other methods treated as supplementary and instead consider ways (and examples of good practice) in which these other approaches may provide the principal methodological focus in the field yet still retain the depth of understanding and the purchase on the lives of real people that is the characteristic strength of ethnographic research.

This shift in theoretical focus and the move away from traditional bounded field sites, with the related changes required in research methods, was seen as desirable for ethical and political reasons in the 1960s and 1970s. By the 1980s and 1990s, it was increasingly presented as unavoidable in order for anthropology to respond adequately to a fundamentally altered world in which global forces of production and consumption, as well as the influence of electronic media, force researchers to recognize that many of the old bases on which they organized their research questions and selected their field sites no longer pertain. These new forces are subsumed most often under the label of globalization (cf. Appadurai 1990; Hannerz 1990) and one of their markers is the way in which the exotic may be taken into the everyday and vice versa. Fox reports just this kind of experience 'when I watch Pro-Life protesters in North Carolina use present-day versions of Gandhian *satyagraha,* or when animal-rights activists preach a doctrine much like *ahimsa*' (Fox 1991b: 5). At the same time, the phenomenon of the international hotel that could be anywhere in the world, the availability of ever more exotic locations and experiences to the international tourist, as well as the ubiquity of a huge variety of consumer items, makes anthropological claims to authority on the basis of having 'been there' (Geertz 1988) unimpressive at best and essentially irrelevant. Appadurai (1991) argues that with the breakdown of the viability of a localized ethnography, a new focus on what he calls 'global ethnoscapes', whose boundaries are permeable to people and ideas, becomes both possible and desirable. For example, because the imagining of other lives made possible by the globalization of ideas as well as commodities has real social consequences, in formats such as new collectivities and political movements, he suggests that 'ethnography must redefine itself as that practice of representation which illuminates the power of large-scale, imagined life possibilities over specific life trajectories' (ibid.: 200) and calls on ethnographers 'to find new ways to represent the links between the imagination and social life' (ibid.: 199).

Thus, globalization poses a challenge to the pursuit of ethnographic research and to a large extent discredits its continuance in its classic format. Clearly, if ethnographers are doing no more than reporting their experiences of other ways of life, no matter how exotic, whether at home or abroad, then they are offering no more than what thousands of tourists have experienced directly and millions more vicariously by means of electronic media. Ethnographic research must be capable of adding value to such personal experiences and reports. It does so by the theoretically informed nature of its investigations and the deployment of research methods that provide greater depth and validity to the explanations it develops. Good ethnographic research encourages a continual interplay and tension between theory and on-the-ground methods and experiences. The next section considers methodology, which essentially is the relationship between these two realms, theory and method.

Methodologies

Social research must be concerned with methodology throughout the research process. In the initial stage of formation of research questions, as we have seen, the research must be located within on-going theoretical debates. Furthermore, data collection is guided by the theoretical orientation of the researcher, so that the methods selected, the kinds of things that are observed in the field, the way in which they are problematized and the kinds of middle-level theoretical explanations eventually proposed are all related to the broader theoretical orientations of the researcher. The contrasting ethnographies produced by the distinctive theoretical positions of British structural functionalism and American culture complexes have already been noted above. But consider two other studies from within the same disciplinary climate and even addressing the same general research question concerning child-raising practices among black ghetto families. One of these is Liebow's (1967) study of black street-corner men and the ways in which they construct self-respect in social circumstances that remove most material means of success. The other is Stack's (1974) study of matrifocal black families, one of the first studies to treat this household form as anything other than dysfunctional. The main reason for the differences in the perspectives developed and insights produced by these two studies is not simply the gender of their respective authors but the related yet broader factor of the influence of feminism on Stack's theoretical perspective. Feminism, both as a political movement and a theoretical perspective, has been a profound influence on social research since the 1970s, and I want to consider briefly the variety of ways in which this influence has been felt as a means of illustrating some of the ways that methodology can affect research practice.

The initial effect of the women's movement on social research was in encouraging women's entry into the research process in two ways, as the subjects of research and as researchers themselves. Clearly these processes were linked – women researchers were both more likely to study other women and better placed to do so. This orientation produced a lot of studies of women in other societies (e.g. Weiner 1976; Wolf 1972) as anthropologists came to recognize that the bulk of traditional ethnography had virtually ignored half of the social world by discussing only the lives of men and using mainly male informants; women, when they were visible at all in classic ethnographies, were viewed from male perspectives, both that of the ethnographer and of his male informants (cf. Moore 1988). The altered perspective deriving from feminism did not simply add to the existing ethnographic knowledge base about gender relations, but also often challenged it and developed some far-reaching theoretical insights. For example, studies of women traders in West Africa brought out the relative autonomy based in economic power of some women under particular social circumstances and helped to undermine ideas of women's universal oppression and passivity (Moore 1988: 91–2). And such an altered perspective, with its greater attention to women's activities, also contributed to the revelation that among hunter-gatherers women's gathering activities were not just supplementary and peripheral to men's hunting large animals but were central to subsistence and often responsible for well over half of the group's caloric intake. In studies of women in Western societies, it has already been noted that Stack's (1974) research on black women provided a very different picture of ghetto life than that presented in ethnographies by male ethnographers who had tended to concentrate on public life rather than households and whose perspective on families as unstable reflected their male informants' peripheral relationship to these family groups that coalesced around women (Liebow 1967). This feminist theoretical orientation also produced a shift in the kinds of topics that were considered appropriate for social research, with Oakley's (1974) study of housewives and housework providing an influential example of this change in what is considered legitimate subject matter for research (also cf. Charles and Kerr 1988).

Thus in its efforts to include women in the research process, the feminist movement not only expanded its subject matter but also developed new theoretical insights and began to challenge some long-standing theoretical perspectives. Nevertheless, for the most part, both female researchers and the new subject matter were still fully incorporated within existing methodologies. However, these methodologies were to come under much closer scrutiny, with both methods and theoretical perspectives being subjected to critical evaluation as the feminist movement changed in the 1970s and 1980s. Feminism is both an intellectual critique and a political movement (see Chapter 3) and these two aspects have interacted throughout its development. Just as the political movement went from a liberal position of trying to include women as equals in society to a more radical analysis which maintained that social structures were themselves inherently sexist and had to be transformed, so feminist research moved away from the idea that women could simply be added to the personnel and subject matter of social research and argued that genuinely to include women and women's concerns requires a transformation of methodologies, affecting both methods and theoretical perspectives.

One of the main research methods to be selected by feminist researchers as needing a fundamentally new approach was ethnographic interviewing. In an influential article, Oakley (1981) argued that it is impossible for a feminist interviewing women to follow the precepts for good interview technique that had been developed within a male-dominated tradition of social research. She objects to admonitions to guard against over-rapport and revealing her own opinion, and maintains instead that the interviewer has to become involved, to answer questions as well as ask them and to accept, indeed welcome, her effect on the relationship with her informants. As this suggests, feminists have tended to favour and advocate the more qualitative and reflexive research methods characteristic of ethnographic fieldwork. However, there is no necessary connection between feminist theory and qualitative methods (Reinharz 1992), and examples can be found of feminist research using more structured and quantitative methods (Jayaratne 1993 [1983]; Pugh 1990). Nor is the use of ethnographic methods any guarantee of a feminist theoretical perspective. Nevertheless, the fact that feminist researchers tended to advocate the use of ethnographic methods, the complex of methods long central to anthropological research, is probably one reason why the subject was not overly affected by feminist research methods per se. However, feminist anthropologists began to be uneasy about the process of just mechanically adding women to the research situation and to question whether traditional methodology was adequate to accommodate feminist concerns. Specifically they asked whether the theories within which feminists work might themselves be sexist and hence distort their research on women and women's issues, so that they still reproduce an essentially male-biased anthropology. Thus the feminist challenge to social research moved from choice of individual topics and methods to the relationship between them and the theories within which they are selected – that is, it moved to the level of methodology. Rosaldo (1989), for example, argues that the male bias of anthropological theory forced feminist research into working with and within various dichotomies – for example nature/nurture, expressive/ instrumental, domestic/jural–political – whether trying to refute them or reinterpret them in feminist terms, instead of developing a radical revision of such categories and the dichotomizing that accompanies them.

Another example of feminist methodology challenging the basic theoretical categories that inform social research is the debate about the inadequacies of the concept of social class (cf. Delphy 1981; Llewellyn 1981). The traditional approach using the household as the basic unit of stratification ignores women as individuals and assigns them to a social class based on the occupational status of their husbands (or fathers, if unmarried) – often even after the relationship has been terminated by death or divorce – and even when women themselves are the primary focus of the study (Roberts 1981). However, rectifying this approach involves much more than simply allowing women's occupational status to inform the determination of their class position. Because women's relationship to the labour market is so different from that of men, fully assimilating it requires rethinking and reconstituting the entire classificatory system in order, for example, to find meaningful ways to include part-time work and home working, to make finer distinctions among women's occupations, and to incorporate housework and other forms of unwaged labour.

A more recent study that addresses some of these concerns advanced by the development of feminist methodologies is Cockburn's (1991) research on the implementation of equal opportunity policies in four different organizations. In her study, she explicitly problematizes discourses about men and women based in concepts of sameness and difference and examines their effects in the workplace. She rejects both essentialist treatments of women's biological difference as explanatory of social inequalities and liberal dismissals of this difference as inconsequential. Her study instead analyses the ways in which concepts of sameness and difference are used to support a patriarchal system of dominance; for example, to be successful, women are expected to display what are considered to be male characteristics, but are criticized for doing so. Her analysis of the effects of this form of dichotomizing discourse is further strengthened by extending it to other such discourses based on race, class and disability.

A final example of the ways in which methodology may affect the focus and methods of research is found in a comparison of symbolic interactionism and ethnomethodology. Both of these methodological approaches derive much of their fundamental theoretical perspective from that of phenomenology. Developed in the 1930s and 1940s by Schutz (1967), phenomenology maintains that the social world which researchers investigate is pre-interpreted in that all social actors work within a set of preconceptions about that world and these must be uncovered in order to understand their actions. Symbolic interactionism, as developed primarily by Herbert Blumer (1969), emphasized that social researchers must get at the meanings behind social actions – that is, the symbolic content of interaction. Thus they must attempt to see the world first through the eyes of their informants, and this can be accomplished by talking to them and developing in-depth descriptive accounts of their interactions, seen as on-going creative processes that construct social realities through the meanings they develop. Clearly such a theoretical perspective is more compatible with relatively open forms of ethnographic research, such as semi-structured interviewing, than with surveys based on structured questionnaires. Furthermore, it has stimulated a great deal of work on the topic of deviance, investigating how acts and individuals come to be defined as deviant through the meanings assigned to certain kinds of interactions. For example, the middle-level theory most closely associated with this area, usually referred to as labelling theory, argues that the meanings given to behaviour and negotiated through social, especially verbal, interaction at various points in the criminal justice system will result in a young person being labelled a delinquent or otherwise (Cicourel 1968). Another area of investigation encouraged by a symbolic interactionist perspective is the social basis of personal identities, a reflection of the influence of G. H. Mead, stimulating research on 'moral careers' as in Becker's (1963 [1953]) classic study of how an individual becomes a marijuana user.

Ethnomethodology also was heavily influenced by phenomenology (Heritage 1984) and, as a consequence, its basic tenets are quite similar to those of symbolic interactionism. However, the differences between these two methodologies are responsible for some quite striking divergences in methods and topics, and as such they provide an instructive example of the ways in which theoretical perspective affects the more mundane aspects of social research. Ethnomethodology, as developed mainly in the work of Garfinkel (1984 [1967]), in common with symbolic interactionism maintains that the researcher must uncover the preconceptions with which social actors interpret their circumstances and decide on actions. However, unlike symbolic interactionists, ethnomethodologists regard these underlying assumptions, which Garfinkel calls 'sense-assembly equipment', as taken for granted by social actors and hence not in their conscious awareness. This means that they cannot be accessed by simply asking informants to discuss meanings and interpretations. One of the best-known approaches that Garfinkel used to uncover such assumptions was to act in ways that challenged them. For example, he instructed his students to behave at home as if they were boarders (ibid.: 47–9), with the responses of their families to their breach of expected forms of interaction serving to make these assumptions visible. In another experiment 'counsellors' were instructed to respond with 'yes' or 'no' randomly to individuals who were describing their problems and asking for advice. When these individuals were asked subsequently to explain the answers they had received, they provided an example of the ways in which sense was constructed around essentially nonsensical occurrences (ibid.: 79–94). As these examples illustrate, ethnomethodologists tend to concentrate on everyday activities, rather than the unusual, or deviant, that formed so large a part of the interests of symbolic interactionists. And in another contrast, while both make a great deal of use of verbal interaction, ethnomethodologists tend to concentrate on naturally occurring talk and to analyse complete transcripts of relatively short segments of such talk, especially in the ethnomethodological subfield of conversation analysis, whereas symbolic interactionists make greater use of extensive interviewing and selection of significant passages to construct their analyses. This contrast is perhaps particularly striking in a comparison of two studies of death and dying in the context of a hospital ward: Glaser and Strauss (1968) using a symbolic interactionist approach develop an interpretation of how the social meanings of deaths are constructed on the basis of the social roles of the dying; Sudnow (1967), an ethnomethodologist, concentrates on the way in which hospital staff talk about deaths in relationship to their organization of work.

In considering these various methodologies and some of the research within these theoretical perspectives, it should become apparent that there is no simple and direct link between choice of topics and methods and the theoretical perspectives that guide the researcher. But neither are they totally independent. Certainly it may be possible to develop new perspectives simply by applying methods not customarily adopted within a given theoretical perspective – for example, structured interviewing in a feminist or symbolic interactionist study – or by applying a particular theoretical perspective to hitherto untouched topical areas. But however flexible the relationship between topics, methods and methodologies may be, it is nevertheless essential that researchers be aware of the theoretical perspective that underlies their approach and that their choice of topics and methods be informed by and answerable to their reflexive awareness of where they are situated both personally and theoretically.

Chapter 3

Ethics and politics

Along with increasing reflexivity in the conduct of social research inevitably comes greater awareness of ethical questions and political considerations regarding the conduct of research. For example, the 1960s saw a growing recognition of the ways in which anthropologists had aided the colonial enterprise, if only by their concentration on so-called traditional sociocultural forms at the expense of contemporary contacts and conflicts, and, in so doing, inadvertently bolstered racial prejudice at home and abroad (Willis 1969). Although most critics agree that anthropological research contributed very little directly to colonial domination, its indirect contribution to the maintenance of the status quo raises fundamental ethical questions about the nature of social research and its exploitative potential, as well as about the viability of a politically neutral position on the part of researchers (Asad 1973b, 1991).

Furthermore, in 1965 came the public exposure and cancellation of Project Camelot, a social science research project funded by the US Army, whose objectives were to assess conditions leading to internal conflict in other countries, notably initially in Chile, and to uncover means of preventing such conflict. This was followed in the 1970s with the revelation that ethnographic information had been used by the CIA to select bombing targets in Indo-China (Barnes 1977: 50–6; Horowitz 1967). These discoveries fuelled debates about the responsibilities of social researchers regarding the uses to which their findings may be put, in particular any harm that might come to participants in the research as a consequence of it. Professional organizations responded by developing ethical codes covering the conduct of social research as well as other aspects of professional ethics. It should be noted that in some countries the ethical requirements of research are mandated by legislation. For example, since 1974 the federal government in the United States has required that research review boards be established at all universities which receive federal funding in areas of research that involve human subjects to assess the ethical bases of all such projects (cf. Sieber 1992 for a full discussion of these boards, their activities and expectations). This chapter considers some of the central features of such codes for ethical practice in social research, along with the ambiguities and debates surrounding them, in particular the areas of informed consent, covert research and questions of confidentiality. It then looks at the related area of politics in social research and, finally, considers briefly various assessments of the nature and significance of policy research.

Informed consent

Social research may be said to involve relationships among a variety of individuals and collectivities: between researchers and sponsors; researchers and various gatekeepers (those who control access to research sites or to information); researchers and their colleagues and the discipline more broadly; researchers and the general public; and researchers and research participants (Barnes 1979: 14; Association of Social Anthropologists 1987). Informed consent is primarily concerned with this latter relationship – that is, with the interactions that constitute the research encounter – and the ethical standard of informed consent is the one that is most relevant for this relationship. This standard was first developed in the area of medical research prompted particularly by the revelations concerning Nazi experimentation on human subjects during World War II (Homan 1991: 9–16). Although the exact formulation may vary slightly, the definition of informed consent is fairly constant across disciplines involved in social research. The following from the British Sociological Association is representative:

> As far as possible sociological research should be based on the freely given informed consent of those studied. This implies a responsibility on the sociologist to explain as fully as possible, and in terms meaningful to participants, what the research is about, who is undertaking and financing it, why it is being undertaken, and how it is to be disseminated.
>
> (British Sociological Association 1996)

Researchers should become familiar in detail with the ethical code promulgated by their professional association. These codes specify more fully the implications of informed consent and some of the difficulties that arise in practice. It will be helpful here to consider these as two elements: first, informing participants of the nature and likely consequences of their participation in the research in a way that is comprehensible to them; and, secondly, obtaining consent that is based on their understanding of this explanation and free of any coercion or undue influence (Homan 1991: 71–4).

There are two sets of difficulties that researchers face in deciding on how to present their research to potential participants. The first has to do with the relatively technical question of how to present their research in a manner that is meaningful to their particular audience of participants; the second is related to the effect on the research of any such disclosure. Although some research participants may be informed and knowledgeable about the theoretical debates and terminologies in which the research questions are grounded, many will not be, and consideration must be given to how to express these questions in language that is meaningful to participants. A particular problem may arise when researchers are using terms that have both popular meanings and a rather different specialized interpretation; for example, the distinction between sex and gender which a researcher can easily take for granted will not be clear to many informants. The problem of comprehensibility may be increased with cultural distance – not to be confused with geographic distance. Strathern contrasts Okely's (1983) study of traveller Gypsies in Britain with her own two studies in Malay and in an English village and suggests, 'while Travellers and Malay villagers are not so at home, in their talk about "community", "socialization", or "class" ... Elmdoners [English villagers] are' (1987: 17).

Another difficulty with the explanation of research to participants is that, particularly with the more open research designs characteristic of ethnographic methods, researchers do not know at the outset what are all the pertinent aspects; in fact, the theoretical focus may shift and different sorts of data become relevant as the research proceeds. Certainly participants do not need to be consulted about all developing theoretical perspectives; in any case, they should be informed that research is always a process of discovery so that its consequences can never be fully known at the outset. However, if changes in the research focus and design are likely to affect the consequences of the research for participants or have a bearing on their willingness to participate, then their consent needs to be renegotiated. Furthermore, in forms of research that extend over a period of time, particularly participant observation, people will not keep foremost in their minds in all social interactions that the researcher's primary purpose is collecting data, and they have a right to be reminded or consulted again about the use of information gained in informal encounters and perhaps based in ties of friendship or putative kinship. 'Consent in fieldwork studies ... is a process, not a one-off event, and may require renegotiation over time' (ASA 1987: 3). It is equally the case that during a series of interviews with the same individuals, their continued willingness to participate should be ascertained before each session. In interviewing people with learning disabilities, I tried to ask regularly, even during the course of a single interview, if they were willing to continue. Another aspect of informing this particular set of participants about the research was ensuring that they understood the function of a tape recorder, which I frequently did by replaying our initial conversation before beginning the interview.

Thus careful consideration must be given to the kind of discourse which frames the presentation of information about the research and when it occurs. However, these introductory explanations should not be regarded as primarily an exercise in persuasion. The purpose is to provide information that will enable people to assess the likely effects of the research on them and to make an informed decision about whether or not they are willing to participate. Certainly, the positive aspects of participating in the research can be presented. For example, people often agree to participate for altruistic reasons, that it will help others; however, any assessments of the beneficial effects of the research must be as realistic as is possible. Many individuals find participation in research a positive experience personally in that it gives them a chance to express their opinion or unburden themselves to a sympathetic outsider. However, Finch (1984), who felt that her identity as a former clergyman's wife made her interviews with women in this category much more frank and informative, warns that while it is legitimate for researchers to offer such positive inducement for participation, it is not always possible to ensure that other researchers who will have access to the material after publication will deal with their disclosures as sympathetically. Thus participants must also be made aware that there are some risks in any research, in that no one is able fully to control future use and interpretations of their research findings.

A secondary consideration is the effect of disclosure of the aims of the research on the conduct of the research itself – that is, the reflexivity inherent in the process of informing participants about the research. As has already been argued, all social research is reflexive, and this reflexivity occurs at various levels. Thus the reflexivity that is a part of the ethical procedure of informed consent is not something to be regretted and certainly not to be deliberately reduced but rather to be recognized and included in the research process and accounted for in subsequent analysis. In determining the way in which research is to be presented, researchers must consider the effects of this disclosure in terms of whether it is comprehensible, how it is likely to be interpreted and how it may affect the subsequent behaviour and ideas of participants. For example, presentation of the research topic as questions may give informants the impression that their role is to supply answers directly. This is particularly the case with interview-based studies and is probably more likely to occur with relatively high status interviewees. For example, when I described research I was conducting as a study of the transition to adulthood of people with learning disabilities to service providers, they assumed the aim of the research was to assess whether or not this category of young people achieve adulthood, and their contribution was to offer opinions on this point rather than contribute to more informative (for me) discussions of social activities, employment prospects, family relationships, and so on. In fact, since the study problematized the concept of adulthood in any case, I found it more helpful to present it as research about the problems these young people encounter as they reach chronological maturity. This was slightly disingenuous in that the research would eventually assess the question of their adult status, but it was not deliberately misleading about the researchers' interests.

A more difficult problem was how to explain the research to the young people themselves. In the first place, there was the question of how to refer to them as a collectivity. It was not at all clear whether reference to them using any of the terms then in common use by professionals (whether mental handicap, learning disabilities, learning difficulties) was acceptable. In fact, once research was under way it became clear that the understanding of these terms and the degree to which they were a part of people's self-identity was highly variable (Davies and Jenkins 1997), and the research eventually led me to problematize the entire category (Davies 1998b). Thus clearly it would have been inappropriate to use such terms in the presentation of the research to these young people even though they were used in explanations to other categories of participants. The problem was solved by the fact that the young people were all contacted through various day centres and other services for people with learning disabilities, and I was able to contact and invite to participate – in a research project looking at problems encountered by young adults – everyone within a specified age range in each of these facilities or in receipt of the particular service.

The second set of considerations regarding informed consent has to do with ensuring that consent is based in understanding and free of coercion. Certain categories of people may be less competent to comprehend the explanation of the research and to make an informed decision in their own interests, such as children or people with mental illnesses or learning disabilities. In these cases, it is common procedure to obtain consent from others who have some degree of responsibility for the welfare of these individuals – for example from children's parents or guardians. In the research on young people with learning disabilities referred to above, this procedure in fact presented a rather ticklish problem. All of the young people I sought to interview were 18 or older, and thus legal adults and empowered to make their own decisions about such matters. Asking parental permission to interview them would have been yet another way in which their status as adults was being undermined. At the same time, problems might easily arise if parents were not informed, given that most of the young people were living at home and dependent on parental care. The compromise reached was to send a letter addressed to the young person, but also to be seen by parents, asking the young person's consent to participate but noting that I would also like to interview parents. Ideally the decision to participate would have been a joint one between parents and young people, although clearly this did not always occur in practice. The fact that two young people elected to be interviewed even though their parents declined to participate suggests that the strategy was partially successful and in some cases seemed to enhance the young person's experience of adult autonomy.

As was noted above, it is common practice to obtain consent from gatekeepers for certain categories of people. It is also necessary to go through gatekeepers for research in virtually any institutional setting, such as schools or business organizations. Since such gatekeepers usually have authority over other individuals, their consent does not always signal the agreement of these others, and researchers should seek consent from them directly to ensure that their participation is in fact free of undue coercion. Furthermore, researchers should be sensitive to the ongoing relationship that exists between gatekeepers and other participants and endeavour not to disturb it.

A final consideration regarding undue influence is the question of gifts and payments to participants. Certainly informants should not be exploited and a fair return should be made for their assistance. On the other hand, the use of material or other rewards to persuade individuals to take part, when there is an indication that they consider it against their interests, should be avoided.

Confidentiality

The question of confidentiality essentially concerns the treatment of information gained about individuals in the course of research. It overlaps with considerations of privacy and assurances of anonymity (cf. Sieber 1992: 44–63). People will feel that their personal privacy has been invaded when information about them is obtained without their knowledge and consent or used in ways of which they disapprove. Since ideas about what aspects of a person's beliefs and activities should be considered private will obviously vary according to a host of factors – for example cultural background, religious belief, age, gender, social class – researchers must make themselves aware of these differences and respond accordingly. Much social research depends on the researcher's ability to gain information about areas of life that are considered to be private, and there are numerous examples where this has been successful. Leaving aside temporarily the question of deception and covertness in research, the usual reason for such success is that researchers have been able to offer their informants assurances of confidentiality regarding the use of the data they supply and anonymity in any publications. Normally such assurances are given at the outset of data collection, particularly so in the case of interviewing. However, in research such as participant observation, based on long-term and multi-stranded social relationships, discussions of confidentiality are normally inappropriate in the early stages since researchers usually only have access to the public life of their informants; instead it needs to be included in ongoing negotiations and explanations about the nature of the research and the conditions under which people are participating. In any case, researchers must be cautious about the degree of confidentiality they promise and realistic about their own abilities to protect their informants' anonymity. For example, the usual practice of using pseudonyms and altering some details of an individual's biography in referring to research subjects does prevent their being unambiguously identified. However, the individuality that is preserved in linguistic habits means that the use of extensive direct quotations makes informants recognizable, at least to themselves, and often to others who know them well. They should be informed of this in explaining how confidentiality is to be provided. Anonymity is not always possible to provide when doing research on public figures. That is, the research sometimes necessitates that respondents be identified in terms of their public position – the town mayor or the prospective parliamentary candidate for a named constituency. Even if there is enough time-lapse prior to publication in which the individuals occupying such positions may have changed, earlier occupants can usually be identified. In such cases, it should be made clear that it is not possible to protect anonymity. Certainly the ability to promise confidentiality to anyone, whether a public personage or not, is further compromised when using photographs and film. In these cases, it is probably most important to be able to specify how the materials are to be used. Asch (1992) stresses the importance of obtaining control over the distribution and subsequent use of any film, noting that his failure to do this in one case, when he was filming among nomadic groups in Afghanistan, meant that the film was never used for educational purposes as promised and subsequent use of footage for news broadcasts after invasion by the Soviet Army may have endangered some of his informants.

A further complication in assurances of confidentiality is that the data collected by social researchers do not have the same privileged status as communications between doctors and patients or solicitors and clients, and research subjects should be warned against self-incrimination if there is any likelihood of this occurring. On the other hand, researchers should clarify with their sponsors at the outset of research who owns their field notes and other data in order to be able to guarantee their control over the information collected (Cassell and Jacobs 1987: 22–3). This also needs to be clarified with gatekeepers; that is, researchers should not be expected to supply them with information about subordinates: Goffman (1961) was careful about clarifying this in his study of asylums in spite of his adopting a clandestine role on the wards; similarly, on several occasions I had to refuse to divulge to parents what their sons or daughters had discussed with me in interviews. A recent serious ethical consideration regarding the viability of assurances of confidentiality has grown out of the increasing importance being given to archiving datasets, with emphasis on making available complete raw data sources such as full transcripts of interviews and the sound recordings on which they are based. Such practices have been common with survey datasets for decades. However, the sanitizing of survey datasets so that individuals are genuinely anonymous is fairly readily accomplished by replacing identifying responses such as names and addresses with case numbers. With ethnographic data, personal characteristics such as speech mannerisms, as well as ways of expressing opinions, uses of anecdotal material, and detailed personal narratives, are not so readily expunged, and so individual identities are not easy to disguise completely. Furthermore, while it might well appeal to informants to think that the information they provided could be of more extensive use and influence than in a single project, the degree to which they can be informed about the likely future uses of such data in order to enable them to make a decision that does not undermine their own interests is much more problematic. Thus concern has been expressed by one researcher interviewing 'adults with genetic conditions about the value and quality of their lives' as to whether such transcripts might in future be 'used, for example and perhaps inadvertently, in racist or eugenic ways' (Alderson 1998: 7).

A final point about anonymity is that sometimes it is not desired, and research participants may be disappointed and feel that much of the benefit of participating in the research is lost if they are not identified (Cassell and Jacobs 1987: 24–7; Crick 1992). Obviously if the research is about a collectivity then the wishes of individuals may conflict in this regard and the issue may have to be resolved by the researcher, if possible in some negotiation with participants. However, even if all the individuals who directly participated in the research decline anonymity, it behoves the researcher to take into account any possible effect either immediately or stemming from future publications drawing on the data that could adversely affect a larger collectivity.

Covert research

Covert research involves investigation in which the researchers deliberately conceal their identity as researchers, along with their intention of conducting research, and present themselves in another guise in order to collect data for this secret and unacknowledged research project. Under this definition it is clear that covert research can only be undertaken using observation or participant observation; it is not possible, for example, to conduct an interview covertly. On the other hand, in reconsidering some of the discussion above regarding informed consent, it is certainly possible to mislead informants in ways that maintain a degree of covertness about the research. And there is also a difficulty in ensuring that even the most open researchers do not, during long-term participant observation, tend virtually to disappear from their research role as other social relationships established in the field take precedence. Furthermore, some researchers have argued that deception in conducting research is part and parcel of the impression management that is integral to social life (Berreman 1962). Thus, to a degree, covert research can be viewed as one end of a spectrum that spans various shades of openness in research design and comprehensibility of research aims. Significantly, most ethical codes appear to acknowledge this difficulty. The Association of Social Anthropologists states:

> The deliberate deception of subjects is hard to defend but to outlaw all deception in social inquiry would be as unrealistic as it would be to outlaw it in social interaction. But in cases where informed consent cannot be acquired in advance there is usually a strong case for making it post hoc ... It should, however, be recognized that, even where no deception is intended, it is particularly difficult under the conditions of anthropological fieldwork for research participants to remember or even perhaps to realize that they are being studied all or most of the time.
>
> (ASA 1987: 4)

Nevertheless, in spite of these qualifications, the deliberate assumption of another social role for the primary purpose of conducting research, while at the same time concealing that research from those who are its subjects, is qualitatively very different from the difficulties that inhere in fully guaranteeing informed consent discussed above or even from such minor dishonesties in the field as pretending to be older, or to be married, in order to ensure better relationships. There are numerous compelling reasons why such covertness should be eschewed in the conduct of social research (cf. Bulmer 1982a). In the first place, it is a clear and unambiguous violation of the principle of informed consent, which is a central pillar of most ethical codes regarding relationships with research participants. Furthermore, the covert collection of information is also a form of exploitation as well as a betrayal of trust in personal relationships. While there may be an analogy with the obtaining of data through ties of personal friendship in the course of long-term fieldwork, the use of covert methods involves a deliberate intent to conceal and deceive whereas the latter, while it sometimes produces feelings of betrayal, is a result of misunderstanding rather than intentional deceit.

Covert research also involves risks to the subjects, as does all research, but when it is covert subjects do not have the opportunity to determine for themselves whether they are willing to accept such risks. For example, in what is one of the most widely discussed examples of the extensive use of covert methods, Humphreys (1975) undertook to observe male homosexual activities in public toilets. To do this he adopted the role of watchqueen, that is, a voyeur who also acted as a lookout. This was an established role in these social circumstances and cannot be said in itself to increase the risks in this inherently risky activity. On the other hand, when he undertook to obtain car licence numbers in order to trace the men to their homes, he was exposing them to very great and, I would maintain, unacceptable risk entirely without their knowledge or consent. Besides the risks to research subjects, those adopting covert research also expose themselves to a variety of risks, either from retaliation upon being exposed as a researcher or from being pressured into risky behaviour, such as illegal activities, in order to protect their disguise.

Another set of considerations is whether covert research is practical or effective as a research strategy in any case. Certainly the inability to either record observations openly or to ask questions of informants severely limits the accuracy and scope of the data obtained. The argument that there are many situations that simply could not be studied by more open methods is not fully convincing. Certainly, successful studies have been undertaken in sensitive areas such as drug dealing without resorting to covert methods, or even without making unrealistic promises or representations. For example, Adler and Adler note of their research among drug dealers: 'Although we had forged no bargains in gaining entrée to this loosely organized group, we did promise individuals anonymity and confidentiality at the point when we began our taped life-history interviews (though we made it clear that we were unwilling to go to jail to protect them)' (1991: 179). Furthermore, the distortion considered to be introduced by the presence of a researcher is not something to be eliminated but rather considered as a part of the reflexive element inherent in all research. Thus again in the example of the Adlers' research, the way in which they were treated by their informants was itself informative:

> Our subjects dealt with us on the basis of individual trust and negotiation. They came to recognize that we were willing to maintain relations by doing them favors. They knew, also, that we held a different set of ethical standards from theirs. Although they felt comfortable stretching the truth, fudging the rules, and borrowing objects or money from us, they knew that we would not do this in return. We could not afford to treat them as they treated us because we needed them. They therefore, gradually, began to take advantage of us. Money they gave us to hold, they knew they could always rely on having returned. Money we lent them in desperate times was never repaid, even when they were affluent again. Favors from us were expected by them, without any further reciprocation than openness about their activities.
>
> (Ibid.: 177–8)

The use of covert methods does not eliminate such reflexivity but rather drives it underground and renders it less predictable and informative in the conduct of research. For example, the infiltration, by several researchers posing as converts, into a small religious sect predicting the end of the world (Festinger, Riecken and Schachter 1956) can hardly be said to have been without effect in strengthening their belief in the prophecy. Nor does the argument that covert research is necessary to conduct research on powerful and secretive groups convince. In fact, covert research has probably more frequently been conducted on relatively powerless collectivities, and the potential for a researcher successfully penetrating powerful organizations is quite limited.

The final set of considerations regarding covertness in research has to do with its effects on the disciplines that allow it and on the researchers themselves. Certainly the widespread use of covert methods could very quickly pollute the research environment making more open research methods highly suspect and less likely to gain the cooperation of potential subjects. Nor is the effect on the individual researcher of the constant deception required by such methods to be lightly dismissed. A habit of deception, no matter for what reasons it is cultivated, may encourage a rather broader cynicism and callousness in human relations which is not desirable – certainly not in those who study other human beings, individually or collectively (cf. Mead 1969). A striking and compelling example of the high price to be paid by the researcher using covert methods is Mitchell's account of an incident during research on survivalist groups. 'Alone, two thousand miles away from home, on the third day of the Christian Patriots Survival Conference, I volunteered for guard duty' (1991: 106). In the course of the evening he found himself standing around a campfire with three other guards, in a social situation in which displays of their common commitment were expected. There ensued a discussion of how to handle what was perceived as the problem of homosexuals in the future, with proffered solutions of increasingly violent forms being offered by each of the other three guards as turn-taking in the conversation moved clockwise around the circle.

> It grew quiet. It was Nine O'clock. My turn. I told a story, too.
>
> As I began a new man joined us. He listened to my idea and approved, introduced himself, then told me things not everyone knew, about plans being made, and action soon to be taken. He said they could use men like me and told me to be ready to join. I took him seriously. Others did, too. He was on the FBI's 'Ten Most Wanted' list.
>
> If there are researchers who can participate in such business without feeling, I am not one of them nor do I ever hope to be. What I do hope is someday to forget, forget those unmistakable sounds, my own voice, my own words, telling that Nine O'clock story.
>
> (Ibid.: 107)

The above discussion takes a definition of covert research in its least problematic form, that is, when there is a deliberate assumption of a disguise in order to undertake research unknown to the research subjects. There are forms of research that are also covert but do not always carry the same ethical objections. Research in public places – for example observations of public rituals or performances – does not require notification of the presence and intent of the researcher, although some forms of recording these events may require permission of the organizers. Nevertheless, anonymity of those being observed, aside from publicly identified performers, must be preserved. It is furthermore important to recognize that definitions of what is public will vary cross-culturally, and also that people do sometimes carry out private acts in public places and these distinctions must be noted and respected.

Another form of covert research is retrospective analysis of experiences as a participant in a social setting prior to contemplating research on that setting or collectivity. This should fall under the admonition to seek permission post hoc and before publication, and when, as is common, it is accompanied by subsequent follow-up research, the expectations of informed consent clearly apply. A variant of this is research undertaken on a collectivity or in a setting to which the researcher legitimately belongs. There are numerous examples of researchers using a period of hospitalization or other medical treatment as an occasion for social research (Davis and Horobin 1977; Homan 1986) but such research need not remain, or ever be, clandestine (cf. Homan 1991: 98–9).

Politics and research

The role of politics in social research can be interpreted in a narrow technical sense as having to do with the practical questions of obtaining the financial backing and necessary official permission to carry out research. It is therefore concerned with convincing those in positions of power either to provide the funds for the research or to use their influence to obtain permission for it to be carried out among a particular collectivity or in a given location. This kind of politics also includes the various manipulations, and uses of contacts and sponsors at all levels of government, to gain access to a research site or to specific individuals or particular documents. There is also the micropolitics of making contacts and having the research project accepted by participants on the ground. Politics in these forms is certainly not unique to social research but is generally a part of many kinds of social settings and relationships. However, the various political manipulations can raise serious ethical questions for researchers at all stages of the research process, from determination of the focus of research through questions of access to informants and other data sources to eventual publications. Punch (1986) provides an informative case study of the interrelationships of ethics and politics in research in which permission to study an experimental school and promises of cooperation were initially given, then withdrawn following some changes in personnel as well as disagreement about the direction his research appeared to be taking. While it is important that such activities be undertaken in accord with professional ethical standards, the various other concerns that they raise are addressed elsewhere, for example, in Chapter 2 in discussing choice of research topics and locations, as well as in chapters on research methods that discuss such concerns as selection of informants.

However, there is a broader interpretation of the questions raised by the relationship between politics and social research having to do with the relationship of researchers and research with those in positions of power, and with the ideologies of power and their influence on the policies that they develop and the practices which put those policies into effect. This section concentrates on this broader interpretation of politics. Even in this second sense, there is a fairly clear division between those concerned with the politics of social research primarily in terms of its applicability to the formation of social policy and those who argue that recognizing the significance of politics for social research means fundamentally transforming the way in which research is conducted.

Debates about the relationship between research and social policy ask whether social research can or should be directly applicable to the formation of policy and related practice or useful for its evaluation. The main question is whether specific research projects should be developed for the express purpose of answering policy-relevant questions or whether research should be concerned with more general theoretical issues, closer to so-called pure research, and simply provide a bank of research-based social knowledge on which policy makers can draw to make informed decisions. As discussed in Chapter 2, the increasing involvement of anthropologists in policy research appears to be guaranteed by the changing conditions of anthropological work, and thus an open reflexive engagement with debates about the nature of such applied research will benefit both individual practitioners and the discipline more broadly. Bulmer (1982b) discusses three models of policy research, rejecting the first two and advocating the third. In the empiricist model, researchers simply collect facts for administrators to use in their policy decisions; such a model founders on the recognition that such facts are not theoretically neutral and the approach misses all the insights social research has to offer while also risking serious distortion in its assumption that facts are unproblematic. In the engineering model, policy makers supply specific questions and researchers carry out the research and make recommendations. The problem with this model is that such precise formulation of questions tends to foreclose the possible answers, basically restricting the research to choosing between a few known options, a choice that might well be better made on the basis of practitioner knowledge rather than social research. In any case this model essentially eliminates a central component of research, its ability to surprise, to produce unexpected findings. Bulmer's third model, the enlightenment model, sees the purpose of social research as providing alternative possibilities and enlightening policy makers through their interaction with researchers and exposure to new perspectives. Hammersley basically agrees with this perspective, arguing that research should be of 'general rather than specific relevance' (1992: 131–2). He further argues that social research is essentially a collective process, rather than a matter of individual problem-solving, in the sense that research is submitted to a broader professional community for critical scrutiny and development. Thus, the time scale of social research precludes its applicability to the short-term goals of policy makers.

As appealing as this enlightenment model might be in terms of its holding out for a development of social research in an independent intellectual mode, it faces some serious drawbacks as a definitive approach to policy research. In the first place, it is impractical and naive to imagine that policy makers are likely to have the time, resources or inclination to consult the findings and professional debates growing out of research that is of potential relevance for their concerns. At the very least, researchers must be ready to bring relevant points to their attention, in an accessible format and non-technical language. In reality researchers are much more likely to have some input into policy formation when they do research directed towards particular policy issues and, usually therefore, sponsored by organizations involved in making and implementing social policy. However imperfect this approach to social research may be, it is arguably better when undertaken by those who have professional training and broader research experience than by specialist researchers internal to the organizations. It could be argued that it is only through such links that the enlightenment available through generalized social research can be brought into the public policy arena. And some will even argue that such policy research will produce more robust conclusions because it is more likely to be interdisciplinary and multimethod and because it has to face up to the immediate rigorous testing of its recommendations by implementation in policy and practice (Hakim 1987).

Okely's (1987) experiences in carrying out policy research on traveller Gypsies in Britain are instructive as a warning about difficulties and drawbacks as well as exemplary of the positive reasons and features of undertaking such research. She notes that at the time of the research, in the early 1970s, few anthropologists were involved in policy research and she had constantly to argue the case for the use of more open ethnographic methods, in particular participant observation. It should be noted that, although ethnography has become a relatively favoured form of research since then, anthropologists are still not as engaged in policy research as are those from other social disciplines, perhaps partly due to a continuing reluctance about altering 'its conventional objects of study and developing new domains and methods of enquiry that are commensurate with the new subjects and social forces that are emerging in the contemporary world' (Ahmed and Shore 1995: 15–16). On the other hand, Okely was able to vindicate her use of ethnographic fieldwork through the quality of the data she produced and their capacity to explain, for example, travellers' resistance to social provisions that involved their permanent settlement. Furthermore, this was accomplished in spite of the fact that 'the Gypsy project was only supported in the upper echelons of the research centre because it was sincerely believed that a policy of assimilation into the majority society was the inevitable outcome' (1987: 62). As this latter point indicates, it is possible to produce findings that do not simply confirm the expectations of sponsors in policy research. However, such an outcome requires a willingness to search out and challenge these expectations and the researcher will not always succeed in obtaining a hearing. Okely notes that her research report finally reached policy advisers by a circuitous route, and further that 'it remains largely unread by racist councillors and journalists who have vested interests in stereotypes and myths' (ibid.: 64); furthermore, some subsequent conflicts over ownership of data put individual informants at potential risk. A final unexpected indirect advantage of undertaking such policy research is the opportunity it may provide to study up, to study the policy makers as well as those who are the objects of such policies. Okely, for example, found that through reading local government reports on traveller Gypsies, she 'gained significant insights into non-Gypsy classifications of Gypsies and attitudes which guided the dominant society's policies' (ibid.: 69).

These considerations introduce another critique of the enlightenment model of applied social research, namely, that it is politically naive to ignore the influence of the politics and values of the broader social institutions within which researchers are located on every aspect of their research, from selection of problems to analysis and writing up. In this view, research cannot be value neutral any more than it can be theory neutral and, furthermore, the vast majority of research that does not have an explicit value commitment does in fact have an implicit value orientation and political position in support of the status quo of existing power relationships. This critique has been developed from various perspectives, among them in the work of Habermas (1971), who argues that there are three forms of social enquiry: one based on a natural science model (empirical–analytic); one found in history and interpretative sociology (historical–hermeneutic); and critical theory. Critical theory, which is regarded as the only valid form of social enquiry, is research that is grounded in a concern to overcome social oppression, particularly those forms that are characteristic of advanced capitalism. Thus the only way to produce valid knowledge through social research is through engagement with struggles against oppression.

Feminist critiques of social research have developed a similar position regarding the researcher's political engagement with the subjects of research and their experience of oppression, but this epistemological critique concentrates on the distortions introduced by the gendered nature of knowledge about the social world. As was discussed in Chapter 2, the initial feminist objection to the absence of women from social research developed into a much more fundamental set of challenges to the methodological – and epistemological – bases of such research. Thus it was argued that the basic theoretical categories and perspectives within which social research has been conducted, while treated as universally valid, are actually partial and present a male perspective as if it were objective truth. Various feminist epistemologies responded in different ways to this critique (Harding 1987). Among the most influential and relevant for our considerations of the relationship between research and politics is that of feminist standpoint theory, which has its fullest expression in the work of Dorothy Smith (1987, 1988). Smith argues that there has been a total discordancy between the everyday world of material existence and theorizing about the social world, with women inhabiting the former and mediating for men between it and the conceptual world that men create and inhabit. This women's world is not accommodated in male theorizing about the social world because of its status as not only separate but subordinate to the conceptual world created by men. Research undertaken from this subservient perspective will of necessity fundamentally alter theoretical understandings of the social world. Such an altered perspective will also be a truer one, because it incorporates awareness of the dominant perspective as a condition of its survival, whereas the dominant perspective remains completely unaware of the other and in fact imagines itself to be universal and absolute truth. However, this altered perspective is not available to a researcher simply because she happens to be a woman or to belong to an oppressed category. Rather than being ascribed as a product of a particular social position, such a perspective must be achieved in the process of struggle against such oppression. Hence research methodology is intertwined with politics, with the validity of its findings dependent in part on the political position and experiences of the researcher.

A major difficulty faced by feminist standpoint theory is the question of which subaltern position provides the clearest vision. This question became particularly acute not simply in terms of theory but also in practical political terms with the fragmentation of the movement in the late 1970s under the criticisms of black women and lesbian women that the movement really only represented the concerns of white, middle-class heterosexual women. Thus one of the major difficulties faced by this methodological perspective in the end is the question of which standpoint to privilege. Smith makes clear that she eschews both a total relativism and a complete subjectivism. However, some feminists have tended to move towards a postmodern denial of the possibility of making an informed choice between possible viewpoints. Such a move can be seen as the next logical step in the feminist critique in that there are numerous convergences between it and postmodernism (Farganis 1994), convergences which centre around postmodern criticisms of all universalizing positions and meta-narratives and reject the privileging of any one discourse over another. Nevertheless the political roots of the feminist critique distinguish it and ultimately make it incompatible with the extreme relativist position, which, by making all voices equally valid or invalid, erases difference 'implying that all stories are really about one experience: the decentering and fragmentation that is the current experience of Western white males' (Mascia-Lees, Sharpe and Cohen 1989: 29; see Chapter 12 for a further discussion of these issues).

Such a perspective on politically grounded research has numerous implications and raises some important questions. In the first place, it raises the question of who can do research on oppressed groups in the sense of what constitutes political experience of resistance to such oppression. As already noted, simply being a female researcher does not necessarily produce feminist research. Motzafi-Haller (1997) makes a similar point with respect to so-called native ethnography, arguing that the anthropologist from a non-Western society has neither an inherent sense of oppression nor a greater moral right to carry out ethnographic research on that society. 'I find little use in this kind of argument, not only because it opens itself to charges of the purity of the essentialized identity of the writer. ("How native are you, Smadar?" And what about class and other defining criteria that make the writer a "representative" of the "oppressed"?)' (ibid.: 214–15). Rather, she argues that it is the combination of experiencing some form of oppression and becoming conscious of it in ways that also inform research which has the capacity to produce politically engaged and socially relevant research. Such political engagement, it is argued from a feminist epistemological position, also provides 'a ground for reclaiming objectivity for our enterprise while at the same time recognizing the partiality of truth claims' (Mascia-Lees, Sharpe and Cohen 1989: 28). A similar argument, inspired largely by feminist epistemology, has been advanced in respect to disability research, in which researchers are urged to develop an emancipatory research paradigm based on the experiences of people with disabilities that facilitates their attempts at self-empowerment and responds to their research agenda – as, for example, in directing research attention to 'institutional disabilism' (Oliver 1992: 112). It is worth noting that the criticism of research that does not make its political commitment explicit is not restricted to traditional ethnographic methods; for example, in a critique of the kind of official statistics that have been collected on people with disabilities, Abberley argues that they continue to fail to recognize social models of disability and notes that 'information gathered on the basis of an oppressive theory, unless handled with circumspection, is itself one of the mechanisms of oppression' (1996: 182–3).

The implications of such politically committed research are a narrowing of the gap between researcher and research subjects in that research is undertaken from an examined perspective in cooperation with the members of an oppressed category. Such a perspective encourages, indeed requires, the reflexivity that I have argued is an unavoidable and, when properly employed, a beneficial part of social research, without descending into total self-absorption. It also clearly emphasizes the view from below, although this often entails researching up – that is, researching the powerful – and it implies involvement of the research subjects in the research process at all stages from selection of research problems through analysis to final product (cf. Mies 1993 [1983]; Papadakis 1989).

Part II
In the field

Chapter 4

Observing, participating

Participant observation is usually taken as the archetypal form of research employed by ethnographers. It is more properly conceived of as a research strategy than a unitary research method in that it is always made up of a variety of methods. In its classic form participant observation consists of a single researcher spending an extended period of time (usually at least a year) living among the people he or she is studying, participating in their daily lives in order to gain as complete an understanding as possible of the cultural meanings and social structures of the group and how these are interrelated. Clearly such a goal seems more readily achievable if the group selected for study is small and relatively isolated. Stereotypically, members of 'simple' societies, in the sense of being preliterate and having a subsistence economy, have been favoured subjects and many classical ethnographic studies deal with subjects of this nature (e.g. Evans-Pritchard 1940; Firth 1936; Malinowski 1922; Mead 1943; Turnbull 1961). However, participant observation has also been widely employed for community studies in complex industrial societies. Most commonly, the communities selected have either been rural backwaters, usually with a peasant economy (e.g. Arensberg and Kimball 1940; Friedl 1962), or urban ghetto communities, often with a distinctive cultural identity (e.g. Gans 1962; Whyte 1955). Furthermore, a somewhat modified participant observation has frequently been used for studies in institutional settings, such as schools, hospitals or prisons, in complex societies (e.g. Goffman 1961; Myerhoff 1978).

Participant observation became, and to a large extent remains, the hallmark of anthropology (but see Chapter 2). Even more than a distinctive body of knowledge, and certainly more than any theoretical position, participant observation carried out among a culturally alien community became to outsiders the distinguishing characteristic of the field that in some quarters produced a romantic, even heroic, image (Sontag 1966). And to anthropologists themselves it became virtually a rite of passage: without experiencing the trials of this sort of fieldwork, one could not really become an anthropologist (Stocking 1983b). Because of this centrality of a particular sort of research experience, it has been suggested that participant observation became 'the legitimizing basis for anthropology's claim to special cognitive authority' (ibid.: 8). Another version of this tendency to accord legitimacy on the basis of participant observation may be seen in Geertz's (1988) analysis of the varying textual resources which classic ethnographers have used to establish that they had really 'been there'.

Nevertheless, participant observation has not always been the chosen research strategy of anthropologists. Anthropology emerged as a recognizable field of study towards the middle of the nineteenth century with the creation in Europe and America of various ethnological societies. The formation of these societies had been stimulated by discoveries consequent upon colonial expansion and their main intellectual objective was to collect information about the other cultures and 'races' which were being brought into Euro-American consciousness in such astonishing numbers and varieties. The orientation of this interest was very similar to that of the natural historian. Thus the emphasis was on collecting and cataloguing, and the theoretical orientation was comparative, either to trace historical diffusion of specific customs and institutions (e.g. Rivers 1914) or to establish the evolutionary course of various social and cultural forms, as in the work of the nineteenth-century theorists Lewis Henry Morgan and Sir J. G. Frazer. Initially, the main method employed was the questionnaire which was designed to direct the observations of amateurs on the ground (colonial administrators, traders, missionaries) so as to obtain data that could be analysed by the armchair ethnologist back in the colonial centres. Given the natural science ethos, as well as the scientific background of many early ethnologists, this approach was replaced towards the end of the century by the survey expedition. On such expeditions the ethnologists themselves collected their own data about the peoples and cultures of the area being surveyed; their investigations were normally guided by predetermined sets of questions, with the best known of these, *Notes and Queries on Anthropology*, being developed under the auspices of the British Association for the Advancement of Science and appearing in six editions between 1874 and 1951 (Urry

1984). These experiences produced a growing dissatisfaction with the superficiality of the information that could be obtained through survey techniques and the increasing emphasis on what was called intensive study can be seen in the content of subsequent editions, going from lists of simple questions to relatively lengthy articles on such things as the importance of obtaining as full a knowledge of the native language as possible (Stocking 1983a).

This development towards more intensive and long-term involvement with peoples being studied was transformed in the early decades of the twentieth century into the fieldwork based on long-term participant observation that has become so intrinsic a part of the making of professional anthropologists. The transformation in research methods is associated primarily with the work of two men, Bronislaw Malinowski in Britain and Franz Boas in America, and their students. The emphasis was somewhat different in the two areas, but they shared some theoretical orientations and motivations for advocating this form of research. Both had come to recognize the complexity of the so-called 'primitive' and to link this with both an attack on cultural evolutionism and a deep and genuine (if sometimes naive and unreflective) opposition to ethnocentrism (Benthall 1995: 9). Furthermore, both were concerned to recognize and include in their analyses the interconnectedness of each individual society's cultural forms and social structures; in British social anthropology, this came to be expressed theoretically by Radcliffe-Brown's structural functionalism; in American anthropology, its fullest expression took the form of an interest in culture complexes.

Malinowski, and his students even more so, put very great emphasis on living among the people they studied. The purpose of this daily contact was to enable them to collect concrete evidence about their subjects' lives. Particular emphasis was placed upon a census (often the first task ethnographers set themselves) as well as on technologies; the concern with kinship was due more to the subsequent influence of Radcliffe-Brown. Furthermore, these living arrangements allowed them to observe at first hand the minute and superficially insignificant details of everyday living. Great emphasis was also placed on the acquisition of competence in the native language in order to understand the perspective of peoples being studied. The American experience was rather different, due in part to their somewhat different relationship to colonial expansion (cf. Asad 1973b). In the first half of the twentieth century, the colonized peoples most accessible to American anthropologists, both in terms of distance and research funding, were American Indians. Their societies were regarded as being in disarray and their cultures were considered corrupted by the nature of the American conquest, hence anthropologists tended to place a greater emphasis on the recording of native texts and on intensive work with a few informants who could assist them to reconstruct life ways prior to white contact. Clearly, given this interest, especially in native texts, there was a great emphasis on language, not simply as a medium of communication, but as itself containing cultural meanings. Some American anthropologists, Margaret Mead among them, were more heavily influenced by the British school of social anthropology and as a consequence placed a greater emphasis on that fieldwork model, in particular living among the people being studied. In the decades after World War II, America's emergence as a world power greatly expanded the possible fieldwork sites for American anthropologists, and the model of long-term participant observation by an individual anthropologist in a single fieldwork site became virtually universal.

Another tradition of participant observation in social research was that developed by Robert Park and his associates at the Chicago School in the 1920s and 1930s. This tradition has influenced and been influenced by anthropologists, an early example being Robert Redfield. There, researchers were urged to use the city as a social laboratory. They tended to concentrate on particular and fairly readily distinguished subcultural groups in the city, for example hobos and street gangs. They tried to study and present the perspective of the social actors, making use of a range of methods from participation through recording of life histories and collection of documentary evidence like court records and newspapers. There are some clear differences in this form of participant observation – researchers are to some degree already a part of the native culture, they share a common language and have access to a wider range of sources of information. In some situations, effective research can be carried out over a shorter period of time. Usually the interaction is neither as intensive (the ethnographer is not as isolated) nor sustained over as long a period.

Nevertheless, it is worth noting that all three of these sources for the development of participant observation as a style of social research had a positivist orientation in their basic assumptions. All assumed that there were social facts to be discovered and a major concern was to reduce any distortion that might be introduced by the presence of the ethnographer. The familiarity with the ethnographer generated by long-term participant observation was believed to help accomplish this. At the same time, ethnographers were warned against the dangers of 'going native', since such over-involvement would jeopardize their ability to analyse or even to notice native cultural assumptions. The claims to such objectivity came to be presented more in terms of the style of classical ethnographies than in actual fieldwork practices, which were seldom discussed, and almost never written about. This style was one in which the distanced observer was in fact made invisible in the text, while the activities of people were presented in terms of rule-following behaviour with consequent neglect of emotions and individualistic behaviour and attitudes (Rosaldo 1993 [1989]). This foundation in relatively unexamined positivist assumptions left ethnographic practice quite vulnerable to the critiques initially from the hermeneutic tradition and subsequently from feminists and various poststructuralist and postmodernist perspectives. As a consequence of these critiques, the expected role of the ethnographer has been transformed so that reflexive considerations are central to practice and analysis.

The hallmark of participant observation is long-term personal involvement with those being studied, including participation in their lives to the extent that the researcher comes to understand the culture as an insider. However, participant observation consists of a cluster of techniques and the researcher chooses those that are most fruitful in the given situation. In point of fact, participation is almost certainly not the major data-gathering technique. Rather, participation in the everyday lives of people is a means of facilitating observation of particular behaviours and events and of enabling more open and meaningful discussions with informants. Without ethnographers' participation as some kind of member of the society, they might not be allowed to observe or would simply not know what to observe or how to go about it. In addition, even over the course of a year or more, it is not possible to observe everything of interest. So ethnographers virtually always develop key informants, individuals who for various reasons are either very effective at relating cultural practices or simply more willing than most to take the time to do so. Thus a great deal of use is made of unstructured interviewing, a conversation in which the researcher still has particular questions or direction of inquiry in mind. In addition, participant observers may collect life histories, do surveys, take photographs and videos, and so forth.

Many of these particular research methods I will consider more fully in subsequent chapters in that they are not unique to participant observation. However, in the remainder of this chapter, I want to look at several issues and practices that are either unique or particularly central to participant observation, namely: the balance of observation and participation and their respective roles; the importance of language; the selection and significance of key informants; and some of the practical difficulties of doing participant observation. I will conclude by considering criticisms of participant observation regarding its reliability, validity and generalizability.

Participating or (mainly) observing?

The expression 'participant observation' may appear oxymoronic, in that the two activities, or the roles they suggest, cannot be pursued simultaneously. Gold (1958) has suggested that in fieldwork the ethnographer may adopt one of four possible roles: complete observer; observer-as-participant; participant-as-observer; or complete participant. These four roles are sometimes conceived as if on a scale measuring degree of acceptance by the people being studied, gradually achieved in the course of long-term fieldwork. Whyte (1955), in his study of an urban Italian neighbourhood in Boston, said that he moved from complete observer (and also a virtually complete outsider) who could not understand the significance of the social relationships of those around him to complete participant when he became involved in a political campaign, and crowned the experience by 'repeating', voting more than once under assumed identities in the election (ibid.: 309–17). While it is certainly true that opportunities to participate will normally increase as ethnographers develop a social network within their research sites, it is fallacious to take participation as the only, or even the principal, measure of the success of the research. In fact, the degree of participation may be abnormally high at the onset of fieldwork as people attempt to find out who these researchers are and why they are there, then fall off as they become more a part of everyday life, no longer a curiosity, and finally increase again (although not to the frenetic level of the introductory period) but be of a very different quality in that the ethnographers are involved with particular informants whom they have come to know well as assistants and sometimes as friends. Rabinow, in his reflections on the relationship between these two aspects of ethnographic fieldwork, provides a more useful and realistic spiral, rather than linear, model.

> Observation ... is the governing term in the pair, since it situates the anthropologists' activities. However much one moves in the direction of participation, it is always the case that one is still both an outsider and an observer ... In the dialectic between the poles of observation and participation, participation changes the anthropologist and leads him to new observation, whereupon new observation changes how he participates. But this dialectical spiral is governed in its motion by the starting point, which is observation.
>
> (Rabinow 1977: 79–80)

Whereas anthropologists have frequently placed the greatest emphasis on their level of participation as an indication of the quality of their research, in particular suggesting that participation shows the ethnographer has been fully accepted and hence the degree of reactivity (the degree to which research findings were influenced by the ethnographer) is very slight, I want to argue that the more important indication of good research is the nature, circumstances and quality of the observation. Such observation must also include reflexive observation – that is, the ethnographer needs to be sensitive to the nature of, and conditions governing, their own participation as a part of their developing understanding of the people they study. Complete participation, even when the researcher's identity is disguised, is not a guarantee that the researcher is not unduly influencing the data. For example, the study *When Prophecy Fails* (Festinger, Riecken and Schachter 1956) of the disconfirmation of belief looked at a religious sect predicting the imminent end of the world; the method used was infiltration of the group by researchers pretending to be converts. Leaving aside temporarily the ethical questions this raises, the sudden appearance of several new converts not recruited through existing members' social networks must have had a powerful confirmatory influence on members' beliefs and probably strengthened the group's solidarity as it approached the prophesied date. Thus the researchers' presence, even though they were unacknowledged in that role, was likely to distort their observations. On the other hand, the presence of a researcher in a large public spectacle or religious ceremony may represent the same level of participation as experienced by most of the audience, yet the quality of observation is unlikely to be very high unless the ethnographer has previously discussed meanings and interpretations with informants which can help to guide observations and lead to more informative questions subsequently.

Thus the tendency of both ethnographers and readers of ethnography to evaluate the quality, and validity, of ethnographic findings on the degree of participation which an ethnographer is able to achieve is unfortunate. A more useful guide is the way in which ethnographers ground their observations in critical reflection on the nature of their participation and its suitability to the particular research circumstances, and the relationship between researcher and subjects. A sensitive study based primarily on observation is certainly preferable to one in which participation is forced and self-aggrandizing. Consider, for example, the ethnographic study of people with 'severe and profound mental and physical handicaps and multiple handicaps' undertaken by Gleason (1989), who spent approximately 15 months in two periods of intensive observation in the living areas of three residential homes. He describes the kinds of observations he made and some of the considerations that structured them:

> I adjusted to the sights and sounds of the residents, attempting to interpret their movements, actions, giggles, gurgles, waves, and handshakes. I was interested in residents' response to the cycles of the day as well as to different individuals. I watched resident reaction to different members of the staff for contrasts and differences in the context of their interactions.
>
> ... I watched interaction among residents. I was interested in the touching, holding, playing, or mirroring one another's rhythmic sounds in their vocalizations and movements. I watched and listened to the direct care staff. I was interested in their casual comments, which indicated how they interpreted a particular situation.
>
> (Ibid.: 4)

Thus Gleason was prompted to pay attention to a particular toy, a Fisher-Price lawn mower, by attendants' comments that it is a 'favourite toy' of one of the boys and that they will 'kill' for it. Although staff are aware of the importance of the toy to two of the boys in their care, Gleason's observations allow him to interpret its significance differently and imbue it with a very different meaning.

He describes a play event lasting over two hours in which the boys, lying on mats next to one another, initiate a series of interactions using the lawn mower to attract one another's attention and to engage in a sort of friendly combat. In the midst of this, a staff attendant, seeing that one of the boys has rolled into the aisle and completely unaware of the reasons for it, moves him to another mat at the opposite end of the room. There then ensues a series of movements in which the two boys, only able to inch themselves along the floor, finally manage to resume their interaction lying head-to-toe with the lawn mower between them. In his second period of research, Gleason observes the introduction of a new programme in which developmental skills such as social interaction and communication are deliberately taught. In particular, he describes a socialization class in which the same two boys are being taught to work together in a way determined by the teacher. From previous observation, he recognizes their attempts both to resist some of the activities mandated as cooperative play by the teacher and to reestablish their normal play activities during brief breaks. 'The teacher focuses on their explicit behaviour in the context of the lesson, and misses the underlying meaning implicit in how they perform' (ibid.: 135).

It could be argued that had Gleason chosen fuller participation, as a member of staff for example, he might well never have recognized the extent and nature of the social interactions going on between residents because he would have been too fully involved in the considerations of the staff and their relationships with residents. In this instance, less participation, but more open, long-term and patient observation, allowed the development of a greater insight and better understanding of the social position and perspective of residents.

In a contrasting study, in which participation is central to the research, Kondo (1990) describes how she went to Japan with the intention of studying kinship and economics in the context of family-owned businesses. Her initial social structural orientation was transformed by her fieldwork experiences into a focus on 'what I perceived to be even more basic cultural assumptions: how *selfhood* is constructed in the arenas of company and family' (ibid.: 9). One of the main reasons for this shift in her research interests was her direct experience of having her own self as a Japanese-American woman and a researcher remade into an acceptable Japanese self, a reconstruction in which she almost inadvertently colluded with her informants. This transformation of self was so successful that it provided the principal means through which she developed her understanding of self and the social world in these Japanese workplaces. At the same time, she experienced it as a fragmentation of her identity and it produced quite considerable internal conflict: 'I became "the Other" in my own mind' (ibid.: 16). On two occasions she left the field fearing a collapse of her American professional identity: once when she did not recognize her own reflection while out shopping, seeing instead 'a typical young housewife, clad in slip-on sandals and the loose, cotton shift called "home wear" *(homu wea)*, a woman walking with a characteristically Japanese bend to the knees and a sliding of the feet' (ibid.: 16–17); and a second time after being praised for performing the tea ceremony flawlessly, not like the awkward American she had been on arrival (ibid.: 23). Through her own experiences of crafting a Japanese self, she developed her understanding of the power relations and how they operated within the context of family and workplace.

> We participated in each other's lives and sought to make sense of one another. In that attempt to understand, power inevitably came into play as we tried to force each other into appropriately comprehensible categories ... The sites of these struggles for understanding were located in what we might call salient features of 'identity' both in America and in Japan: race, gender, and age.
>
> (Ibid.: 10–11)

Thus the near complete participation that Kondo adopted in her research was essential to the kind of understanding and explanations she develops of a particular nexus of power and personal identities in Japanese society. Her participation, far from being superficially displayed to support the validity of findings, is an integral part of both her data and analysis.

In Passaro's (1996) research on homelessness – a study whose methods challenge the classical assumption of the field as a unitary bounded site – the approach to this issue of the balance between participation and observation is similar to the one I advocate in that she treats 'participation and observation as elements in dialectical tension' (ibid.: 4). Passaro resisted the considerable pressure from other anthropologists to do an ethnography of a well-defined group, such as a homeless shelter, or to focus theoretically on the discovery of a subculture of homeless people (1997: 148–52). Instead she carried out a multi-sited ethnography over a range of locations that required different levels of participation and observation, from volunteering at emergency shelters to observing at meetings and demonstrations, thus treating participation and observation as lying at either end of a continuum with their actualization contingent on specific research circumstances and liable to vary significantly even within a single study.

Language

Learning the language of the people being studied has been one of the main common emphases of both of the major schools of ethnographic fieldwork. Malinowski was a talented linguist and stressed learning the language as an important insight into 'native mentality'; most of his students adopted a more pragmatic approach to language, seeing it primarily as a tool for collecting data rather than of any intrinsic interest. Boas put great stress on language and native texts, and most of his students had at least basic training in linguistics (Urry 1984: 50–1, 55–6). Certainly, speaking the native language is part of the anthropological mystique associated with ethnographic fieldwork. And there are very good reasons for this stress on language. 'One of the most profoundly transforming experiences a person can have is learning another language' (Becker 1991: 226). For the ethnographer attempting to understand another social world, the process of learning the language in which that world is lived out is fundamentally insightful. Working entirely through translators, an ethnographer is tied to processes of encoding and decoding that inevitably leave out much of the meaning that utterances carry for native speakers (see Chapter 5). This is not primarily because concepts in one language cannot be fully explicated in another, but rather that they will not be – the process would be too cumbersome and time consuming – so much of what is taken for granted by native speakers is omitted or explained so superficially as to appear meaningless. In the process of learning another language, ethnographers enter 'another history of interactions'; initially this means that they face 'what is basically a problem of memory' (ibid.: 230), a collective memory. And much of the process of learning the language is linked to building up a set of shared cultural memories.

Thus the importance of language cannot really be over-emphasized, and ideally instruction should begin quite some time before going into the field. Nevertheless practical considerations, in particular time constraints, often mean that ethnographers must do the best they can with a somewhat lower linguistic competence than is ideal (Tonkin 1984) – although not attempting to learn the local language is totally unacceptable in ethnographic research. Mead (1939) was one of the first to suggest that language competence did not have to reach total mastery for effective fieldwork, but that being able to follow everyday conversation and ask basic questions was sufficient for many research purposes. The process of language acquisition in the field does not necessarily have to be time taken from the actual research. At the very least, it helps to establish rapport and provides a reason to interact with people. And experiences in language learning can become important data (cf. Kondo 1990). When I began fieldwork in Wales, doing research on ethnic nationalism, I found learning Welsh to be an invaluable experience, in spite of the fact that all my informants also spoke English. In addition to the changing character of my relationships with Welsh speakers as my fluency increased, and the opening to me (both in terms of awareness and access) of a variety of political and social occasions, I also came to understand much more directly my informants' expressed feelings about their language and its relationship to various aspects of political and cultural activism (cf. McDonald 1989 for a rather different set of experiences in learning Breton). Occasionally it is necessary to work through a third language, or a pidgin, that is not native to either ethnographer or informant. This seemingly most undesirable situation can be turned to advantage if it heightens the sensitivity of both partners to the ways in which translation is affecting how they interact and what they say, so that they make greater efforts than in normal conversation to explicate meanings and discuss possible misinterpretations.

Choosing informants – and being chosen

Ethnographic research is based in and depends upon social interaction. Such interaction takes place between specific individuals, however much it may be interpreted in more general collective or structural terms. A major part of the interaction will be between the ethnographer and other individuals, and much of this will be verbal, whether informal conversations or more directed attempts to gain information through questioning and interviews. Thus informants are of central importance to any study. Their social identities will influence the ethnographer's access to others, opening some doors and firmly closing others. And their cultural knowledge is the basis on which ethnographers build an understanding of the peoples and societies they study. In classical anthropological studies this was often interpreted as finding individuals in particular roles that meant they could speak with authority about specific aspects of their society (e.g. priests about religious beliefs, headmen about political power). More recent perspectives resist any such uniformist understanding of the nature of culture and suggest that the information provided by informants must be understood in the light of their particular set of relationships within their society and taken as indicative of its characteristics rather than as representative.

Thus, clearly, selection of informants is of critical significance for the ethnographic researcher. In participant observation, the ethnographer will normally interact with many different individuals. Like most human interactions some of these will be very brief, superficial or highly focused on a particular type of relationship or activity. Others will be much more diffuse, covering a broad range of interests and activities. In many studies, a single key informant may be so important to the conduct of the research that their contribution is clearly predominant in the analysis (e.g. Casagrande 1960; Liebow 1967; Whyte 1955) which may even tend towards a form of biographical interpretation (e.g. Crapanzano 1985; Shostak 1990 [1981]; see Chapter 9).

In spite of the very critical importance of informants, especially key informants, the process of selecting them is not a one-way procedure. Ethnographers should continually bear in mind the requirements of the research and seek out and evaluate informants in this light. Nevertheless, they are often as much selected by their informants as the reverse. Selection of informants depends upon factors such as their accessibility and willingness to assist in the research, as well as their knowledge and insight and their skill at understanding ethnographic queries. The process of working with informants thus becomes one of a mutual search for understanding that bridges, or mediates, between the social worlds of informant and ethnographer. In order for ethnographers sensitively to interpret this interaction, they must develop a reflexive understanding of their relationship with their informants. The information provided is affected by the positions of both ethnographer and informant within their own social worlds, as well as by their evolving personal relationship and understanding of one another's social worlds. Thus ethnographers must interrogate and explore not just the information being obtained but also the social dynamics that lead to certain individuals becoming central to their study and others not.

It has frequently been noted that good informants are often 'marginal' in some respects in their own society (cf. Rabinow 1977: 73–5). Probably the main reason why this particular characteristic is so common among those who become key informants is that it places them in a position not dissimilar to that of the ethnographer as a kind of outsider who thus becomes more aware of the assumptions and expectations of their own society, often because they flaunt them or fail to fulfil them. The process of working with an ethnographer further develops and enhances this reflexive capacity. Thus Rabinow says of his key informant:

> This highlighting, identification, and analysis also disturbed Ali's usual patterns of experience. He was constantly being forced to reflect on his own activities and objectify them. Because he was a good informant, he seemed to enjoy this process and soon began to develop an art of presenting his world to me. The better he became at it, the more we shared together. But the more we engaged in such activity, the more he experienced aspects of his own life in new ways. Under my systematic questioning, Ali was taking realms of his own world and interpreting them for an outsider. This meant that he, too, was spending more time in this liminal, self-conscious world between cultures.
>
> (Rabinow 1977: 38–9)

Duneier's (1999) ethnography of sidewalk vendors in New York's Greenwich Village was made possible in the first instance and facilitated throughout by his striking up an acquaintance with Hakim, one of the vendors whose stand Duneier frequented. Hakim was an example of just such a 'marginal native' in that he was both erudite and had formal qualifications but had elected a life on the streets after becoming disillusioned by his employment experiences in a white corporate environment. He used his influence with other vendors to negotiate access for Duneier to carry out extensive participant observation on the stand of one of his acquaintances, a used magazine seller. He also collaborated significantly in Duneier's development of his ethnography, including reading drafts of the manuscript and co-teaching a university seminar on urban street life; and he confessed to having himself learned a great deal about street life from the research (Hasan 1999). Thus the process of fieldwork is a transforming experience for both ethnographer and informants, particularly so for key informants, and the development of understanding is a creative process in which both are engaged.

Scattered through the history of the discipline are a few key informants who, like Hakim, became collaborators in ethnographic research on their social group. Boas's relationship with his Kwakiutl informant, George Hunt, was of this kind, with Hunt carrying out interviews and corresponding with Boas over a period of years. This was also the case with Whyte's informant, Doc: 'I discussed with him quite frankly what I was trying to do, what problems were puzzling me, and so on ... so that Doc became, in a very real sense, a collaborator in the research' (Whyte 1955: 301). Nevertheless, these collaborations appear to be that of a junior partner, based on a teacher–pupil model, in contrast to the more equitable intellectual partnership that seems to pertain between Duneier and Hakim. A somewhat more common experience is the development of friendships between ethnographers and their informants. Indeed Powdermaker maintains, 'In all my fieldwork, except in Hollywood, there has been one person ... with whom I have had an exceptionally close friendship, who has helped me, more than I can say, to understand the people and their society. Each was dedicated to the project and to me. The friendships lasted whether or not we ever saw each other again. They became a permanent part of my life and, apparently, I of theirs' (1966: 261–2). In contrast, Jay (1969) argued that the degree to which ethnographic research depended upon close personal relationships rendered it inappropriate for the exploration of analytical concepts of culture or social structure. More common, and more in keeping with Powdermaker's approach, is the belief that these close personal relationships with informants enhance and deepen analysis, while helping to protect against the tendency to present others as rule-following robots.

Not all ethnographers regard close friendships in the field as possible or desirable. Geertz (1968) suggests that much of the reported emotional leave-takings of anthropologists are figments of their imaginations, necessary for both self-respect and professional standing and rest on a slim fiction regarding the possibility of cross-cultural communication. Certainly Crick (1992), while wanting to regard Ali as his friend, was too aware of the ambiguities in their relationship to feel he could confidently claim an unproblematic friendship. While they apparently developed a relationship that was mutually beneficial and emotionally satisfying, at another level,

Crick had to ask whether Ali still saw him as just another type of tourist and if indeed it made any difference since it was precisely that – the relationships between tourists and locals who exploited them – he had come to study. For others, attempts to use a friend as an informant adversely affected a friendship that predated their fieldwork (Hendry 1992). In his study of crime in London's East End, Hobbs (1988) was returning to his home area and one of his principal informants was Jacko, who was already a friend prior to undertaking the study.

> But when I finished the study, and became, in Jacko's own words 'Dr Dick the Academic Prick', I became somewhat removed from Jacko's reality. In his eyes I had made it, and while he viewed my progress with some paternal pride, my cultural bolt was shot. Eventually we entered into a business deal together and he 'did a runner' owing me a considerable sum of money.
>
> (Hobbs 1993: 47–8)

Clearly the ethnographer must be sensitive to the inevitable ambiguities in social relationships; such ambiguities inevitably mean that surface interactions are sometimes misleading and readily misinterpreted. The development of multifaceted relationships with some individuals in the field helps to sensitize ethnographers to the possibilities not simply for deliberate deception, but for mutual misunderstandings arising from cultural and sometimes personal differences. These latter may be among the most informative for analysis, particularly when the ethnographer and informants manage to uncover and move beyond them. All human relationships develop and those in the field are no exception. Thus ethnographers must continually reflect upon and reevaluate these relationships with informants, an evaluation that should include recognition of changes that the contact has induced both in others and selves. While such constant and deliberate reflection upon social relationships may appear to make the social situation overly analysed with some neglect of natural human emotions, it is really only a somewhat heightened self-consciousness about a process that, as suggested in Chapter 1, is continually under way in the production and reproduction of selves, that is, an ongoing evaluation and restructuring of self in the light of interaction with others and reflection upon that interaction.

A final point could be made regarding the question of informants who are lying. Lying is, of course, common in many social circumstances – not just during fieldwork – and lies can themselves be as useful as other kinds of information. Powdermaker argues that the lies told to her by white residents in a Mississippi community about their aristocratic planter backgrounds were significant for her understanding of their position, in particular, 'the absence of a middle-class tradition, and the white peoples' burden in carrying a tradition that did not belong to them' (1966: 186). I had a similar experience when working with young people with learning disabilities; a large number of them developed quite elaborate fantasies about romantic relationships with a staff member at the day centres they attended. I did not challenge these fantasies nor discuss them with staff, although they made occasional joking references to various current attachments. On reflection I felt that the prevalence of such fantasies indicated the extreme social deprivation and lack of autonomy with which these young people had to cope and the joking response to them was yet another indication of the social obstacles to their being accorded full adult status.

To some extent the question of the relationship of ethnographers with their informants and, in particular, the belief that these relationships should include close personal friendships among them is another version of the question of participating versus observing. The reporting of these relationships has to some extent been used to establish the validity of a study, sometimes in place of the more open reflexively based analysis which should in fact do so. The important methodological point for ethnographers is that their personal relationships with informants are a part of their data, a very fundamental basis of their analysis and, as such, cannot be glossed simply as 'close'. A relationship of very close personal friendship neither guarantees nor precludes good ethnography. It may produce excellent analysis if it also allows for an understanding of the way such friendship was developed and mediated in culturally based differences. It could also produce very bad ethnography if it degenerates into a highly individualized and particularistic account made without consideration of the processes of mediating between social and cultural differences. Furthermore, a more distanced or even hostile set of relationships may be highly informative so long as the more general social processes that can be discerned at work in such a situation are not presented as overriding the individual differences that we recognize are inherent in any social grouping. Briggs (1970) provides an example of good ethnography based on relationships which were fraught with tension and which eventually broke down entirely. The important point for good ethnography is that the relationship with one's informants is an examined one, that its input into the analysis and more general conclusions is made clear to the reader, and that the levels of analysis are transparent so that statements about general social processes, while grounded in individual relationships, are not seen as fully accounting for or explained by such relationships.

Some practical considerations

There are numerous sources of advice about preparations prior to embarking on fieldwork (e.g. Ellen 1984: 155–212). The variety of field sites and forms of participant observation that might be undertaken are so great as to make specific advice virtually impossible. The more general injunctions about intellectual preparation through familiarizing yourself with literature of all sorts about the area (not just anthropological studies, but also travel, journalistic, geographic and economic source materials) clearly holds, as does trying to commence language study prior to entry into the field. Ideally you should have acquired a level of fluency that will enable you to converse in most everyday social situations without great difficulty. The practicalities of so doing, both in terms of available time and funding and, for less widely spoken languages, of learning resources are of course a major set of stumbling blocks to the realization of this particular goal. However, you should attempt to carry it out to the furthest extent possible, and also assess the ways in which failure to do so will affect your proposed research and consider possible alternative strategies for addressing these drawbacks.

Other practical considerations that all researchers about to embark on fieldwork, particularly any long-term close involvement with another culture, should give their attention to are those that concern the personal stresses to which they are likely to be subject. It is important to remember that virtually all fieldworkers report experiencing emotional extremes, from great exhilaration to serious feelings of inadequacy and self-doubt. It will be helpful to read widely from the by now quite extensive literature on the experience of fieldwork (e.g. Bell, Caplan and Karim 1993; Hobbs and May 1993; Shaffir and Stebbins 1991). Thought should be given to how to retain contacts that will allow discussion of problems and provide an available source of advice. It is also important, if at all feasible, to develop and maintain contacts with local academics. This can provide a very helpful local perspective and one which can also link into the ethnographer's academic culture, and there are sound ethical reasons for making such academic contacts and retaining them after returning from the field.

Finally, ethnographers must be prepared to examine as honestly and carefully as possible their personal reasons for undertaking the research and their feelings about it. Many anthropologists have discussed (with hindsight) their rather inappropriately romantic reasons for going to a particular location or undertaking a specific form of research (e.g. Chagnon 1992: 10–13) which at least initially produced quite severe culture shock, with feelings of revulsion and associated guilt. Others (Powdermaker 1966) have been able to assess more honestly their own reasons for seeking out particular sorts of research experiences. In any case, it is important that researchers are aware of their own feelings towards those they research, particularly since, in this age of limited funding, fewer and fewer researchers are able to pursue research interests without regard to other considerations. This was my situation prior to undertaking research on people with learning disabilities. As I read the literature, I gradually became aware that I was in fact very uncomfortable at the prospect of interviewing such people. I had to do a considerable amount of self-questioning, calling up all recollections of prior experiences with individuals with learning disabilities, before being able to confront if not fully dispel my own unease at how they might react to me – not to mention my fear that I would not be able to understand their speech. Having gone through this process – and accepted that I probably would not understand them all and that some might well, indeed did, reject me – I was better equipped to resist the pressures others put on me, when I did go into the field, to work only with those who had good social and communication skills. In the end, some of the most rewarding interactions, both personally and in terms of research data, were with individuals whom I had dreaded having to interview (Davies 1998b).

Reliability, validity, generalizability

Ethnographic research, and most especially participant observation, has often been judged – both criticized and praised – in the light of arguments about its satisfying the three criteria of reliability, validity and generalizability. In general, it has been judged deficient as regards its reliability as well as the generalizability of its findings, while given high marks for validity. The first two concepts in this triad are particularly closely associated with measurements in the natural sciences. Reliability refers to the repeatability of research findings and their accessibility to other researchers; that is, it is concerned with whether another researcher under the same circumstances would make the same observations leading to the same set of conclusions. Validity refers to the truth or correctness of the findings. The two are clearly related, but not identical. The classic illustration used to distinguish them is that of a thermometer which consistently records the temperature of boiling water under standard atmospheric conditions as 97°C. This measurement is reliable, but not valid. Moving into the realm of social research, these two concepts are of considerable utility in the design and evaluation of social surveys. For example, it is conceivable that one might obtain very reliable (in terms of consistent) responses to questions about certain activities such as drug-taking or extra-marital sex, without such responses reflecting social behaviour (what people actually do) accurately. On the other hand, they might reflect social mores (what they think they should do) or particular conventions (what it is appropriate to reveal to strangers). Thus the validity of these results would depend on how they were interpreted and hence refers to the correctness of the theory developed to explain them. A researcher might be able to decide on the best interpretation of such survey results through getting to know the respondents better, thus being in a position to observe their behaviour, or by talking to them informally and in a less directed manner to obtain their own views and interpretations – in other words by doing some ethnographic research.

Considerations such as these are the basis for most arguments that ethnography can lay claim to greater validity than most other forms of social research. In fact, participant observation satisfies more fully most of the formal criteria for ensuring validity. It is generally argued that validity is more likely if a variety of methods are used and, as already noted, participant observation is by its nature multimethod; ethnographers in the field employ a wide range of methods from surveys to observation to interviews. Another source of validity comes from the side of participation by the ethnographer in the social context being studied; ethnographers are compelled to cope with social interactions that are, for the most part, on someone else's terms and understandings; their ability to do so, even their experience of miscommunications and misunderstandings, lends the validity of practice to their conclusions and interpretations. In fact, doubts about the validity of ethnographic research focus more on epistemological issues, in particular, questioning the degree to which ethnographers can know anything other than that which expresses their personal standpoint and experiences (see Chapter 11 for a further discussion of these issues) as well as on whether they can attain intersubjective agreement, that is reliability, and whether they can say anything of broader significance, that is the question of generalizability.

Fieldworkers must be concerned about reliability within the confines of their own research projects in the sense of continually cross-checking information they obtain and interpretations they develop. This can be accomplished by returning to the same topic, even asking the same question, under varying circumstances, and checking verbal assertions with observations. Of course reliability within the context of a given ethnographic study should not be interpreted to mean absolute consistency. Even the most homogeneous group will contain varying perspectives, and ethnographers should be aware of alternative perspectives, even those to which they may not have access, for example due to their gender (Bell 1983). Furthermore, individuals are not fully consistent and may vary their own explanations and interpretations. Such variation, if it can be explained, may be as informative as great agreement on a particular interpretation. In fact too much consistency in responses may indicate carefully rehearsed answers that are intended to conceal rather than clarify. Kirk and Miller (1986) report on just such an occurrence in their study to ascertain the kinds of knowledge of coca (a plant which is the source of cocaine) that was current among the urban lower middle class in Peru. Across representatives of a variety of occupational categories, they received very consistent answers to the effect that chewing coca leaves was an Indian vice, but that it was also used by the airlines for a tea that could prevent travel sickness. It was the very reliability, in the sense of consistency, of these answers that led them to question their validity and to suspect that they were receiving an official version of the social uses of coca. It was only by varying their approach and asking somewhat bizarre questions such as 'When would you give coca to animals?' that they began to elicit information that showed most of their informants had a wide knowledge of the various uses of coca as well as some first-hand experience of its use. Their approach, which relied on their suggesting that they already had some insider information and could therefore be given access to more, is a fairly common one in ethnographic research. It is one of the advantages that long-term residence as well as participation often gives. It is also often used to obtain additional information when informants are concerned to correct what they regard as errors or misrepresentations likely to have been supplied by others. However, it is not always an effective or acceptable approach. Bell (1983), for example, in her study of Australian Aboriginal rites, deliberately did not attempt to find out about the rituals of men because she felt this would prejudice her perspective regarding women's rituals.

I found a similar sort of artificial consistency to that discussed above in my research with young people with learning disabilities when I asked them about meanings of adulthood. In this case, they were not trying to hide information, but it soon became clear that their responses were drawn primarily from their having been told or deliberately taught by social services personnel that they were adults, and not from any other discussions about, or lifestyle indications of, adult status. 'Kids, we're not!' proclaimed one of the young women in the words of a song the unit she attended had developed. That this was an unexamined and unsupported assertion of adulthood became clear in subsequent discussions of meanings of adulthood and participation in activities that are commonly taken as markers of social adulthood. Thus clearly ethnographers must treat reliability within their fieldwork experiences with considerable circumspection, and not as a desirable end in itself.

The other place to look for reliability in ethnographic research is between ethnographers. However, given the inherently high reflexivity of ethnographic fieldwork, it is important to begin by recognizing that no ethnographic study is repeatable, either by another ethnographer or even by the same ethnographer at another time. On the other hand, I have argued for acceptance of the public and shared nature of ethnographic knowledge. As such we should be able to expect, if not complete consistency between an ethnographic study and a so-called restudy, at least a degree of overlap or agreement, and, where there is disagreement, a reinterpretation in the light of the reflexive components of the two studies that either allows for a more comprehensive understanding or a way of selecting between them, rejecting one and favouring the other. Certainly the best known example of a controversy stemming from an ethnographic restudy is that surrounding Freeman's (1983) restudy of Samoa in which he attempted to refute and discredit Mead's classic study of adolescence, *Coming of Age in Samoa* (1943 [1928]). Freeman argued that Mead was so concerned to demonstrate her theoretical position – that adolescence was not universally a difficult transition but was made so in American society mainly because of repressive attitudes towards sexuality – that she was misled by her informants who were mainly girls and young women. On the other hand, Freeman's main motivation in his attack on Mead was to support his own particular theoretical perspective rooted in sociobiological anthropology, particularly the greater determinative force of genetic inheritance over culture on human behaviour (Harris 1983; Marcus 1983; Turnbull 1983).

Another restudy of Samoa, undertaken by Lowell Holmes, predated Freeman's work but was available only as a PhD thesis and hence did not attract the same kind of interest. Nevertheless, it provides a much better example of how reliability can be sought in different ethnographic accounts, while still allowing for reflexive differences, and how informed choices can be made as to the better interpretation. This study and Holmes's subsequent research in Samoa spanning 35 years was the basis for an assessment of the Mead–Freeman controversy that provides a balanced approach to the question of reliability. Holmes notes that what prompted his restudy was the recognition of the methodological difficulties Mead faced as 'a twenty-three-year-old woman investigating a male-dominated society that venerates age' (Holmes and Holmes 1992: 139). Thus the ways in which the ethnographer affects the study are given fuller consideration, recognizing that it may produce perspectives that are not so much incorrect as partial. He discusses differences in their findings – noting that he found plenty of evidence (in the form of illegitimate children and claims of adultery) for considerable sexual activity, although he still disagrees with the degree of sexual freedom that Mead attributed to the Samoans. On the other hand, he found even less evidence to support Freeman's depiction of extreme sexual prudery. Furthermore, he notes the considerable difficulties he faced in investigating sexual matters in the face of opposition from the London Missionary Society church and accepts that 'Mead was better able to identify with, and therefore establish rapport with, adolescents and young adults on issues of sexuality than either I (at age 29, married with a wife and child) or Freeman, ten years my senior' (Holmes and Holmes 1992: 143). Thus in Holmes's evaluation, Mead's analysis included errors, overstatements and misinterpretations which he is able to correct and improve upon, yet he agrees with her central conclusion regarding the differences between Samoan and American adolescence and argues that her characterization is more valid than that of Freeman. Certainly Freeman's uncritical use of the assertion by one of Mead's informants that she had lied to her without ever considering the very considerable motivation for lying to him suggests a much more questionable lack of reflexively based knowledge than is required for good ethnographic research.

Other examples of classic restudies are Redfield's and Lewis's very different interpretations of the Mexican village they both studied (Redfield 1930; Lewis 1970 [1953]). This again appears to be an instance of too great a commitment to a particular hypothesis (in this case, Redfield's folk-urban continuum) to the point that it was overly directive regarding the data that were collected. As Lewis was to observe:

> [T]he concept of the folk culture and folk-urban continuum was Redfield's organizing principle in the research. Perhaps this helps to explain his emphasis on the formal and ritualistic aspects of life rather than the everyday life of the people and their problems, on evidence of homogeneity rather than heterogeneity and the range of custom, on the weight of tradition rather than deviation and innovation, on unity and integration rather than tensions and conflict.
>
> (Lewis 1970 [1953]: 41–2)

Not all restudies have produced such profound disagreement, although it would hardly be expected that any restudy would simply confirm the findings of an ethnographic predecessor. Even setting out simply to obtain a different perspective will normally also lead to a reevaluation of other aspects of previous ethnographies. For example, Weiner (1988) found that her interest in women's productive work in the Trobriands, which Malinowski had not considered, or apparently not even noticed, 'not only brought women as the neglected half of society clearly into the ethnographic picture but also forced me to revise many of Malinowski's assumptions about Trobriand men' (ibid.: 5). However, she regards these revisions as improved interpretations reflecting the current state of anthropological knowledge, rather than as refutations. In yet another and particularly reflexive example of a restudy, Larcom found herself following somewhat unwillingly in the footsteps of Bernard Deacon whose *Malekula: A Vanishing People in the New*

Hebrides (1934) had been produced from his field notes after he died at the end of his fieldwork. What she found is that both of them in the course of their fieldwork had in fact been led, by practical observations on the ground, away from the theoretical orientations they had brought with them – the organizational primacy of kinship in Deacon's case and a model of social change in hers. 'While he grew toward a tentative interest in place as a significant part of descent systems, I went in the direction of a fresh appreciation of the tenacity of ideology ... Thus his notes, his letters, and his book helped me to achieve both a new sense of the meaning of place and an understanding of the ideology persisting behind that concept of locality' (Larcom 1983: 190–1).

Thus given the fundamental importance of reflexivity to ethnographic research, it is clear that in the strictest sense the criterion of reliability is not applicable, in that no study is formally or perfectly repeatable. Even the same ethnographer is a different person on subsequent field trips to the same research site (e.g. Kenna 1992). Furthermore, it is easy to exaggerate the replicability of more structured methods, such as social surveys, especially if restudies are undertaken some time after the original (Davies and Charles 2002). On the other hand, we can expect that taking reflexivity fully into account does allow the critical comparison of various ethnographies to arrive at some determination of which one, or what combination of their findings, gives the most valid interpretation available to date. As with all knowledge, we must accept its incomplete and contingent character but this can be done without sinking into a relativistic hole in which no evaluation or improvement in knowledge is possible.

The third criticism often raised against ethnographic research is that of its lack of generalizability. It may be argued that this is inappropriate as a criterion for an interpretive, or idiographic, field. But it can also be argued that without the promise of generalizable findings, ethnography and indeed social anthropology has little to offer (cf. Ingold 1989). A critical realist perspective contends that the development of generalizations in the form of law-like statements is possible in social research. However, it also maintains that the objects of social research 'only ever manifest themselves in open systems; that is, in systems where invariant empirical regularities do not obtain. For social systems are not spontaneously, and cannot be experimentally, closed' (Bhaskar 1998: 45). This means that the generalizations of social research can be explanatory but not predictive. This has important implications for the bases of generalization and the kinds of generalization that are possible in ethnographic social research. Essentially it means that the utility of measurement and in particular the use of statistical inference is limited. One advocate of critical realism has gone so far as to suggest that the use of statistics in the social sciences is 'an inappropriate aping of features of the experimental sciences which make no sense in the absence of experiments' (Collier 1994: 252). There are two main forms of generalization employed in ethnographic research, empirical generalization and theoretical inference. The first form is closest to the sort of generalization criticized by critical realist philosophy. It simply means that the findings of a study are extended to other cases, judged to be similar, but which were not included in the fieldwork of the original study. The main difficulty and the source of most criticisms of this form of generalization is the necessity to specify its boundaries, that is, the extent to which it may be judged valid. For example, many ethnographic studies, based on intensive fieldwork in a single community, have generalized, sometimes without even making this generalizing process explicit, about a much larger population. In fact the definition of the boundaries of either the peoples or geographic areas to which these generalizations were to apply often were more a product of past colonial administration than of any real basis for generalizing found on the ground, in people's own social understandings. In contrast, Leach's (1954) study of highland Burma is a good example of an attempt to avoid this reification of boundaries and to emphasize the contingent and transitory nature of named social groupings while still generalizing about them. In a more recent example, Metcalf (2002) discusses the complex tangle of ethnicities he encountered among the people of the longhouses of central northern Borneo. He considers historical and more contemporary movements of peoples, intermarriages and consequent tangled genealogies, and the intermixture of languages. He also acknowledges the degree to which some ethnic identities have their origins outside the peoples they name, often in ethnographers' struggles to systematize their data, and recognizes the ambiguity of his own position in his representation of the particular cultural tradition of one of his key informants.

Another problem often encountered in ethnographic use of empirical generalization is the degeneration to stereotypes, for example, in the use of national characterizations that ignores internal divisions and individual variation (Ingold 1989: 9). On the other hand, Benedict's work on Japanese society (1967 [1945]) is one of the few examples that suggests that such generalization need not be overly deterministic and insensitive. There are a few other examples, such as peasant studies, that generalize to the national community or to a culture area without suggesting the uniformity of statistical inference (cf. Cowan 1996).

How are these more acceptable examples of generalization achieved? Basically they depend on the adoption of the second form of generalization, that of theoretical inference. That is, the conclusions of ethnographic analysis are seen to be generalizable in the context of a particular theoretical debate rather than being primarily concerned to extend them to a larger collectivity. Thus Cockburn's (1991) study of the introduction of Equal Opportunities policies, based on ethnographic fieldwork in four different organizations, offers some empirical generalization in that it is not restricted to the specific four organizations she studied but is meant to be applicable to other similar organizations in British society, and, perhaps with some modifications, to other Western industrial societies. On the other hand, her more significant generalizations have to do with the forms of resistance both formal and informal that characterize the introduction of such policies. Such generalizations are likely to be of much greater explanatory value in quite disparate situations because they can be adapted to the particularities of these other situations rather than relying on intrinsically inaccurate assumptions about the identity of a set of abstract characteristics on which empirical generalization depends.

This sort of generalization relies upon a case-study method in a very different way than as a representative of a class of cases. Thus, from a critical realist perspective, 'the deep analysis of the minute particulars of some concrete conjuncture, rather than superficial knowledge of great statistical populations, should occupy the foreground of the picture of the human sciences' (Collier 1994: 259). In other words, ethnographic analysis within a single study, as well as theorizing based on several studies, proceeds by a gradual accumulation and 'constant comparison' (Glaser and Strauss 1967) of cases in which, rather than seeking to show repeated instances of particular conjunctures of occurrences leading to a predictive causal statement, the ethnographer actively seeks the differences and variations whose explanation will refine, strengthen and make more profound the developing explanations that constitute valid generalization in ethnographic research (cf. Baszanger and Dodier 1997; also see Chapter 11).

Thus, these three criteria – validity, reliability and generalizability – are indeed important and useful considerations for ethnographic research once they are removed from their positivist frame and interpreted in the light of a critical realist epistemological basis for such research. Doubts about the validity of ethnographic research have come primarily from an unexamined assumption that it rests primarily on the ethnographer becoming a part of the group being studied. Once this assumption was considered more honestly it became clear that few ethnographers achieve the requisite level of intimacy and insider knowledge to carry this burden of authority, and this realization prompted a tendency to despair of making any claims at all for the validity of ethnographic research. Instead there was a turn towards viewing ethnography as primarily a personal literary activity or emphasizing various experimental forms of textual presentation. What I argue here is that ethnographic methods may produce valid knowledge without complete participation and total acquisition of local knowledge by ethnographers so long as they honestly examine, and make visible in their analysis, the basis of their knowledge claims in reflexive experience. This is not to remove as the ideal the achievement, usually over a long period of multiple visits to a field site, of the level of intimacy and insight suggested by classical participant observation. But this level of participation is not the only source of good ethnography nor is it, in and of itself, sufficient to guarantee the validity of ethnographic knowledge. The second criterion, reliability, both within and between ethnographic studies, must be reinterpreted to incorporate a recognition that the reflexivity intrinsic to ethnographic research does not permit or even make desirable the superficial consistency that a classical positivist position would dictate. Finally, the third criterion, generalizability, while highly desirable, is to be sought in terms of theoretical, rather than statistical, inference.

Chapter 5

Interviewing

Interviewing is probably the most widely used method of investigating the social world. However, the actual interview formats adopted by social researchers vary widely. Interviewing carried out by ethnographers whose principal research strategy is participant observation is often virtually unstructured, that is, very close to a 'naturally occurring' conversation. However, even in such unstructured interviews ethnographers have in mind topics they wish to explore and questions they would like to pose; thus they tend to direct the conversation with the research in mind, without imposing much structure on the interaction. Furthermore, unstructured interviews nearly always take place between individuals who share more than simply the interview encounter; usually the ethnographer will have established an ongoing relationship with the person being interviewed, one that precedes the encounter and will continue after it. Thus points made during the interview are usually with reference to both a shared history of a relationship and with awareness of a future connection. At the other extreme is the structured interview frequently employed in conducting survey research. In the structured interview, a series of predetermined questions are asked, often by interviewers other than the researcher, trained to use invariant wording and to standardize forms of clarification and other responses to queries by interviewees. These interviewees may be allowed considerable freedom in answering, but in the most highly structured formats they will be asked to select their answers from a set of possible responses provided by the interviewer. Usually the interview is a one-off occurrence, and there is no presumption of a continuing relationship between interviewer and interviewee.

Between these two extremes may be found another form of interviewing, semi-structured interviewing. Researchers conducting semi-structured interviews will normally make special arrangements to do so – that is, the interviews are formally bracketed, and set off in time and space as something different from usual social interaction between ethnographer and informant, in contrast to unstructured interviews which often just happen. Furthermore, the researcher goes to the interview with some sort of interview schedule: it may be as structured as a set of written questions or it may be a very informal list, perhaps memorized, of topics. However, in contrast to structured interviews, researchers may alter the wording and order of these questions, perhaps omitting some that seem inappropriate; they may introduce new topics and supplementary questions not included on the list, and respondents are encouraged to expand on a response, or digress, or even go off the particular topic and introduce their own concerns. Most important, their responses are open-ended, in their own words and not restricted to the preconceived notions of the ethnographer.

Research based primarily on such semi-structured interviewing has become a very popular and important form of qualitative research across the social sciences, especially in anthropology (Edgerton 1993; Spradley 1979), sociology (Cockburn 1991; Laws 1990), psychology and various applied social sciences. In very many of these studies, the relationship between researcher and respondents, while not meeting the extensive time involvement of classical participant observation, extends beyond the immediate parameters of the interview. Many researchers who use this method combine it with participant observation and thus their relationship with interviewees goes beyond the particular interview, which is often a series of interviews rather than a single event in any case. At the very minimum, semi-structured interviewing requires attention to the interview context and the relationship between participants beyond simply what is said. For these reasons research based on this form of interviewing is also sometimes referred to as ethnographic interviewing. Ethnographic interviews are usually conducted by the researcher with just one individual at a time. However, a common and frequently employed variant are group interviews in which ethnographers interview several individuals at the same time so that they interact with one another as well as with the ethnographer. Group interviews in which the format is somewhat more structured and the topic rather more directed are referred to as focus groups, a form of ethnographic interviewing that is particularly popular in policy-oriented research. Ethnographic interviewing is also employed with single individuals when collecting life histories and is heavily relied on for studies of myth and ritual; these uses are discussed further in Chapter 9. In this chapter I will be concentrating on the use of a series of such interviews as the main research method in a given project.

The ways in which interviewing provides knowledge about the social world may be variously conceived. The traditional assumption is that those being interviewed have access to knowledge which they can share with the researcher when they are asked to do so in ways that help them to remember and organize the presentation of their knowledge. In this view, what the respondent says is a representation of social and cultural realities. The task of the interviewer is to direct these revelations to topics of interest and to avoid unduly influencing their narrative. Normally this is accomplished by adopting a neutral position and refraining from expressing an opinion or assisting in interpretation. The main difficulties faced by the interviewer are conceived, in this view of interviewing, as either incomplete and/or incorrect knowledge or deliberate deception on the part of their respondents. These problems are to be addressed by comparing what a number of informants may say on the same topic.

There are a number of difficulties with this model of interviewing. At a practical level, the goal of open and free-flowing discussion is not readily attainable when one party to the discussion is clearly holding back, not expressing any opinions, or even interacting except in the most minimalist form. More seriously, at a theoretical level, it is clear to anyone who has done some interviewing or just reflected on everyday conversations that, except for relatively trivial uncomplicated information, individuals are not able simply to provide uncontested knowledge about their social world. Much more commonly, interviews contain apparent contradictions, probings, suggestions. Consider the following extract from an interview with the parents of a young man with learning disabilities. Their son was 21 years old and attended an adult training centre, a day-care facility for people with learning disabilities which at the time of the interview offered a combination of work contracted by the centre (such as filling plastic bags with screws) and a variety of educational experiences. (In this and subsequent interview transcripts from my research: ... indicates a longer than usual pause; ... // ... material omitted.)

CD: Do you think that being unemployed has an effect on him now?

LYN REES: No, I don't think he realizes, you know, to be honest with you.

CD: What do you think he would do with the extra money if he had a job?

LR: Well, the point is that he've got no value of the money. So if, he wouldn't really know, would he?

MURIEL REES: He saves, he puts money in his money box.

LR: He saves, like, you know.

MR: You know and ... He do have sweets at the weekend.

LR: But he don't know the value of money, so you know he wouldn't, you know, like if he had extra money, he wouldn't know what to do with it anyway.

...//...

MR Only thing, when he did start [in the adult training centre] they were giving him one pound something in a pay packet.

LR: Now he was pleased about this.

MR: My money' he was going.

LR: Only a pound.

MR: 'Job'. Well, of course, they stopped that now, haven't they.

LR Cutbacks.

MR See, he did say, 'no money, I've no money'. Well, more or less, he's going to work and he's not having nothing for it.

CD: Yes, yes.

MR: So he was thinking he was having a pay packet. 'It's my money', he was going, innit. So he was putting it in the money box. His money.

LR: And we had to put that by for him then. You see, he could spend that like, it was his money.

MR: They've stopped that.

LR: So I contradict myself now like, innit. In that respect, yes, perhaps he would. [I can see] the question [you're on about]. Yes, probably he would value a bit of money, if he was having it in a pay packet every week.

What this suggests and what numerous analysts (e.g. Chirban 1996; Holstein and Gubrium 1995; Rubin and Rubin 1995) have come to argue about interviewing is that it is better understood as a process in which interviewer and interviewee are both involved in developing understanding, that is in constructing their knowledge of the social world.

> Both parties to the interview are necessarily and unavoidably *active*. Each is involved in meaning–making work. Meaning is not merely elicited by apt questioning nor simply transported through respondent replies; it is actively and communicatively assembled in the interview encounter.
>
> (Holstein and Gubrium 1995: 4)

This model of the interviewing process can be interpreted as suggesting that the only knowledge accessible via interviewing is knowledge about the interview itself, that is, about the bases on which interviewer and interviewee construct their interaction. In this interpretation, the interview does not provide access to any other ontological level but only reveals its own set of rules and relationships as it constructs them.

Critical realism rejects both the purely representational and the totally constructed models of the interview process. I would argue that while interviews cannot be taken as a straightforward reflection of the level of the social, as opposed to individual interaction, there is a connection, an interdependency between the two levels that allows interviewing to provide access to the social world beyond the individual. This can be accomplished by ensuring that the analytical process takes into account the nature of the links and the inherently reflexive character of the knowledge. Thus both interviewer and interviewee begin with some necessarily incomplete knowledge about another level of reality – the social – and through an analysis of the character of their interaction including, but not limited to, the content of the verbal interaction, they may develop this knowledge. A researcher may further increase and deepen such understanding through interactions with a range of interviewees focusing on a given area of interest (cf. Miller and Glassner 1997). This raises the issue of sampling, that is, of locating respondents for an interview-based study. Clearly any selection of respondents should be based primarily on theoretical considerations, in particular keeping in mind that the purpose of ethnographic interviewing is to obtain a variety of interpretations rather than to seek consistencies in responses in order to develop statistical generalizations (cf. Johnson 1990). It is often the case that the research requires that respondents come from a range of social positions, based on gender, class, age, ethnicity and so forth, but they are normally selected to cover this range and not on any criteria for statistical representativeness.

In what follows I consider a number of issues raised by this understanding of the nature of ethnographic interviewing and its role in social research. First, I look at the implications inherent in an interactive approach to interviewing, particularly as regards the roles of interviewer and interviewee in developing understanding. Second, I consider the importance of context in generating and interpreting interview data. Third, various linguistic issues, such as translation, levels of meaning of verbal utterances, language and power and nonverbal communication, and their effect on the research, are examined. Finally, I consider issues involved in saving talk, through recording, transcribing and reporting.

Interviewing interactively

Fairclough (1989) suggests that the interview must be understood at three levels: the level of discourse produced, the text; the level of interaction, that is, the processes of production and interpretation that go on between the individuals involved in the interview; and the level of context, that is, the social conditions that affect both interaction and text. These three levels are not fully separable. Interactions are fundamentally affected by social conditions – for example, those that structure gender relations – in that individuals embody these conditions and carry presumptions about such relationships into the interview encounter. Any differences – such as those based in gender, class, age, status – which have implications for differential access to power in the wider society will affect interaction during the interview; in particular, such differences tend to undermine what is sometimes regarded as a fundamental distinction of research interviews (as opposed to other types of interviews), namely, the presumption of equality of the participants within the context of the interview itself (cf. Benney and Hughes 1984). Any such presumption needs to be accompanied by a suspension of overly judgemental attitudes by the researcher in order to allow for a mutual exploration of the area of research. Such a presumption of equality will be more difficult to establish in some situations than others – for example when interviewing children, people with learning disabilities, people whose lifestyles are regarded as deviant. Nevertheless, it is not impossible to overcome or at least mitigate such structurally determined differences through careful interaction. One researcher interviewing female gang members found that the difference in age, race and class did not preclude meaningful interaction. She notes that the experience of being listened to and taken seriously by a researcher possessing high social status can be experienced as both empowering and reflexively enlightening and, as such, is not necessarily a barrier to communication (Miller and Glassner 1997: 105–10). The opposite problem may arise when interviewing high status individuals, who do not respond to the ethnographer's questions, but rather give lectures on what they believe the researcher should be told. One researcher on a project looking at postgraduate research in sociology reported that 'I found many examples of the status of the respondent being used to deny me interviews or to control the interview itself ... One senior woman academic controlled the interview by behaving as if it wasn't an interview at all but just a general chat, ... A male professor said he was so busy he could only give me fifteen minutes and then proceeded to fill the time with his views on research training' (Scott 1984: 171). Thus the social positions of interviewer and interviewee may distort or undermine the egalitarian ethos of the research interview and ethnographers must be aware of such difficulties and make attempts to compensate through their interactions.

At the same time, it is important to recognize that shared social statuses, for example shared gender, do not guarantee understanding or make possible a presumption of equality and associated openness in responses. Riessman (1987) considers an interview about the experience of marital separation carried out by a middle-class white female interviewer with Marta, a working-class Hispanic woman. She is able to document the growth of intimacy between them based on gender and strengthened by the interviewer's participation in some aspects of Marta's everyday life; 'a woman-to-woman bond starts to develop as the interviewer steps outside the traditional professional role of interviewer and enters Marta's world' (ibid.: 179). However, this is not enough to overcome communication difficulties springing from cultural and class differences.

> The interviewer held onto the white, middle-class model of temporal organization and thus could not make sense of the episodic form that Marta used – the dramatic unfolding of a series of topics that were stitched together by theme rather than by time. The narrator did not understand the interviewer's

> implicit expectations about discourse form, and the interviewer did not understand the narrator's allusion to meaningful themes of kin and cultural conflict. As a result, they were unable to collaborate.
>
> (Ibid.: 190)

In fact, interviewers would be wise to problematize all statuses, whether shared or disparate, in terms of how they may affect their interaction with interviewees. Lal (1996) notes that from an unexamined perspective, her social identity as an Indian woman researching women factory workers in Delhi, a city that had been her home prior to postgraduate education in America, should secure her insider relationships. However, the reality of arranging and conducting her interviews in factories, as well as class differences, left her more often aligned, however unwillingly, with her interviewees' employers.

It may generally be acknowledged that ethnographers retain a degree of control over the interview interaction in that they introduce both the general area of discussion and more specific topics. However, a good interviewer needs to be open to the possibility that respondents will not be able to discuss the subject in the terms that they suggest. They may, for example, openly reject a line of questioning as nonsensical and perhaps try to redefine what is being discussed; or they may simply not respond, which requires that interviewers try to elicit their respondents' frame of reference and perhaps alter their own system of categorization in order to reconstruct a shared understanding (Holstein and Gubrium 1995: 56). DeVault (1990) argues, for example, that women's experiences do not always fit readily into existing theoretical categories due to the male-dominated nature of these categories. She suggests the distinction between work and leisure may be particularly blurred, and hence these terms will be problematic for women. Thus, she advocates that interviewing be conducted so as to allow interviewer and interviewee to cooperate in a search for topics that are meaningful to both.

Traditional forms of interviewing have specifically prohibited interviewers from expressing an opinion and have advocated that they strive to prevent their own views from affecting the interaction. Even those advocating a more interactionist style of interviewing, and arguing that the interview must be seen as a situated encounter whose specifics affect what is communicated, often still regard self-disclosures on the part of the interviewer as part of a controlled strategy to get the interviewee to open up (cf. Douglas 1985). Another approach to the question of self-disclosure is Oakley's (1981) argument that both for ethical reasons and for the efficacy of the interview, interviewers must be prepared to share their own knowledge; she suggests that the interviewing process can only develop effectively 'when the interviewer is prepared to invest his or her personal identity in the relationship' (ibid.: 41). Others suggest that personal experience should be called upon not just to develop empathy or fulfil ethical expectations but also to challenge and contrast as another means of developing understanding. DeVault (1990) notes that difficulties in developing empathetic understanding, when examined as to why such empathy is not forthcoming, may be equally helpful in interpreting interviewees' perspectives.

The endeavour to see the interview in terms of interaction means that ethnographers need to be sensitive to how they are being perceived by interviewees. At one level there is the question of various status differences and how these affect interactions. But the more personal and individualistic dynamics are also significant. While virtually all interviewers will form opinions about interviewees as individuals, what sort of people they are, the impressions they want to create, and so forth, it is also important to try to develop an idea of how you, the interviewer, are being perceived. This may, for example, be a product of the kinds of topics you are researching. Jorgenson (1991) reports that during her research on family, guesses were made as to her expectations regarding family relationships that led to some interviewees apologizing for not displaying more family feeling.

Interactive interviewing also implies that understanding may develop and alter during the course of an interview. In the context of interviews for my project on the transition to adulthood of young people with learning disabilities, I found parents often searched their own feelings about what constituted growing up and that their ideas about the adulthood of their sons and daughters would alter as we talked. Comments made in the course of a three-hour interview with Susan James, the mother of a 20-year-old woman with Down's Syndrome, illustrate this process. In reference to her worries about her daughter Ellen's romantic interest in a man in his thirties, she said, 'We were really worried, you know, that, 'cause Ellen is the type of child, you see, that anybody shows a little bit of affection – I think most of the Down's children are – you know, they thrive on that.' Later she expressed concern about the way other people tended to indulge her daughter:

> I mean, all children need discipline, you know, don't they. And I mean we're far from hard, too soft we've been really, but we find, oh, you know, when she should be told off, or she should be, say, 'Oh, Ellen, you shouldn't say that, that's not nice', or 'you shouldn't do that', you'll find they say, 'Oh no'. Because she's, she is as she is, she – I'm getting a little bit mixed up now – because Ellen is the way she is then, they want to ... be silly, where they wouldn't put up with it from another child, you know.

Yet as the interview progressed, she developed a relatively strong position *vis-à-vis* her husband regarding their daughter's adulthood.

CD: Do you think of her as a child or as an adult? How do you think of her?

RONALD JAMES: Oh, how do I think, I still think of her as a child.

SUSAN JAMES: I think you more than me, Ron, don't you? I mean, perhaps I do to a certain extent, but then she'll say, I mean like I notice things like with jewellery and, I mean different to a man, I obviously see, well, you know, she's growing up and she's taking an interest more in what a teenager would. I mean what, dealings that Ron doesn't have with her, you know, that way, clothes and what have you.

RJ: I don't know, because I never thought of it, other than the question, until now, very often going down in the car on a Sunday morning, she'd say to me, 'How do I look?' I'd say, 'Terrible. How do you feel?' 'Daddy, how do I look?'

SJ: Oh yes, she's quite concerned.

RJ: I'd say, 'Oh you're looking lovely'. 'Oh, that's good.' But, mind you, I never thought, beyond that, never thought beyond that, that she'd say, but now that you're forcing the question like, I mean perhaps she is ...

SJ: Oh yes.

RJ: taking that interest.

Similarly, from this interactionist perspective whereby ethnographer and interviewee are engaged in knowledge creation, it is naive to look for consistency. Holstein and Gubrium (1995) argue that the knowledge base on which interviewees draw may shift significantly within the course of an interview as they adopt different social identities – for example as adult caregiver or as spouse – and respond from these varied perspectives. And quite new interpretations and understandings may emerge in the course of the interaction. It is important, as well, to see these developing understandings in terms of the various perspectives on which they are based rather than as some gradual move towards the truth. Thus, in the interview extract with Lyn and Muriel Rees quoted above, there is no single simple answer to the question of whether or not their son is concerned about being unemployed; rather the response is highly contingent upon how employment is interpreted by him and by his parents, as well as on the status of monetary remuneration in the adult training centre.

Although the usual model of ethnographic interviewing is of a dyadic interaction, it is not uncommon that social circumstances dictate that other people are present. For example, when interviewing in people's homes, it is sometimes impossible to exclude other members of the household; and if they are excluded, this exclusion and their presence in another part of the house will still affect the interaction. Even if they do not formally take part in the interview, their presence affects the interaction of researcher and interviewee and it is essential that they be noted as part of the context of the interview (see next section). However, more commonly, if others are present, they will make comments engaging both researcher and interviewee in conversation. By such informal mechanisms traditional one-on-one ethnographic interviews are not uncommonly converted into a form of group interview. The experience of ethnographic interviewing with more than one respondent can have its own virtues. For example, in interviewing couples together, you sometimes find that differing perspectives and conflicts they report individually are performed in their interactions with one another during the interview. Of course, it may be that one partner is dominant and can control what is said, either through doing most of the talking or sometimes simply through their presence, without saying much, affecting what their partner feels able to say. In any case, it is clear that the interaction between interviewees can be very informative for the ethnographer. Furthermore, in interviews with more than one respondent, ethnographers frequently find they can be much less directive during the interview, in the sense of having to probe for more information on a given topic, as respondents often stimulate one another's responses and even pose questions to one another. Given these kinds of considerations, researchers may choose to conduct an interview with a group rather than with an individual. Such group interviews are quite common in this type of research and are often combined with interviewing members of the group individually as well. This combination of group and individual interviews was used by Mac an Ghaill (1994) in his study of masculinities and schooling. He includes numerous examples of discussions where boys respond to one another's comments and explore a topic with minimal intervention from the ethnographer (e.g. ibid.: 98–192). Group interviews are particularly helpful when working with people, such as adolescents, who may be more reluctant to talk freely when alone with the researcher (cf. Jarrett 1994; Morgan and Krueger 1993). As this suggests, such group interviewing, like the more traditional forms of ethnographic interviewing, involves only some formalizing and structuring of a process that also is used in participant observation.

The main difficulties associated with group interviewing are the much greater complexity of the interactions to which the ethnographer needs to attend and the difficulty in trying to direct the discussion to topics relevant to the research without disrupting the social dynamics of the group. Focus groups, which are based on concepts of group interviewing, are one way of addressing some of these concerns (Morgan 1997; Stewart and Shamdasani 1990). Focus groups consist usually of between six and 12 individuals whom the researcher contacts and asks to participate in a group discussion on topics of interest to the research. The group is assembled in a location arranged by the researcher, normally a small conference room, with recording facilities. Thus, in contrast to most ethnographic interviewing, respondents are likely to feel that they are on the researcher's territory rather than the reverse. Usually the members of the focus group are strangers to one another. This has the effect of simplifying, to a degree, the observation of interactions among them since they will not be based in some (unknown to the researcher) history of their relationship. The researcher takes the role of moderator, facilitating initial interactions among group members and introducing the topic to be discussed. The degree of researcher involvement subsequently may vary between particular researchers and projects but typically they are quite non-directive, allowing the group discussion to develop its own dynamic and pursue topics as they arise and capture the interest of the group. 'The hallmark of focus groups is their explicit use of group interaction to produce data and insights that would be less accessible without the interaction found in a group' (Morgan 1997: 2). There are several concerns about the nature of this interaction and how it affects what people say within a group, as opposed to what they say in individual interviews (Albrecht, Johnson and Walther 1993). One possible group response is to create consensus, to the extent that individuals refrain from saying things they might say in a one-on-one interview. Moderators try to avoid this by stressing that they are looking for a range of different responses to a given situation rather than presenting the research as a question or series of questions for which answers are sought, so giving the group an expectation of varying perspectives and little incentive to seek definitive answers. Another possible group response is to polarize so that some participants, in the heat of argument, may present rather more extreme views than they would in an individual discussion (cf. Kitzinger 1994; Wight 1994). This potential difficulty is believed to be most effectively defused by the sampling process which attempts to set up homogeneous groups – whether based on class, gender, ethnicity, age, social roles or whatever – in terms of what are perceived to be likely fault lines in the topic to be discussed. This sampling strategy seeks homogeneity within groups and segmentation between groups. Thus a study of the social conditions of declining fertility rates in village Thailand (Knodel, Havanon and Pramualratana 1984) used focus groups homogeneous in terms of age and gender.

While such strategies may minimize the differences between what respondents might say in group as opposed to individual interviews, it is neither necessary nor desirable to eliminate all such disparities. If we adopt a genuinely reflexive perspective in social research, we must accept that different methods of data gathering will necessarily produce different results. But these results need not be regarded as irreconcilable. The challenge to the researcher – who, after all, has the opportunity to participate in the widest variety of these interactive attempts to understand the social world – is to see how such varied results may indeed contribute to a more complete and valid analysis.

One interview-based study that used both individual semi-structured and focus group interviewing is Laws (1990), *Issues of Blood*, which looked at the way in which women's experience of menstruation in British society is constructed by men's attitudes towards it. This study raises a number of interesting methodological issues. Laws' means of locating her comparatively small sample of 14 men meant that they represented a relatively progressive liberal group (e.g. several volunteers had been contacted through a request made in a course on sexual politics that they attended). This particular approach gave her what is sometimes termed a belwether sample, that is, one that might be presumed to represent the leading edge of current social trends – in this case, a liberalization of attitudes about menstruation. Clearly, with such a topic and with the status differences between herself and her interviewees, Laws had to be particularly aware of the degree to which discussion was inhibited by these differences. She notes that none of her informants 'said they were embarrassed, or seemed embarrassed, at the time, although quite a few had expected to be' (ibid.: 41). She suggests that the relative openness of the interviews was due, in part, to the way in which the topic was raised, and also to factors in the broader social context: 'It is also well understood by all the respondents that social propriety in relation to menstruation is at present in a state of crisis and change' (ibid.: 42). At the same time, she felt that her presence might still be inhibiting her informants' disclosures, 'limiting them to what could be said to a woman's face, if you like, so I also asked a "men's group" to tape a discussion about menstruation for me' (ibid.: 8). This use of a form of focus group, but without a moderator present, is one strength of her study, and in fact produced responses that were very similar to the interviews. A related weakness is the fact that she does not make clear the degree of overlap between group members and individual interviewees. The other aspect of the interaction with which she deals very effectively is in assessing her own responses, her personal discomfort, and occasionally anger, with the attitudes of her informants. Thus, in analysing her interview material, she had to work through these responses which were produced by her relatively less powerful social position.

> There are two kinds of understanding involved here, an understanding as a woman, what you might call 'getting the message' which often led me into a reaction of anger or despair, and also an understanding with the men, of what their words meant to them. The difficulty was that I had in a sense to overcome my hearing of 'the message' in order to understand in any other way – to 'make sense' of what they said.
>
> (Ibid.: 217)

Certainly, this study provides a useful example of the way in which interactive interviewing can effectively employ reflexively sensitive research without becoming self-absorbed, and can enhance eventual understanding of a social phenomenon not directly known by the researcher and, in fact, one to which her social position made access quite problematic.

Semi-structured interviewing tends to be the method of choice for ethnographic research on elite groups, where access is likely to be strictly controlled and hence participant observation is problematic. In his study examining the efforts by elites in the European Union to encourage the development of a common European consciousness, Shore (2000) used a range of methods including participant observation and archival research but noted that 'given the nature of this enquiry, the most frequently used strategy was that of the in-depth interview combined with cross-check or follow-up interviews' (ibid.: 8). The effectiveness of this strategy can be seen, for example, in his discussion of how the European Commission went about trying to prepare the European population for the introduction of the single currency. Commission employees maintained in interviews that their role was not to persuade but to inform, that the euro was widely accepted. However, further questioning revealed that these employees 'were professional marketing agents but wished to conceal this because the campaign was not supposed to be about "selling" the euro' (ibid.: 105).

Contextualizing

The researcher's awareness and understanding of the context of interviews needs to be developed on multiple levels. At the most general level, interviewers must have some basic knowledge of the structure of social relationships and the complex of underlying cultural meanings in the society in which they are working. For many anthropologists, this society is not their own and hence they usually require a period of participant observation before interviewing is likely to produce anything but very rudimentary knowledge. Certainly, in Apache culture, the belief that asking direct questions about another's feelings is intrusive (Basso 1972, 1979) means that interviews cannot have the accepted question and answer format but must be structured for a less direct conversational mode. For ethnographers doing research in their own society, the difficulty is to guard against assuming that their particular perspective is shared by their informants. They must attempt to make the broader context visible by a process of defamiliarization. Often informants will do this for them by rejecting and redefining the terms of the interview; sometimes this can be facilitated by comparative reading and juxtaposing and problematizing quite disparate social and cultural forms.

It is also essential to be sensitive to differential power relationships; these are commonly linked to social divisions such as class, gender, ethnicity, race, age or professional status, and will almost certainly affect the interview interaction. It is also quite common for differential social statuses to be interpreted differently by interviewers and informants. For example, most ethnographers carry with them into the field a belief in the importance of their research and an assumption that within the context of an agreed interview, the topics they deem relevant to this research will be given due attention. They are not uncommonly met by high status and knowledgeable individuals who interpret their own role as one of instructing the ethnographer in those aspects of their society which they believe to be important (cf. Briggs 1986) rather than responding to apparently peripheral questions posed by the ethnographer. Such a situation will be frustrating at best and could render the research impossible, unless the ethnographer is sensitive to what is occurring. Possible responses might be alternative methods, use of other informants or redefining the research questions. In any case, sensitivity to power relationships and how they are affecting the interaction is essential. In addition, such sensitivity needs to be examined – that is, the interviewer must ask how status and power differences are being signalled. They must take note of specific markers such as dress, accent, household furnishings and surroundings. At the same time, ethnographers must interrogate their own assumptions about the significance of such markers and be aware of the signals they themselves are projecting.

Moving down a level with respect to the context, ethnographers need to consider the degree to which interviewing is, or is not, a known cultural activity. Certainly interviewing is widely known and employed in many contexts in Western societies. This can be helpful in that interviewees are familiar with the expectations of an interview process in which they respond to concerns raised by the interviewer. However, because the interview is used in many other contexts, such as employment interviews, where a hierarchical relationship is intrinsic to the process, ethnographic interviewers may find their respondents adopting a similar mode, undermining the internal egalitarianism they strive to create. I found in interviewing some young people with mental handicaps that the combination of an interview format in a college setting produced a very strong attitude of deference marked by extreme politeness in their responses. Being unable to alter the setting, I had to attempt to undermine my association with college staff by hanging around with students in less formal contexts, primarily the canteen. This, along with making the interview interaction itself as informal as possible, helped to mitigate, but did not entirely eliminate, this deferential response. Another technique often used with young people to overcome this very common difficulty is the group interview as noted above. Such a context has several advantages. It breaks the association of the research interview with interrogations by teachers and counsellors; it means that the young people can interact with one another in a relatively informal and open manner; and it makes it more likely that they will feel able as a group to challenge the interviewer's assumptions or disagree with a suggested interpretation, something few will be confident enough to do in an individual interaction.

Another way in which ethnographers may be able to affect the informant's interpretation of the interview relationship is in explaining at the outset what it is designed to accomplish. This introduction should attempt to present the interview as a joint exploration of the topic of the research, rather than a mining of the interviewee for information, and this approach should of course be reflected in the subsequent interactions. Furthermore, careful thought should be given to the way in which the topic being investigated is portrayed; if it is presented as a fairly specific research question, informants may feel obliged to provide answers rather than reflect on their own relevant experiences. Such a response closes the area being studied when it might need to be altered or expanded, defeating much of the purpose of ethnographic interviewing. (See Chapter 3 for a discussion of the ethical implications of informing participants about the nature of research.)

If the ethnographic interview format may be misinterpreted in societies where it is a relatively common social occurrence, the possibility of misunderstanding in societies where it is less widely known or accepted is great indeed. In research among Spanish speakers in New Mexico, Briggs (1986: 57–9) found that his questions were turned away with very brief and dismissive responses; he eventually came to understand that his relative youth and unmarried status meant that he was not considered fully adult, hence that it was inappropriate for him to ask questions, and that what he perceived as interviews, his respondents regarded as pedagogic occasions to instruct him about their society. Once he recognized the nature of their resistance to his research, in terms of their very different meta-communication strategies, he was able to develop the valuable insights that this provided. 'If the category of "interview" is not shared by the respondent or if the latter does not utilize this frame in defining such interactions, then he or she may apply norms of interaction and canons of interpretation that differ from those of the interviewer' (ibid.: 48).

As already noted, the immediate setting in which an interview takes place, its location in time and space, is also of consequence for the way in which interactions proceed as well as affecting the ethnographer's interpretation of what is said. 'It matters a great deal, for example, whether the social construction of agedness – such as construing possible dementia in the forgetfulness of a parent – is done in the context of being a chapter member of the Alzheimer's association or in the context of a family network' (Gubrium and Holstein 1994: 178–9). In the course of a study of the relationship between gender and cultural identities (Charles and Davies 1997), a colleague and I conducted interviews with women refuge workers in Welsh-speaking areas. Our findings that 'an organizational and political commitment of women who are homeless as a result of domestic violence took precedence over other, potentially contradictory, identities' (ibid.: 433) must be seen in light of the fact that the interviews were conducted in the refuges. Although we were unable to alter the setting, we attempted to mitigate undue influence by carrying out all interviews with Welsh speakers in Welsh, thus signaling to both Welsh and English speakers that we valued their cultural identities as well as their work-based identity.

In using ethnographic interviewing in research, therefore, it is as important that researchers be aware of the contexts in which the interview is set as that they attend to the actual interactions which make up the interview. This implies not just awareness, but deliberate taking note of and problematizing the possible effects of these contexts. Thus the data produced by an interview should include not just a record of what is said (the text to which I now turn), but full notes as to the contexts and how these various contexts are likely to affect the interactions that formally constitute the interview.

Edgerton's (1993) study of 48 former residents of an institution for people with mental retardation, who, in the early 1960s, had been released on 'work placements', was ground-breaking in that it was based primarily on interviews with these people themselves rather than with parents, guardians, employers or hospital personnel. It is perhaps not surprising for the period in which it was produced that its main methodological weakness may be its failure to utilize fully the interactive nature of such semi-structured ethnographic interviewing. Interviewers were expected to be completely non-committal when asked for their opinion on any matter of consequence and, furthermore, they were instructed not to provide any assistance that might change the circumstances of the interviewees, most of whom had very limited material and social resources. (It should be noted that these instructions were reversed in later restudies (ibid.: xvi).) Such care to limit interaction is apparent in the eventual text produced in that quotations are presented in isolation, never in the context of a dialogue with the interviewer, nor even as a response to a particular question. For example, in presenting a series of statements to exemplify the excuses these people produced for their confessed incompetence (ibid.: 153), it would be particularly informative to know what questions prompted these responses, both confessions and excuses. However, the weaknesses springing from this inattention to the interactive dimension in ethnographic interviewing – and the reason for considering this study here – are very substantially compensated by its sensitive and thorough approach to context. Interviews were supplemented by participant observation, with interviewing occurring around and during activities such as 'trips to recreational areas, grocery shopping, shopping excursions in department stores, sight-seeing drives, social visits in their homes, invitations to restaurants, participation in housework, financial planning, parties, and visits to homes of friends and relatives' (ibid.: 15). Thus the failure to provide adequate data on the verbal interaction leading to discussions of incompetence is largely compensated for by the descriptions of ways in which interviewers observed challenges to competence that arose in everyday social encounters (ibid.: 148–51). Similarly, the description of responses of some of the non-disabled benefactors to the interviewers both contextualizes the study and supports one of its central conclusions:

> Most of these benefactors ... showed remarkable protective fervor when they were first encountered by the research workers from this study. In many instances, they were bellicose and threatening until reassured by proper identification that the researchers were from the hospital, knew the ex-patient's background, had only the best of intentions, and would permit no disclosure of the ex-patient's discrediting past.
>
> (Ibid.: 176)

What this very fine study shows is the central importance of context for research based in ethnographic interviewing. In this case, the particularly extensive and detailed attention given to contextualizing the research goes a long way towards overcoming its inadequacies regarding using and reporting the interview as an interactive occasion.

Text: languaging, recording

Language is central to most forms of ethnographic research and obviously so for ethnographic interviewing. The fundamental importance of learning a people's language in the process of trying to learn about their society and culture was discussed in Chapter 4. This is no less important for a study which is primarily interview based. However, there is a rather greater tendency to make use of translators for assistance with interviewing if only because it is somewhat more practical to do so than when using participant observation. In either case, whether translating for oneself in the process of analysis or using a translator to assist with the actual interviewing, it is essential to consider some of the implications and limitations of the process of translation. First, some levels of meaning are going to be lost in translation.

> Some familiar answers on what cannot be translated include: the poetics ...; humour; puns; a play between different linguistic registers or vocabulary; stylistic qualities ...; multi-levels of meaning, perhaps directed to different audiences; connotations; imagery; and culturally specific allusion.
>
> (Finnegan 1992: 190)

Although it is possible to carry such multiple meanings into another language by means of lengthy exegesis, it would prove impossibly tedious to do so in all instances and such explanations still tend to lose the effect created by such linguistic play. At the same time, the ethnographer must be prepared to recognize these complexities and choose to elaborate upon those that have a bearing on their research topic. Of course, if their own grasp of the language is poor, then most or all such potentially informative linguistic subtleties will be lost in any case. Furthermore, no matter how competent ethnographers are in another language, they must remain aware that translation in any case is far from a theoretically neutral activity and that their own perspective, both professional and personal, will influence their translations (cf. Overing 1987). For these reasons, these perspectives must be examined to make visible theoretical assumptions that lie behind translations. Researchers who work through translators thus add a second level – the translator's – of theoretical assumptions which filter their informants' talk. Temple (1997), in a study of Polish communities in England, found that differences in hers and her translator's versions of interviews, when examined, reflected their very different perceptions of women's social position. She argues that 'researchers who do use translators need to acknowledge their dependence on that translator not just for words but to a certain extent for perspective' (ibid.: 608) and advocates becoming familiar with the intellectual biography of any translators with whom one works.

Even when you share a language with your informants, it is all too easy to assume a congruence of meanings which does not necessarily exist (cf. Spradley 1979). Deutscher (1984) notes that affirmative and negative responses cannot be simply translated and that even within the same linguistic community a so-called simple 'yes' or 'no' can have quite varied meanings, with some groups, based in a profession or region or class, interpreting unemphasized responses to mean their opposite. It is perhaps easier to remain alert to the dangers of unexamined and unshared assumptions among users of a shared language when the collectivity has a distinctive specialized vocabulary. This is frequently the case with marginal groups (e.g. Spradley 1970) as well as with professional groups who use a technical vocabulary. In this case, interviews may be greatly facilitated by asking for explanation of how particular terms are used. However, in many cases different interpretations and understandings may hide behind shared vocabularies. Feminists have alerted researchers to the problems women may face in talking about their lives, given the male-dominated nature of many languages generally and, more particularly, the male bias in much sociological terminology. DeVault (1990) suggests that researchers must be alert to the ways in which women try to communicate through such difficulties; for example she suggests that hesitations and restarts, sections of dialogue that do not make good quotes, may nevertheless provide very important guides to what they are really striving to say.

> As I began to look for these difficulties of expression, I became aware that my transcripts were filled with notations of women saying to me, 'you know,' in sentences like 'I'm more careful about feeding her, you know, kind of a breakfast.' This seems an incidental feature of their speech, but perhaps the phrase is not so empty as it seems. In fact, I did know what she meant. I did not use these phrases systematically in my analyses, but I think now that I could have. Studying the transcripts now, I see that these words often occur in places where they are consequential for the joint production of our talk in the interviews.
>
> (Ibid.: 103)

Clearly, if in analysing interviews the ethnographer concentrates solely on the content – what is said – then they may miss important communications. Apparently meaningless phrases, repetitions, sublinguistic verbalizations, pauses and silences may all be significant in adding to, sometimes even contradicting, the purely semantic content of what is said. This also raises the question of how ethnographers record such a mass of information and what they select for analysis. The use of a tape recorder in ethnographic interviewing is almost universally accepted and unreservedly advocated. It is probably less intrusive and destructive of open and natural conversation than having an ethnographer taking notes, and it is infinitely more reliable than memory, no matter how good, of what was said. Furthermore, its use allows the ethnographer to be much more aware of other aspects of the interaction that cannot be captured by sound recording, and to enter more fully into the development of the interview. However, its use does present the ethnographer with an embarrassment of riches in that the amount of recorded material produced by good ethnographic interviewing of even a small sample is very large indeed and the time required to evaluate, transcribe and analyse it is immense.

The process of transcription itself raises yet another set of methodological questions. Transcription is not a mechanical process of representing speech in written form but, as with translation, is affected by underlying theoretical assumptions. Such assumptions must be made visible and decisions about how transcription is to proceed thus be theoretically informed choices, rather than unconsidered products based on convenience. It is difficult to justify altering actual words and style of speech (e.g. changing regional or class-based dialects into a standardized form) to make it more accessible to the audience. Some consider it acceptable to cut out most occurrences of repetitious phrases such as 'you know', 'like', leaving only a few to suggest personal speaking style (Blauner 1987); others, as discussed above (DeVault 1990), find these phrases themselves may carry meanings for which words were inadequate. Similarly, with the question of recording false starts and hesitations, in some instances these may be precisely the phenomena to be investigated. Decisions on these matters must be made explicitly, and expectations carefully communicated to transcribers if the transcription is being carried out by someone other than the ethnographer. This is not to suggest that transcriptions must include as much detail as can be heard on the tape; such a transcript would be so complex as to make it difficult to interpret; in general, when a very detailed study is required, as with conversation analysis, only a relatively few segments of text can be usefully studied, hence limiting the scope and comparative range of the research. Thus, selectivity in terms of what features are to be included in the transcription is unavoidable and indeed desirable. However, such selectivity should be the result of deliberate and informed choice, and the effects on the research should be consciously evaluated (cf. Ochs 1979). Furthermore, as analysis proceeds (see Chapter 11), ethnographers must be prepared to return not only to the original transcript but to the original recording, if new considerations mean that features omitted begin to seem significant.

Some of the other less commonly recognized assumptions that are made in the course of transcription have to do with the arrangement of the text on the page: traditional vertical organization suggests that each speaker is responding to the immediately preceding one, whereas this may not be the case with some interviewees. For example, in interviewing children it frequently is not even certain 'that an utterance of a child that follows an immediately prior question is necessarily a response to that question' (Ochs 1979: 47). I found, in interviewing young people with learning disabilities, that sometimes their comments were unrelated to my immediate question, while still being related to the broader context of our interaction or occurrences in the immediate vicinity. A somewhat altered form of transcription with speakers and other activities all appearing in separate columns can clarify this and make the utterances of the individual again relevant rather than making them appear inadequate interviewees. In another example of alternative transcription procedures, Mishler (1991) problematizes the usual approach of having speaker turns represent the basic units of transcription. Instead, in a physician–patient interview, he finds different voices (the life world and the medical world) which may speak through either of the two individuals and makes these voices his basic units.

The difficulties of transcription are further compounded when working with focus groups and other forms of group interviews. In the first place, it is rarely possible to identify unambiguously individual voices in a group of any size; if this is attempted it must be approached with great caution. Secondly, the nature of group discussion is such that there will be many more instances of interruptions and speaking simultaneously which render both understanding more difficult and clear representation more complex. Finally, the sequential nature of a dyadic conversation is broken so that speakers are often responding not to the immediately preceding speaker but to an earlier speaker; sometimes this is signalled verbally but more often by eye contact or other non-verbal cues.

A final consideration with respect to recording text has to do with its reporting – that is, its use in the final product of analysis in the reporting of research results. This is yet another level of selectivity and the most stringent in that only a very tiny percentage of what is recorded in ethnographic interviews is ever finally reported. Some of the issues regarding this selectivity for purposes of analysis and writing up will be discussed in Chapters 11 and 12. However, there are a few general principles that can be noted here. In keeping with the emphasis given to context and interaction, it is certainly preferable to include fuller statements and sections of dialogue rather than heavily edited isolated quotations. Furthermore, such text should include the interviewer's questions, comments and other vocalizations to as full an extent as those of the interviewee.

Chapter 6

Using visual methods

There are two ways in which primarily visual materials are employed in ethnographic research (cf. Morphy and Banks 1997). In the first of these, visual records, such as still photographs, film and video, are produced by or at the request of the ethnographer. In this approach, the process of production of these visual materials is itself a central research activity. The product of this research may also be primarily visual, taking the form of an ethnographic film for instance; but such visually focused research may equally lead to a more traditional final product, such as a written ethnography, drawn from and perhaps including some of the visual database. In this latter case, the relationship of visual materials to final product somewhat resembles that of interview transcripts to the eventual ethnography in a primarily interview-based study.

The second use of primarily visual materials in ethnographic research is in the analysis of such materials produced by others, not at the request of the ethnographer, for a variety of purposes. Such visual documentary materials encompass a huge range of sources: family photograph albums and home videos; the work of artists; commercial artefacts such as advertisements; professionally made films and television productions; and in fact virtually all aspects of material culture. This use of such visual archival material has much in common with the use of other documentary materials in ethnographic research, and examples of the use of both visual and written archives will be discussed in Chapter 9. In this chapter, I concentrate on research in which the production of visual materials constitutes part of the process of doing research.

In a frequently quoted reference to anthropology as a 'discipline of words', Margaret Mead (1995 [1974]) urged ethnographers to make greater use of all forms of visual recordings. Ironically, in view of her own pioneering work with Gregory Bateson, she portrayed the main value of such visual recordings as residing in their documenting of disappearing cultures. Yet precisely this attitude, which portrayed the process of visual recordings as a sort of facts-collecting activity, made visual research appear in a positivist light and hence peripheral to the developing central concerns of ethnographic research. Certainly, up to that time, most generally recognized examples of the use of visual recordings were in a decidedly secondary role, both in gathering information and in presenting it, where it was mainly illustrative. At the very time when Mead was suggesting making visual and sound recordings of vanishing cultures for posterity, this approach to ethnography – salvage ethnography – was being rejected as invalid and unviable as well as raising serious ethical concerns. Challenges to positivist and objectivist forms of research were being widely promulgated and replaced by a recognition that the aim and products of ethnographic research were better understood in terms of collaboration between ethnographer and subjects than as an objective discovery of 'others'. These debates about representation and reflexivity, and related political and ethical concerns, quickly became current in visual anthropology as well.

However, one major difference affecting the debates in the use of visual methods in ethnographic research was the very factor that allowed it to be treated as a fact-collecting medium in the first place, namely, its apparent immediacy and transparent factuality. That is, visual representations have a more taken-for-granted obviousness, a greater power to convince. They are granted a greater degree of trust, thus confidence in their validity is normally attained more readily than in the validity of the written word. This belief in the evidence of the visual has both advantages and disadvantages for social research. It has a potential for increasing the immediacy of understanding, but may also impair critical reflection and analysis that can provide explanation. 'In order to be intelligible and explanatory (or articulate) film has to distance itself from its intrinsic "presence" established by the image's insistence on "being there"' (Crawford 1992: 70). To some degree, this difficulty of the presumption of the validity of the visual is addressed from within the processes of production. But it also needs to be considered as a matter of visual literacy, of educating critical viewers.

Photography

Many classic ethnographic studies included photographs. Actually some of these early examples make very effective use of photography: for example, Firth (1936) includes a large number of plates with captions that locate the individuals and activities and supply links to the text. Other examples, however, use photographs primarily for very general illustrative purposes, usually showing aspects of material culture and seldom clearly linked to the text. Their captions, too, are often quite cryptic, treating the illustrations as showing typical aspects of the topography or village life. Evans-Pritchard's study (1940) of the Nuer is amply supplied with some very fine photographs – some that he apparently took himself, but the majority from the collections of others. A selection of their captions – 'Typical savannah'; 'Homesteads on mound'; 'Girl in millet garden'; 'Harpoon-fishing from canoe' (ibid.: xi) – suggests their presentation as representative – that is, based on their typicality – without specific reference to the research in terms of location or individual identities, nor links to the researcher or the completed ethnography. As this tradition of illustrative photography developed, it reflected changing approaches to ethnography, and in particular to the increased specificity in terms of the ethnographer's experiences and relationships with individuals. Thus Turnbull's (1961) study of pygmy society includes a number of photographs all taken by himself with captions that locate, however minimally, the individual or incident – for example, 'Masalito comforts the young Kaoya during the *nkumbi* rites at a Negro village' (one of illustrations following p. 72). The incident which this depicts is also described in the text (ibid.: 221–2), and so there is a much closer link with the written ethnography and the research. However, the photographs remain illustrative and are not themselves either the main focus of the ethnography nor do they contribute to the analysis.

Another use to which photographic illustrations have frequently been put is that of establishing the authenticity of the text through powerfully demonstrating the active presence of the ethnographer in the research setting. This use of photographs can be found in the very earliest ethnographic work: for example the photograph 'Ethnographer with a man in a wig' (plate 68) in Malinowski's *The Sexual Life of Savages* (1929), as well as the extensively discussed photograph of Malinowski writing in his tent while villagers peer in at him (e.g. Clifford 1986a). Another familiar image is that of Margaret Mead in Samoan dress (Mead 1972: 149).

The sociological tradition of photography in ethnographic studies is, if anything, even more meagre (cf. Stasz 1979). The few examples found in ethnographies of the Chicago School tend to be of the same kind as Evans-Pritchard's in selecting typical scenes and presenting them without identifying commentary or captions (cf. Anderson 1923). An exception is Thrasher's (1963 [1927]) study of gangs in Chicago. The photographs in this study are not typical, but specific, as to time, place and identities, which are noted in the more extensive captions; for example we are not given a typical street market but 'The Maxwell Street Market', and in the short paragraph that comprises the caption, its layout is briefly described as is its importance to gangland, while attention is drawn to the fact that 'suggestions of lawlessness are to be found here in stands openly displaying materials for stills and the making of illicit liquor' (ibid.: 11).

The first major study that used photography as an integral part of the research process was the pioneering work *Balinese Character* by Bateson and Mead (1942) on the relationship between child-rearing practices and adult character. They argued that the controlled placidity that is so highly valued as a character trait in Balinese society is produced through particular kinds of child-rearing practices in which emotional responses are stimulated but subsequently ignored. The conclusions were drawn from analysing several thousand still photographs, as well as filming, taken in conjunction with interviewing; they are furthermore supported in the written ethnography with a selection of over 700 of these photographs. Thus, the study shows a very high level of integration of the visual into the research process. Actually obtaining the visual material was central to the methodology; its products stimulated and guided the analysis and were the principal evidence in the final presentation in the form of an ethnographic monograph. This innovative use of photography in research did not, in fact, encourage many ethnographers to follow suit (Ball and Smith 1992, but see their discussion of Strathern and Strathern 1971).

Before looking at another more recent and somewhat contrasting example of the use of photography in ethnographic research, I want to consider some of the more general issues raised by this research method. One of the strengths, as well as a weakness, in the use of photography – and even more so film and video – is the tendency to treat visual evidence as comparatively unproblematic. Thus the products of visual research are sometimes regarded in an uncritically realist perspective that also tends to accord them a very high degree of objectivity. Each of these assumptions needs to be addressed. Certainly there is a naive realism associated with mechanical processes of recording, whether audio or visual, that must be acknowledged. The apparent reality of such recordings and their power to persuade is maximized when they incorporate both sight and sound. Yet a consideration of the evidence produced, and the debate and scepticism regarding UFOs, is itself enough to alert us to the fact that such recordings do not constitute sufficient proof of the reality of phenomena they represent.

What are some of the sources of scepticism regarding visual data? In the first place, all visual recording, whether still photographs or film and video, is restricted in time and space, even in comparison to the spatially and temporally limited observations of ethnographers. A camera does not record what the ethnographer sees and hears, but a mechanically limited selection of it. Spatially the camera sees and records only a very limited selection of what is to be seen by a human in the same position; perhaps most notable is the human awareness of what is just outside the camera's vision, not to mention what is occurring behind the lens, as it were. Furthermore, the camera records a slice of time: in the case of still photography, quite literally an instant; a more extended period for video, but still a brief time span. In addition to spatial and temporal restrictions, there are technical limitations of, for example, lighting or speed. And when these are overcome with the use of more sophisticated equipment, it can be argued that what we see is even further from the experience of a human observer, who sees only very imperfectly in near darkness or whose eye is not quick enough to catch (and freeze) an action. This suggests that one of the central tasks of the visual ethnographer is to contextualize the images, to elaborate on the circumstances in which the recording is made, as well as on the technical improvements in observation. The spatial and temporal limitations can also be partially addressed by utilizing a series of still photographs, perhaps from varying perspectives and taken over time. The approach to space and time restrictions is obviously going to be somewhat different for film and video and will be discussed in the next section.

Another related consideration is the fact that photographs can be staged at the time of shooting or altered during printing.

Although deliberate deception in ethnographic photography is never acceptable, the issue of staging is not as straightforward as it might seem. To take an early example, James Mooney, who was active in studying Native Americans (primarily Cherokee, Cheyenne and Kiowa) during the period 1887–1907, arranged for the Ghost Dance to be performed during daylight in order that it was technically feasible for him to photograph it (Jacknis 1990). This, in fact, must be deemed acceptable practice so long as it is noted in the accompanying ethnographic record. Certainly, Mooney's photographs and related observations have provided a very important and enlightening ethnographic account of this ritual. Their strength lies not in their technical excellence – Mooney was notoriously amateurish, producing out-of-focus photographs, sometimes with his own shadow an obvious feature – but in their ethnographic relevance. Mooney photographed processes, taking multiple shots, and providing extensive contextualizing commentary. His work can be usefully compared with that of his near contemporary Edward S. Curtis, whose widely admired photographs of Native Americans were technically excellent but artistically staged, so that, for example, instances of modern technology or Western dress were removed from the finished plates (Lyman 1982). Mooney, in contrast, while concerned with acculturation, did not eliminate Western dress or other accoutrements from his portraits, and most of his photographs were 'candid, taken in the midst of naturally occurring events' (Jacknis 1990: 205). In both the careful contextualizing of his photographs and his honesty in not manipulating the images as people presented themselves to him, Mooney's work is an early model for good ethnographic practice in the use of photography, in spite of the fact that it was primarily illustrative rather than being an integral part of analysis.

Another consideration closely related to the presumed realism of the photographic image is the assumption of its supposed objectivity. Not only is the visual image technically restricted, it is also the product of an exercise in selectivity by the photographer, thus reflecting a particular vision. Reflexivity inheres in and affects photographically recorded observations as it does more conventional forms of ethnographic observation and must form part of the analysis that derives from them. '[T]he camera creates a photographic realism reflecting the culturally constructed reality of the picture-taker and is not a device that can somehow transcend the photographer's cultural limitations' (Ruby 1982: 125; also cf. Ruby 1980). This inherent reflexivity, or lack of objectivity, is not an invitation to visual ethnographic methods that produce self-absorbed documents of primarily autobiographical relevance. Rather it requires that photographic and other visual materials be situated in the processes of their production, including making the researcher a visible contributor to that production.

There are very few ethnographic studies that integrate still photography into the research process, particularly the processes of analysing or developing understanding. One such is Harper's (1987) study of a rural mechanic in New York state. This study, *Working Knowledge: Skill and Community in a Small Shop*, effectively integrates photography into the total research process, from initial methods through analysis to the final ethnography. Harper began with the relatively unfocused idea of photographing the mechanic in his shop. Initially he attempted to be as inconspicuous as possible in the process, with results that were uninteresting and disappointing. He concluded that he would have to involve Willie more actively and to begin photographing 'in a forthright and even aggressive manner' (ibid.: 11), which in technical terms meant using a strobe with a short telephoto macro lens to allow concentrating on details of hands and materials, supplemented with wide-angle shots to provide context; in terms of interactive research, this meant involving Willie in determinations of what should be photographed, as well as in interpretation. Groups of the resulting photographs then became focal points for interviews with Willie, and this material plus notes made from participant observation in the shop were integrated with the photographs to develop an ethnography that moves from the individual's relationship to work through considerations of the meaning of this work and its role in the definition of a rural community (cf. Harper 1989). Harper (1998) has subsequently argued that this methodology moves beyond so-called photo-elicitation, in which visual material is used to induce responses from interviewees, to a collaborative model of ethnography, in which informants and ethnographer discuss and develop their interpretations of this material. In his study of this rural mechanic, visual material is fully incorporated into the research, as method, in analysis and as an integral part of the completed ethnography. In one section, for example, Harper discusses the relationship between work and the body, noting, 'There is a kinesthetic correctness to Willie's method' (1987: 117) and continues, 'I've chosen a number of conversations and jobs to show how this kinesthetic sense operates.

The photographs isolate a moment in a work process, and they bring from Willie a description of what he ordinarily experiences' (ibid.: 118). In particular, two close-ups of Willie's hands as he sharpens a chain saw are linked to the following dialogue:

> 'What I [Harper] find hard about sharpening a chain saw ... is transferring the pressure from one hand to the other so you ...'
> '... so you're keeping an even pressure going across – so you aren't rocking your file....'
> 'In the photo you see a little of the delicacy.'
> 'Yeah – it looks like I'm holding the file real tender like. But you've got to shift that pressure from one hand to another – as you go across the saw the pressure shifts on your file. If you hold it hard you can't feel the pressure. You're not gripping the file, you're more or less letting it float or glide right through.'
>
> (Ibid.: 118–20)

The study gradually expands to a discussion of the way in which Willie's personal values and his role in the community grow from his work. His dealings with people are likened to his methodical, flexible and unhurried use, repair and modification of machines; and the ongoing relationships produce individual reputations that are the basis of social power in this community.

> But it is a social power that is by no means objective or unquestioned. The community continually redefines the social power around the rise and fall of reputations, such as that emerging from all the deals that move through Willie's shop ... And because Willie's work is invariably needed ... he gains a kind of moral power to define what kinds of actions are proper in the community.
>
> (Ibid.: 151)

A final point is the thoroughgoing reflexivity to be found in the study. But this is not a reflexivity that means the focus is primarily on the ethnographer and his responses and relationships. It is a reflexivity that allows Willie a positive and creative input into the study without having to sacrifice its analytical content. It is Willie's relationship with the research, even more than with the researcher, that gives it authority and depth and is a major strength of the study.

In her study of visual ethnography, Pink (2001) argues that, in addition to developing their professional perspective on the role of visual research methods in data collection and analysis, researchers should be sensitive to the 'uses and understandings of photography in the culture and society of the fieldwork location' (ibid.: 50). This can provide insight into how informants want to be represented, often illuminating their very different priorities in the production of images and illustrating their ideas about social relationships and the meanings they ascribe to material objects (ibid.: 58–64).

Such sensitivity to the meanings of photography among his informants meant that, in carrying out his research among Greenwich Village street vendors, Duneier (1999) did not attempt to include visual data collection until he was in his fourth year of fieldwork (ibid.: 12). As his principal informant explained in an 'Afterword' to Duneier's study, 'People who live and work on the street, as a general rule, do not like, let alone permit, photographs to be taken of them. Some do not like the idea of their lives being reduced to a tourist attraction, while others see photographs as an aspect of police surveillance' (Hasan 1999: 326). Eventually Duneier incorporated photography into this research on street vendors through an intensive collaboration with professional photographer, 'Ovie Carter, an African-American photojournalist who has been taking pictures of the inner city for three decades, ... He visited the blocks year-round and came to know the people in the book intimately. Ovie's photographs helped me to see things that I had not noticed, so that my work has now been influenced by his' (Duneier 1999: 12). One example of the closeness and effectiveness of this collaboration can be found in Duneier's discussion of the support and mentoring that some of the sidewalk vendors are able to provide other men, often with alcohol or drug addictions, with what Duneier describes as a 'Fuck it!' mentality, who have given up on the possibility of social acceptance. He describes the transformation of a young man called Ron under the influence of Marvin, the magazine vendor who had taken him on as an assistant in his sidewalk business and attempted to help him out of his self-destructive behaviour patterns.

> Whereas once he'd had the disheveled appearance of a man who never shaved or showered, now he was clean-cut. He explained that he was still living with his [92 year old] Aunt Naomi, and had continued taking good care of her. ...

> [On a visit to her apartment] Ovie took a number of photographs of Ron and his aunt together, then left. As we waited for the elevator, we heard Ron yell to her: 'Do you want your boiled milk now?'
>
> Ovie went back inside, and before they noticed him he made the accompanying photo of Ron serving the boiled milk. It illustrates, perhaps better than any interview might, the positive changes that Ron was making with the support of Marvin on the street.
>
> (Ibid.: 77–8; cf. Duneier 1992, for a previous example of this collaboration)

This photograph is atypical of most of those in the ethnography in that it is explicitly discussed in the text. Most of the photographs are not, and none are captioned, yet their integration with the text is clear and they contribute substantially to description and analysis. This integration is aided by a two-page spread of photographic portraits of the street vendors, with names attached, arranged on a schematic map of the Greenwich Village streets where the research took place, which appears in the front of the ethnography. The willingness of his informants to be identified in this way, in a study that is clearly sympathetic to them but nevertheless also portrays socially undesirable behaviour, such as harassment of white women pedestrians, attests to the integrity of the ethnography, based on what his principal informant describes as 'the radical willingness of the social scientist to listen' (Hasan 1999: 327).

Film and video

There are several ways in which filming may be used in ethnographic research. The most salient is the production of an ethnographic film as a major product of the research. A second way is to have the subjects of the research film themselves; in this approach the film and the process of its production become the main sources of data for the researcher and its major product is likely to be a written monograph. Another way of using ethnographic film in research is for elicitation – for example when filming by the researcher is shown to those who were filmed, as well as to others, for their responses and interpretations. These uses of filming are not mutually exclusive; they often are combined in a single project. All of these ways of using film in ethnographic research have been affected by

Illustration 6.1 Sidewalk vendor from SIDEWALK by Mitchell Duneier, Photo © Ovie Carter

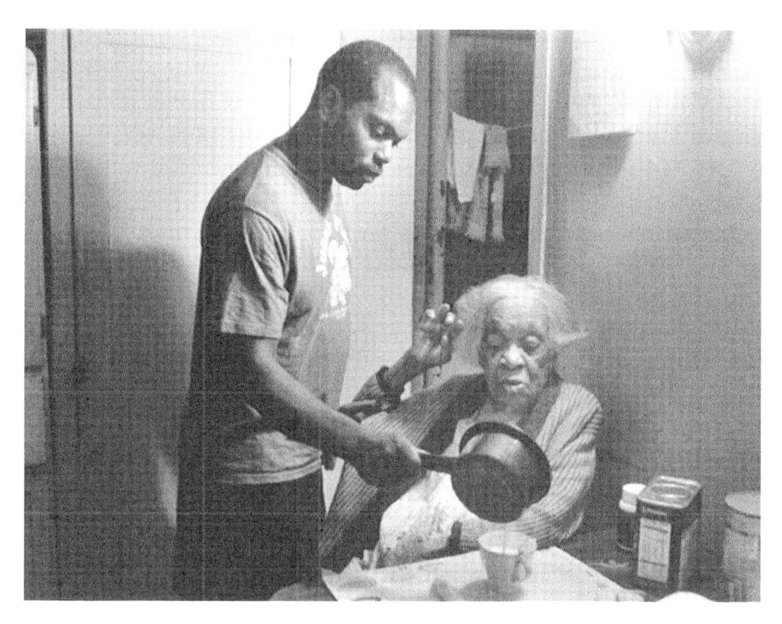

Illustration 6.2 Ron pouring hot milk for his aunt from SIDEWALK by Mitchell Duneier, Photo © Ovie Carter

technical developments as well as ongoing debates about the nature of ethnographic research more broadly.

It is not my purpose here to review the historical development of ethnographic filming (for that see Grimshaw 2001; Heider 1976; Loizos 1993). However, it is worth noting that some of the very earliest recognized examples of ethnographic filming incorporate technical capabilities that lie at the heart of much of the debate about the use of filming for ethnographic purposes – that is, its apparent true-to-life character and related ability to convince. For example, Flaherty's creation of half an oversized igloo to make it possible to show the 'inside' of such a structure in his 1922 production of *Nanook of the North* is a classic example of the way in which props and filming techniques can be used, at the production stage, to deceive the viewer. On the other hand, the film is based on solid ethnographic observation during an extended time in the field (Heider 1976: 21–3). Nor is the capacity for deception limited to the actual production stage. For example, Marshall's film *The Hunters* (1958) which purports to portray a giraffe hunt was actually put together in an editing process that used footage from several different hunts. Similarly, the battle portrayed in Robert Graves's 1963 film *Dead Birds*, perhaps one of the most widely viewed ethnographic films ever, is edited from film sequences of several such occasions; this film also makes use of other techniques, such as imputing specific motivations and thoughts to the subjects of the film, which were considered to introduce practices that undermined the validity of filmic ethnographies.

Criticisms and questions about the validity of the films produced by such techniques began to produce styles of ethnographic filming that eschewed various filming conventions and the capacity of film to produce highly believable images in favour of various filming techniques intended to enhance the observational realism of the production. Such a goal was facilitated by a number of technological developments since the 1960s, in particular, the facility for simultaneous recording of image and sound, subtitling and filming under a variety of natural lighting conditions. The development of easily portable, one-person video cameras that give relatively high quality results with minimal technical knowledge has further extended the possibility for creating a feeling of immediacy and realism in ethnographic films.

One way of seeking observational realism is to try to use the camera as if it were the eyes and ears of the eventual viewer of the film. Clearly, this approach incorporates positivist or simplistic empiricist notions in that it reduces or denies the role and power of the film-maker over the images eventually produced. At its extreme, this style of film-making has been caricatured as one that 'consists of a camera on a tripod which is touched as infrequently as is technically possible and which produces as long takes as possible. These long sequences are spliced together in chronological order' (Ruby 1980: 171). However, a less extreme version advocates avoiding most of the techniques that give films a professional finish: for example minimal or no use of close-ups; no shots that suggest simultaneity of actions, such as shots of an interlocutor nodding at appropriate points in an informant's responses (Heider 1976).

One question that is comparatively vexed in such observational realist filming is that of the role of commentary. The major criticism of commentary is that it is experienced as the voice of authority telling viewers how to interpret the images (but cf. Grimshaw 1995: 35). Thus extensive use of subjects' own voices with translations by means of subtitling is advocated. However, ordinarily, people do not spontaneously explain their behaviour or comment on their motivations and interpretations unless asked, and so a common device has been the introduction of the ethnographer into the film, behaving as an ethnographer by asking questions and participating marginally, but not acting as a presenter. Several of the films of the Maasai made by Melissa Llewellyn-Davies use this device of asking people to explain what is happening around them to good effect. Her 1984 film *The Women's Olamal: The Social Organisation of a Maasai Fertility Ceremony* is particularly noteworthy for its portrayal of conflict between women and men over the ceremony, rather than simply giving a normative account of the way things are supposed to go. Furthermore, in one sequence in particular, the film begins to transcend the observational approach in another way by making the process of filming more apparent to the viewer. This occurs when Llewellyn-Davies asks a question of one of the women at a particularly emotionally charged moment and is rebuked for doing so. Later, in a calmer moment, the woman explains what was happening and why she was unwilling to talk at the time. Leaving this record of the ethnographer's social blunder in the film calls attention to the presence of the ethnographer and film-maker in the ceremony so that 'the distance between film-makers and subjects is reduced, because the intrusiveness of filming has been admitted, and yet transcended' (Loizos 1993:132).

Probably the most influential ethnographic film-maker in stimulating the development of the reflexive potential for filming was Jean Rouch who primarily filmed the Songhay people of West Africa. 'For him, the camera is not confined to the role of a "passive recording instrument", but becomes rather an active agent of investigation and the camera *user* can become an interrogator of the world' (Loizos 1993: 46). Several of the films of David and Judith MacDougall, in particular those made in conjunction with the Australian Institute of Aboriginal Studies, have developed this reflexive potential. David MacDougall argued in 1974 that the ideal of observational reality was based in an artificial separation of film-makers and their films from their subjects, a separation that was both fundamentally dishonest and a reflection of colonialist attitudes. He began to advocate a thoroughgoing reflexivity that meant that the film was based around and displayed this event – that is, the meeting and relationship between film-maker and subjects.

> What is finally disappointing in the ideal of filming 'as if the camera were not there' is not that observation in itself is unimportant, but that as a governing approach it remains far less interesting than exploring the situation that actually exists. The camera IS there, and it is held by a representative of one culture encountering another. Beside such an extraordinary event, the search for isolation and invisibility seems a curiously irrelevant ambition. No ethnographic film is merely a record of another society: it is always a record of the meeting between a filmmaker and that society.
>
> (MacDougall 1995 [1974]: 125)

Thus, in one of his films, *Goodbye, Old Man* (1977), of a Tiwi bereavement and burial ceremony, participants occasionally address the person holding the camera, who responds to them (Loizos 1993: 175–6). In *The House Opening* (1980), Judith MacDougall introduces a reflexive element in a broader sense than the visibility of the film-maker. This film shows the ceremony to reopen a house for a widow and her children to return to it after her husband's death. The widow provides commentary throughout the film, attempting to explain the events to a non-Aboriginal audience. Thus, it is the principal character in the film who reaches beyond it to engage deliberately with the audience. In the process, she also reflects upon changing Aboriginal customs and their responses to European contact and pressures (Myers 1988: 210–12).

As these examples suggest, there is no single way or set of techniques to ensure reflexivity in ethnographic film-making. The ways of making the film-making process visible may vary, but it is essential that the film, insofar as it is to be considered as ethnographic research, visibly include consideration of the reflexivity of the research relationship. Another important aspect of reflexivity in ethnographic film-making is the contextualizing of the film and the process of its construction through the use of supplementary materials. No film, no matter how reflexive, can fully compensate for the limitations of space and time to which the camera is subjected. Additional materials to accompany the film can assist in overcoming these limitations as they also can provide fuller accounts of the circumstances of the film's making. Heider (1976: 68) suggests that even the deliberate distortions of presenting edited versions of several battles as a single encounter, as was done in *Dead Birds*, can be countenanced so long as this is clarified in written accounts.

Asch (1992) goes further and advocates not only the publication of a study guide or monograph to accompany each film, but also making available as an archive an uncut version for research by others. This is analogous to providing interview tapes and/or transcripts and full field notes for inspection and use by other ethnographers, which has various ethical implications that are discussed in Chapter 3. However, it is worth noting that Asch's provision of such archival materials made possible a critique of certain practices, in particular, the general failure to recognize the Western gender, race and class biases that are carried over into ethnographic filming. Kuehnast (1992) examined uncut footage for Asch and Balikci's *Sons of Haji Omar* (1978), along with that for Marshall's *N!ai, The Story of a !Kung Woman, 1952–78* (1980), and argues that evidence of Western technological influence has been systematically edited out, producing representations that deliberately visually obscure the impact of their colonial past on these peoples. Such a critique could not have been made, or made as effectively, without the important evidential base provided by the film-makers.

This critique also points to concerns about the way in which films are viewed, an area that has not been substantially researched (Eidheim 1993) but one where there is some evidence that audiences may decode films in ways that are antithetical to the intentions of the film-makers. Thus, ethnographic films intended to encourage cross-cultural understanding may inadvertently promote higher levels of alienation and distaste and reinforce prejudices about 'primitive' society (Martinez 1992). More specifically, it was found that filming styles based in a less engaged and less reflexive observationalism promoted such negative responses, whereas greater interest, insight and empathy were reported in response to 'emotionally engaging films with humour and narrative drama, made-for-TV documentaries, films using a reflexive style, close-up portrayals of the lives of individuals, and/or filmic attention to topics of general concern (issues of gender, economics, etc.)' (ibid.: 132).

To some degree this may reflect broader changes in documentary styles in the 1980s, when television documentaries began to make greater use of various editing tricks, such as altering background colours, and the influence of drama documentary increased the use of reconstruction as well as the prevalence of interpretative and narrative frameworks. These changes have also begun to influence ethnographic film-makers. Loizos (1997) considers several examples of ethnographic films, all based on some kind of journey, that incorporate some of these more recent trends in documentary filming and appear to move away from the observational realism of the previous two decades. Of the films that he discusses, the one that seems most obviously and drastically to break from recent ethnographic filming traditions is Alan Ereira's *From the Heart of the World: The Elder Brother's Warning* (1990). This film about the Kogi of the Colombian Sierra Nevada interprets the visit by the film-makers to the Kogi as an acting out of a Kogi myth in which they (the film-makers) as the elder brother are sent back with a warning about the destructiveness of capitalist lifestyles. The film makes extensive use of evocative music, as well as repeated close-ups of an enigmatic symbol. It is furthermore inaccurate in its representation of the visit as the first white contact with this society. In spite of its undoubted artistic and emotional appeal, of no small consequence considering the concerns with audience reception, this film has definite limitations as an example of future directions for ethnographic filming. Although it is thoroughly reflexive, in the sense of being about the film-makers and the society they come from much more than about the Kogi, it is an inward-directed reflexivity, which is nevertheless not made clear in the film itself. Also unclear is the Kogi's contribution to the interpretation being placed on their myth. The film-makers seem to appropriate Kogi cultural understandings and apply them to a Western social problem without either obtaining the active participation of the Kogi or acknowledging their own part in developing the particular interpretation they present. As such, it cannot be said to represent good practice in ethnographic film research.

Not all of the films discussed as representing experiments in a more narrative style of ethnographic filming are of this kind, or to be criticized in the same way. Several of the films, Loizos maintains, are examples of ethnographic filming in which the subject is to a large extent the creation of the process of filming. For example, Boonzajer Flaes's film *The Roots of Mexican Accordion Music in South Texas and North Mexico* (1989) deals with the responses of the members of these accordion bands to films of Austrian accordion bands, as well as to films of themselves. This approach represents a creative use of forms of elicitation with films in which the reflexive relationship between film-maker and subjects encompasses aspects of analysis. Another example discussed is *Nice Coloured Girls* (1987) by Tracy Moffatt which uses extensive dramatization to examine the history of white male/black female contact; this film, as the creation of an Australian Aboriginal director, can be seen as an extension of a tradition of ethnographic filming in which cameras are given to the subjects to produce films about their own reality. These two approaches, elicitation using ethnographic filming, and ethnography through subjects' filming of themselves, I now consider in somewhat more detail with reference to several examples.

Perhaps the best known early example of the use of film for elicitation are the two films by Timothy Asch: first, *A Balinese Trance Seance*, filmed in 1978, which shows Jero as a healer working with some of her clients, followed by *Jero on Jero* (1980) in which she watches and comments on the first film. One of the strengths of the second film is its clear inclusion of so-called traditional practices and practitioners in the world of technology rather than its being used to represent them as a world apart. A rather more complex and creative use of film for elicitation may be seen in the work of Robert Boonzajer Flaes, noted above, on the Mexican accordion polka bands of Texas and New Mexico. The film he produced of this research is not a typical ethnographic film 'about' these cultural groups; rather it is itself an exploration of the relationships between these groups and polka bands in Austria (cf. Loizos 1997: 92). In discussing this research, Boonzajer Flaes (1993) notes that video elicitation can be almost too easy to obtain – virtually any video clip will elicit some response; hence it is vital to consider carefully how to get at anthropologically informative responses. In his work, he began with the idea of showing Mexican groups films of Austrian bands, and vice versa. However, he eventually discovered that he learned more by considering how they themselves thought they should be filmed for presentation to the others.

> [T]he players had very specific ideas about how their music should be represented. Moreover these ideas were so different, that I could use this visual self-representation as an important clue when later on analyzing and structuring the interviews. The Austrian players were not satisfied unless I had them in the middle of a picture, surrounded by paraphernalia indicating their social surroundings (the fireplace, the Christmas tree, the dried flowers on the wall). The Chicanes by contrast did not care about things like that at all – I had to concentrate on the minute details of the actual accordion playing. These strangely contrasting pictures corresponded closely with the questions the players would ask about their colleagues across the ocean. Austrian questions invariably boiled down to aspects of social standing and Chicanes were just interested in the notes and the techniques of playing.
>
> (Ibid.: 114)

Boonzajer Flaes came to explain these different ways of choosing to represent what was superficially the same kind of musical performance by considering the different social contexts of Mexican and Austrian performers. For the Chicano performers, he came to realize, the polka circuit was a self-contained, but limiting, social world offering no real prospect of advancement and without any broader significance beyond the music itself. Thus, musical technique was the main thing about themselves that they wanted to portray to others. 'For the Austrian players however, the polka is part of a cherished national heritage, and therefore great care must be taken not to get it represented as dance hall or pub level. The actual notes are only a minor part of the overall social and musical impression the players wanted to present' (ibid.: 15). These two kinds of accordion bands, therefore, both playing polkas, are really giving two different performances; and this understanding of what each is doing was developed through elicitation of their responses to their own representations on film.

Another example in which elicitation helps to develop the focus of the research as well as contributing to the analysis is a comparative study of pre-schools in Japan, China and the United States (Tobin, Wu and Davidson 1989). In this study, as a first step, the researchers produced a 20-minute ethnographic film made of a pre-school in each country based on footage from 'what we hoped would be a more or less typical day, including scenes of arrival and departure, of play both indoors and out ... of more structured learning activities, and of lunch, snack, bathroom, and nap times' (ibid.: 5). The authors are fully cognizant of the influence of their own perspectives; for example, they come to recognize their decision to focus on two or three children in each class as reflecting the attitudes of American pre-school teachers regarding allocation of time. The videotapes are acknowledged to be 'subjective, idiosyncratic, culture-bound – and yet consistent with our method [in that] we were trying not to portray a nation's preschools but instead to begin a dialogue' (ibid.: 7). The researchers then showed and discussed the film with various audiences from the pre-school, parents, children and teachers. Subsequently, the films from pre-schools in the other two countries were shown and discussed; the contrasts thus revealed produced more self-conscious discussions of the perceived aims of pre-school education and the particular and contrasting problems that each of the three groups believed they faced. Finally all three films were shown, not only to audiences from the original three pre-schools, but also to other audiences with an interest in pre-school education outside the three research sites. This extensive comparative and reflexive set of practices – the authors describe the structure of the research as 'dialogic' (ibid.: 4) – ensures that the final ethnographic monograph does not present an overly simplistic version of cultural norms being expressed and reproduced in pre-school education. Rather, it is able to document a spectrum of practices while still developing an informed and informative comparative analytical perspective in which real difference can be recognized and comparative insights developed without either reifying such difference or obscuring internal heterogeneity.

The final way of using ethnographic filming as an integral part of the research process that I discuss in this chapter is when the camera is actually handed over to the research subjects and they create a film for and about themselves. In research like this, observations of the production process are as important for the ethnographer as the content of the final production. Chalfen (1989, 1992) noted that different groups of adolescents in Philadelphia undertook the making of a film in very different ways: black lower-class girls placed their greatest emphasis on before-camera performance and usually made a single shot, whereas their white middle-class contemporaries gave much more prominence to directing and made multiple takes. As this suggests, one of the factors that can affect a study of this sort is the amount and nature of any training in the use of filming and editing equipment that is provided. Clearly, it is vital that the ethnographer reflexively consider such issues and incorporate such considerations into any analysis that results. As this further suggests, ethnographers are not turning the research over to their subjects by this approach; they do not fully relinquish responsibility for analysis and interpretation. But they are attempting to increase their subjects' input and to leave open longer the theoretical or interpretative directions the research may take. David MacDougall, whose series of films on Aboriginal people was a collaborative venture, has since expressed some disquiet with this approach: 'My view of it now is that it was a kind of film-making that rather confused the issues. In those films one never really knows quite who's speaking for whom, and whose interests are being expressed. It is not clear what in the film is coming from us and what is coming from them' (Grimshaw and Papastergiadis 1995: 45). Nevertheless, it could be argued that this dilemma lies at the heart of ethnographic research and should not be taken as either unique to this sort of ethnographic filming or as an argument against it, but rather as a cautionary statement to be aware of the necessity to disentangle these separate voices and views.

One of the earliest extensive studies which adopted this approach, *Through Navajo Eyes* (Worth and Adair 1972), has been very influential and remains an example of good practice. In this project, John Adair, an ethnographer who had been studying the Navajo for a quarter of a century, and Sol Worth, who taught communications and had worked with taking film technology to disadvantaged groups, taught a group of six young Navajos to use cameras and editing equipment in order to explore 'how a group of people structure their view of the world – their reality – through film' (ibid.: 7). One of the study's many strengths is its recognition of the reflexive nature of the project, from initial selection and training through observation (the authors refer to their method as participant intervention and observation) of the filming process and eventual analysis of the meanings of the Navajos' productions. 'We have accepted the obvious: that pretending we are not part of our culture, that we have no preconceived ways of viewing the world or of viewing a film, is impossible' (ibid.: 9). Thus they are visible throughout the study, without being intrusive – that is, in spite of the necessity to refer to their own filming and editing conventions and expectations, it remains primarily a study about the Navajos, their experiences and perspectives, not about the ethnographers. The ethnography describes differences in narrative styles, sequencing, selection of subjects, and use of cameras and editing equipment and relates these differences to various aspects of Navajo culture. For example, 'all but one of the films are without what we would call narrative suspense' (ibid.: 207). In particular, two films, made by different individuals, one about weaving and the other about silver-smithing, begin with the completed product; they then show the process of creation with emphasis, in terms of amount of film footage, on walking to collect materials rather than on the subsequent manipulation of the materials; finally they conclude with a shot similar, but not identical, to the opening shot of the finished product. These filmic statements are linked to Navajo cultural themes of circularity, but without complete closure, and with an emphasis on motion and forms of motion, rather than states of being, an emphasis which is also encoded in their language. Thus, what is important in these films is 'not *what* will happen, but how it happens' (ibid.:207). Worth and Adair identify a similar concentration on, and use of, motion in the Navajos' camera work, where they displayed, virtually from the start of their work, quite sophisticated skills in moving the camera to introduce other forms of motion into their films. '[A]ll of them combined in very intricate patterns the various forms of motion. They played constantly with the speed of the object moving and the speed of the camera movement, sometimes going in the same direction and often going in opposite directions' (ibid.: 202).

In the study, Worth and Adair describe the participants and their relationship to Pine Springs where the study was conducted. Only one of the six came from outside the community – Al Clah was born in another Navajo community and had attended the Institute of American Indian Art, thus combining the attributes of outsider and artist, while still a Navajo. The differences in the film he produced from those of the others in the group are indicative of the influence of Western cultural forms and filmic conventions and expectations. Nevertheless, his product still supports Worth and Adair's analysis in that many of the cultural themes, in particular the concentration on motion and the use of concepts of circularity and balance, can also be seen in his film in spite of its atypical concern with symbolism and exploration of his own position as being between Navajo and Western cultural worlds. Besides strengthening their analysis, this example also suggests that their concern with finding people whose exposure to film or television was minimal for the study, in case they might already have absorbed Western cultural filmic conventions and expectations, was perhaps unnecessary. Certainly, the likelihood of finding such technologically naive peoples has drastically diminished in over 30 years since this study was undertaken. Yet there is every reason to believe on the basis of this study alone that people can adopt and use the technology of visual representations without undermining their own cultural perspectives. As another example, Worth and Adair found their Navajo students very resistant to their suggestions regarding the use of close-ups for cutaways as well as to their objections regarding jumps in action produced by a particular form of cutting. In another example, one with a more political message, the use of media, and particularly video cameras, by the Kayapo, a rainforest people, to assist their political struggle against plans of the Brazilian government to build a dam in their territory appears to be intimately linked to 'not only a new assertiveness about their ritual life and conventional dress, but a new conception of their collective identity' (Turner 1991: 322).

Of course, the use of media for political purposes also sensitizes us to the issue of who is the intended, or imagined, audience for any such production. Worth and Adair's study does suggest at one point that the students may be making their films not only for the Pine Springs community, who are to see the finished products, but also with an idea of another audience. In particular, the two students who make films about artisans both say they want to show how hard the work is and thus justify the cost of the finished products, which are objects often sold to tourists (1972: 101), but this particular theme is not pursued in the study. Nevertheless, it is important that a full analysis of indigenous films must recognize that these films may be expressing not only their makers' own cultural understandings, but also their interpretations of other cultures – in particular, that of the ethnographer's culture – how they want to represent themselves to these others and the ways they develop to communicate with them, a theme that was noted above in the discussion of Judith MacDougall's film *The House Opening*.

Chapter 7

Internet ethnography

The internet can be viewed as simply providing an additional tool for social research, for example, as an effective way of distributing and administering questionnaires, locating potential research subjects or carrying out documentary research on organizations. In these kinds of uses it is supplementary to ethnographic research, but it does not fulfil our expectations that ethnography involves in-depth involvement in the lives of those being studied over an extended period of time. However, even such conventional uses of the internet in research may be extended and adapted to produce studies that are very close to, if not actual examples of ethnographic research. In some cases the openness and flexibility of design that are hallmarks of ethnographic research can arguably be better achieved by conducting the research on-line. In designing her research to look at assisted reproduction from the perspective of women who were involuntarily childless, Illingworth (2001) had originally intended using participant observation and semi-structured interviewing in the Assisted Conception Unit where she had herself received treatment. However, during a discussion of the proposed research, the consultant in the Unit so undermined her position as an academic researcher rather than a patient, and de-legitimized her intended topic of the stigma women experience as a result of childlessness, that she determined ethnographic research in that setting was unlikely to be accomplished without unacceptable control over the project by the medical hierarchy. Having subsequently altered her design to rely primarily on on-line interviews with women located via discussion groups on infertility, she received confirmation of this decision from respondents who said they would have been reluctant to participate in a face-to-face setting for fear it might affect their treatment and even more reluctant to voice any criticisms of their treatment in such a setting. In the end, she felt that had she proceeded with her original design, she would 'unwittingly, have contributed to an enhancement of power relations within the research setting' (ibid.: 6.3), an outcome that was at odds with her feminist methodology. Of course it is legitimate to ask if the change in research design fundamentally altered the original ethnographic intent of the study. Certainly it was no longer clearly an ethnographic study, but it nevertheless retained elements of ethnographic authority. In particular, while she argued that on-line interviews could help democratise the exchange by eliminating some of the visual cues that inform power relations, Illingworth was concerned that the lack of face-to-face interaction sometimes produced misunderstandings that could undermine validity. She tried to counter this effect by conducting two or three interviews with each individual. And she also emphasized her reflexive engagement with the project by providing interviewees with information about her personal attributes and experience of assisted reproduction. Although these measures do not transform this study into an ethnography, they do preserve some of the characteristics of ethnographic research.

The internet, however, is incorporated more fundamentally into much ethnographic research that is conducted wholly or primarily on-line. Such research, variously characterized as 'internethnography' (Tapper 2001), 'virtual ethnography' (Hine 2000) or ethnographies of cybersociety (Jones 1998), may examine topics as varied as the employment experiences of inflammatory bowel disease sufferers (Stewart and Williams 2005) or the meaning of national identity among diasporic communities (Bernal 2005); but it must also address the nature of the internet and its effects on the conduct of ethnographic research and its findings. Thus in addition to the practical considerations of how or whether contacts via the internet can produce ethnographic knowledge, internet research raises fundamental questions about the nature of field sites and of participant observation and about the treatment of context, when that context is the internet itself. It also introduces some new questions regarding research ethics.

Ethnographic knowledge and the internet

Rather than engaging in unproductive discussions of whether various examples of internet-based research do, or do not constitute ethnography, I want to consider how such research produces knowledge that makes validity claims on grounds that are very similar if not identical to those used by more conventional ethnographic methods. One of the characteristics of ethnographic research is its basis in in-depth multi-stranded relationships with informants developed over an extended period of time. Furthermore rather than consisting entirely of a series of binary relationships between the ethnographer and individual informants, it normally also includes observation of relationships between informants, so that the relational data is complex and interconnecting. When one-on-one semi-structured interviewing is conducted via e-mail, as in the Illingworth example above, it is possible to develop quite complex and nuanced relationships with individual informants, but this does not allow testing of emerging ideas in a context that is less controlled by the ethnographer. And restricting research to this form of data collection will almost certainly reduce the potential for surprise and the flexibility that can lead ethnographers in unexpected directions. However, the available forums for internet communication are more varied than simple e-mail and much more complex relationships can be established than these binary conventions. The forums that are most commonly accessed for ethnographic research on the internet are a variety of on-line interactive sites including discussion groups, chat rooms, newsgroups and multi-user domains (muds). These sites allow for multiple participants to contribute to an on-going discussion usually organized around a general topic, such as soap operas (Baym 1998), or catering to a specific interest group, for example the 'Lesbian Café' (Correll 1995). Discussions may be synchronous, that is 'live', with comments displayed in real time as they are being typed; or they may be asynchronous, with messages being composed and then sent to an administrator for subsequent posting. In either case, discussions are retained and accessible on-line for considerable lengths of time, usually for several weeks. Clearly such datasets are multi-vocal, and working with them produces an effect much like being at a party, with different topics and speakers interweaving and competing for attention. The influence of the ethnographer's presence and research agenda can be minimized, although decisions have to be made regarding the desired degree of researcher participation in the site. Researchers may decide to follow specific topics, or conversational threads, over a period of time; they may also take a particular interest in certain individuals, following their contributions and interactions. And most sites also offer the possibility of establishing one-on-one contact with individuals, if they agree, through their private e-mail accounts, thus allowing for follow-up and more in-depth discussion and the potential to develop principal informants along the lines of conventional ethnography.

One of the characteristics of internet-based research is that it moves ethnography's acknowledged high degree of textuality at the level of analysis into the data collection phase, that is, most data consist of typed messages. This has some practical advantages; for example it eliminates the need to transcribe recordings of interviews. But it also raises a major concern in that ethnographers do not have access to the non-verbal cues that often inform their interpretations of what people say. Internet users often attempt to introduce information that would be conveyed non-verbally in face-to-face encounters, for example, with the almost universal use of the smiley face ☺ and the acronym 'lol'. However, all such cues are under the conscious control of the internet user to a much greater extent than are facial expressions and body language in face-to-face encounters. This raises the broader question of on-line identities and the capacity to deceive that the internet offers. Researchers have taken different attitudes towards this issue. Many point to the fact that identity manipulation is a common aspect of social life, both off-line and on-line, and some argue that people have multiple identities some of which they may be able to project more successfully when they are not physically present. In a study of how people with disabilities use computerized communication technology, Lupton and Seymour found that in two of their case studies, its use 'allowed the emergence of an *alter ego* [that the research subjects] considered to be liberating and more expressive of their "true self" than was the self that was defined by the limits of their physicality' (2003: 262). In this instance the internet was not being used to conceal – most of the research subjects spent a great deal of time discussing their disabilities in on-line support groups – but it essentially filtered out the inadvertent non-verbal signals that these individuals believed served to hide rather than to express their identities.

Studies that attempt to adapt ethnographic methods as fully as possible to internet research have tended to argue that participants in the various on-line interactive formats generally are concerned both to project themselves in an integrated and consistent fashion and to be able to recognize others in the same way. Kendall spent three years participating and observing an on-line MUD known as BlueSky, which was a site for socializing that was frequented mainly by computer programmers and system administrators, and concluded that they 'persist in seeking essentialized groundings for the selves they encounter on-line' (1999: 62). They were dismissive of role-playing and their expectations were that participants would provide information about their lives off-line. Thus, far from being a site of multiple and shifting identities, on BlueSky 'people generally have only one character and are known not just by their character name but by their known personality characteristics, their shared history with others in the group, and often by data concerning their off-line lives' (ibid.: 69). In addition, anonymity was definitely discouraged; when new participants came on-line, they were asked about their identity and why they wanted to join the group. Furthermore long-term participant observation on this site, as well as on other such interactive sites, has shown that many attract and hold a regular group of participants, and these regulars develop distinctive patterns of social interaction that are then employed to control the behaviour of newcomers to the site. In the case of BlueSky, the expected form of interaction was built around a masculine style of sexual banter that was often insulting. Women who frequented the site had to be able to hold their own with this abrasive banter. Another example of participants policing a site by means of enforcing expected forms of interaction can be found in Correll's (1995) discussion of the treatment of 'bashers' who log on to harass the regular participants in the Lesbian Café. Although some 'bashers' used male names and were openly hostile, others posted under female names and were only identifiable because their messages – like those of other newcomers to the site – did not follow the conventions that had been built up for appropriate behaviour on entering the bar. When corrected by the regulars, 'bashers' gave themselves away with hostile or negative responses, whereas genuine newcomers tried to adjust their behaviour to fit the site norms.

What these examples suggest is that the problem for ethnographers of the reliability of on-line identities is similar to the dilemmas that they face in conventional participant observation. And the best way to ensure the validity of their on-line observational data is to adopt similar expectations regarding long-term contact with the regulars on any site they are studying. Identities of informants are established through their relationships with other users, and ethnographers must be prepared to evaluate internal evidence regarding the consistency and credibility of their presentation of self on-line.

> Spending time with other participants and getting to know the particular norms and understandings of the group allows

> researchers to build trust and to learn to interpret participants' identity performances in the same way that participants themselves do. In many such forums, shared history of time spent together as well as repetition of on-line performances and stories about that shared history compensate for the relative paucity of interactional cues available on-line.
>
> (Kendall 1999: 70–1)

It is often important to consider as well what can be known regarding their off-line identity. While not an ethnographic study, Donath (1999) looks at various ways in which the likelihood of identity deception can be evaluated by considering the anatomy of an individual's postings, from assessing the significance of account names to examining message content for inconsistencies and inaccuracies.

The concern of ethnographers generally about achieving the best balance of observation and participation in their research is also relevant for research on the internet. The nature of these interactive sites makes it possible for a researcher simply to observe without making their presence known, perhaps the ultimate in pure observation. 'Lurkers', that is individuals who log on to interactive sites but do not participate, are a widely recognized category among internet users, and this clearly provides a possible role for an ethnographer. Leaving ethical considerations aside for the moment, there are some drawbacks to assuming such a role, which are similar to objections to covert research in conventional contexts. Specifically, as a 'lurker', ethnographers cannot ask for clarification nor attempt to move discussions in a direction that is of particular interest to them. Neither is it possible in this role to develop more in-depth relationships with key individuals nor to contemplate organizing one-on-one interviews. In her study of the Lesbian Café, Correll's (1995) on-line participation was minimal, that is she posted weekly notes describing her study and occasionally asked for explanations of observed interactions, but even this low level of participation enabled her to conduct a number of semi-structured interviews on-line and subsequently to meet some of the participants off-line. Kendall's (1999) approach was more interactive, possibly reflecting the much greater length of time, three years as opposed to three months, spent on her study of the BlueSky site. After several months of observing, she began to participate in the group and described how, as a woman, she was nevertheless forced into a masculine style of interaction in which she attempted 'to respond in kind to the common style of obnoxious bantering' (ibid.: 64). This kind of reflexively produced data can provide significant insights into the nature of the social group, in this case giving a powerful lesson in the way the norms of a specific site were enforced on newcomers. It is noteworthy as well that this observation depended on her electing to use her gender identity rather than attempting to conceal it. Another consideration regarding the participation of ethnographers in these interactive sites is that many of the muds are initially entered through public rooms, where 'newbies' (newcomers) always congregate, but they also allow for the construction of private rooms with controlled access. Clearly ethnographers wanting to learn about the population of the site could easily over-estimate the transitory nature of the participants unless they develop contacts that allow them to learn about and negotiate access to these other areas.

Another way of enhancing the validity of internet ethnography is to pursue off-line contacts with some informants. Obviously this is often impossible due to the wide geographic spread of participants in most of these interactive sites. But when it is feasible, it can be very informative. Correll (1995) was able to join in a planned off-line meeting of a number of regulars from the Lesbian Café, carrying out participant observation with the group in a 'real' lesbian bar and conducting two group interviews, each with four participants. These experiences revealed that most of the patrons of the on-line Lesbian Café did not frequent real bars, and indeed were uncomfortable in that setting. As a result of this experience she was able to frame and address another research question, namely why the on-line site was set up to resemble a bar. Another example in which off-line contacts were pursued and were, in fact, essential to the research agenda is a study of the Dehai discussion board for Eritreans in diaspora (Bernal 2005). While this study made extensive use of postings on Dehai, its analysis of the role of this website in constructing Eritrean identity and creating a concept of Eritrean citizenship, as well as affecting real world events, was also based on 'fieldwork in Eritrea, discussions with Eritreans in diaspora, ... and [off-line] interviews ... with readers and contributors to Dehai, including one of the most prolific writers to emerge on the website' (ibid.: 664), who became a principal informant.

Unsurprisingly, when off-line contacts can be incorporated into internet research, they often add depth and extend the scope of the research questions, as well as addressing some of the concerns discussed earlier about identity and deception. However, Hine (2000) has suggested that off-line contacts should be pursued with caution, and only when they are an available option that can also be taken up by on-line participants; otherwise, she argues, 'face-to-face meetings with online informants ... [could] threaten the experiential authenticity that comes from aiming to understand the world the way it is for informants' (ibid.: 49). This is a very restricted view of what ethnographic research can accomplish. From a critical realist perspective we can expect that researchers pursue all available avenues to develop their understanding of social reality, certainly not that they should limit their enquiry only to understanding the perspectives of informants. Furthermore, it is a fallacy to treat on-line research participants as if they exist only in cyberspace, in spite of some of the claims of enthusiasts about their disembodied and decontextualized nature (e.g. Porter 1997). In fact, no one exists entirely in cyberspace; we are all embodied and present in a specific time and place when sitting at the keyboard engaged in on-line activity. 'Individuals exist and participate in off-line social contexts both sequentially and simultaneously with their on-line participation' (Kendall 1999: 60). Thus, for some of the individuals with disabilities in the study discussed above, their local situation was highly significant because, for example, their particular disability meant that they had difficulty participating in synchronous discussion groups. Furthermore the broader off-line context is significant for understanding the dynamics of particular interactive sites. It is important to recognize that BlueSky was primarily frequented by computing professionals, predominantly male, who as a consequence of their employment circumstances had both access to computing accounts and opportunity to log on to this site during their working day. Without this knowledge about off-line context our understanding of the nature of this site and the style of interaction would be much poorer.

This is not to argue that off-line contact must be an intrinsic part of all internet research. Clearly this is neither practical nor always desirable. Lysloff's research (2003) on the mod scene – a network of composers and aficionados of electronic music that they create, exchange and discuss entirely on-line – did not involve any off-line contacts. Nevertheless his involvement with this scene, which he contrasted with the physicality and embodied nature of previous fieldwork in rural Java, still entailed an intensive and long-term relationship with the field.

> Using real-time electronic 'chat' systems and e-mail, I would often stay connected the entire night, traveling from one homepage to another, engaging in a network of far-flung friends, reading and typing messages to electronic musicians and their fans, gazing at images, both still and animated, and listening to random songs that would play automatically at some websites. ... Throughout the night I would check my e-mail to see if my composer friends or fellow enthusiasts had sent their most recent pieces for discussion.
>
> (Ibid.: 235)

He developed key informants, including one who became his tutor in electronic music composition, and his subsequent analysis provides one of the most convincing arguments, based on sound ethnographic evidence, for the interpretation of some on-line networks as communities.

Nature of 'the field' on-line

The changing nature of anthropological understandings of the field and of expectations regarding what constitutes fieldwork (see Chapter 2) has greatly enhanced the acceptability of some forms of internet-based research as ethnography. Thus developments in ethnographic research – conducting fieldwork across multiple sites; the growth of the ethnography of organizations, where research is focused on only one aspect, such as work relationships, of informants' lives; the acceptance of a role for network and discourse analysis; and the use of narrative – all contribute to a positive outlook regarding the potential for on-line ethnography. Certainly research on the internet is by its very nature multi-sited, researchers tend to study groups with some common interest but have little access to other aspects of members' lives, they look at how relational networks develop and change, and they are heavily dependent on interpretation of discourse and narrative presentation.

Although on-line ethnographers cannot claim to study the kinds of clearly defined, territorially bounded social groupings with which ethnographic research was for so long associated, many have made extensive use of the concept of community as an appropriate theoretical description of their research sites. Thus it will be useful to consider how, or whether, internet ethnographers have identified a new type of field site, namely the on-line community. Objections to this possibility have been based in an insistence on the locality bound nature of community and, to a lesser extent, the lack of choice regarding spatially defined community membership. For example:

> A community is bound by place, which always includes complex social and environmental necessities. It is not something you can easily join. You can't subscribe to a community as you subscribe to a discussion group on the net. It must be lived. It is entwined, contradictory, and involves all our senses.
>
> (Doheny-Farina 1996: 37)

Expectations like these regarding the nature of community and of community participation clearly eliminate many internet sites from any such consideration. However, while access to on-line sites may be easily achieved – just as visitors can pass through or sometimes even settle in spatially defined communities without actually belonging – the question of whether the social relationships established within on-line groups can be understood as community cannot be dismissed out of hand but rather must be addressed by ethnographic investigation of particular cases. The issue of the relationship between community and the internet is also implicated in the numerous examples of off-line social groups which are supported by on-line interactions, both those who live in fairly close proximity to one another (Baym 1998: 37–8; Wellman and Gulia 1999: 181–3) as well as disasporic groups (Bernal 2005).

The interpretation of some internet sites as communities has been facilitated by the critique of the concept of community from the 1970s onwards as well as by some aspects of the on-going debate about the nature of community and the utility of the concept in off-line contexts (Davies and Jones 2003). One of the main criticisms of the concept as it was applied in traditional community studies was its tendency to over-emphasize homogeneity and to ignore the existence of conflict and oppressive relations, a tendency that reflected the social characteristics delineated in Tönnies' (1955 [1887]) *gemeinschaft/gesellschaft* distinction and subsequently elaborated with ethnographic example in Redfield's (1930) folk/urban continuum. Many of the early enthusiasts for the potential of the internet as a basis for community (e.g. Rheingold 1993) argued that on-line communities would be able to avoid the oppressive and intolerant aspects of traditional communities because of what they felt was the inherently egalitarian nature of the internet and its potential to conceal most of the characteristics, such as gender, age, ethnicity, social class, on which hierarchical relationships depend. As a consequence they repeated the error of earlier theorists of romanticizing community, ignoring the potential for alternative forms of hierarchy and social control in an on-line context. They also tended to adopt the traditional view of community as transforming locality into meaningful 'place' by arguing that new kinds of places outside geographic localities were being created in cyberspace.

Ethnographic studies of on-line sites as potential communities have undermined some of these assumptions about the likely nature of cyber-communities. Kendall's (1999) study of the BlueSky network demonstrated that gender and ethnicity remained important attributes affecting the culture of this site. And numerous studies (Correll 1995; Lysloff 2003) have shown that social control mechanisms are developed which can be used effectively to exclude participants. One of the best examples of an attempt to create a meaningful 'place' in cyberspace is found in Correll's discussion of the Lesbian Café site. This site was built around a fantasy, created entirely through verbal descriptions, of a bar with various accoutrements such as a pool table and fireplace; when patrons first came on-line they would post a note ordering a drink and perhaps indicate where they intended to place themselves in the bar, behaviour both announcing their presence and showing their familiarity with the café and its rules. This fantasy was sustained by patrons at least over the three months of the fieldwork, and Correll argues it demonstrates that 'a locale need not be confined to a specific geographical location but can instead be created and maintained in cyberspace' (ibid.: 298). On the other hand, its status as fantasy was acknowledged as such by the participants in e-mail and face-to-face interviews and it was not used in their personal e-mail contacts with one another. More recent access to this site suggests that the bar fantasy is no longer a predominant feature. It may be that this particular device of constructing a fantasy locale was primarily useful in the early stages of creating the site, when Correll's fieldwork took place, but became unnecessary once a network of regular participants was established. New technology that allows the construction of graphical muds, so that multiple users, in addition to their text-based communication, can also be represented by characters in an on-screen landscape, may enhance the sense of an on-line 'place'. This technology has been used in the conduct of on-line focus groups (Stewart and Williams 2005) and the researchers claim that it created a greater sense among participants of being in the same location. In addition, they argue,

> ... forms of visual communication, until recently void in online communication, allow for a richer form of social interaction. ... For example, each avatar is ascribed a detailed set of animated emotions, so if someone in the group was in disagreement of an opinion they could shake their head; likewise, if someone agreed with another avatar's statement, they could jump for joy.
>
> (Ibid.: 407–8)

While this clearly adds a visual dimension to textual data, this representation of body language is no more spontaneous or involuntary than is the smiley face inserted in text commentary. Nevertheless, based on participant observation in an on-line virtual environment (Cyberworlds), which contains thousands of public and private spaces and encourages participants to build their own space, Williams (2007) argues that users form impressions of one another based as much on the appearance and actions of their avatars as on their text messages, and hence that a similar attentiveness to graphical as well as textual representations is essential for ethnographers of cyberspace.

Rather than pursuing the analogy to locality-based communities through attempts to discover cyberplaces on-line, other ethnographic studies of on-line sites have adopted more contemporary understandings of community as primarily network-based rather than spatially defined. It can be argued that most modern communities are spatially dispersed, not entirely, or even primarily face-to-face, and individuals participate in multiple, sometimes overlapping communities. An excellent study of a network-based on-line community is Lysloff's (2003) research on the mod scene. As a consequence of his long-term participation and in-depth involvement with these digital music composers and their fans, Lysloff was able to document a social structure based on expertise in the computing complexities of this particular musical genre – with new composers often subjected to stringent reviews published on the internet – as well as on the popularity of the compositions (mods) that were widely circulated. Although there is no equivalent mod scene in the off-line world, on-line 'it resembles a prestige economy constituted through the circulation and exchange of valued objects [mods]' (ibid.: 244). There are also mechanisms to control plagiarism, which is the most serious infringement of group mores, through 'humiliation and banishment from the scene' (ibid.: 251), a punishment that can be very effectively enforced by virtue of the programming expertise of many mod composers. Thus Lysloff argues that the internet provides a new kind of materiality that can become the basis of a complex social network which he interprets as community.

Although there can never be any presumption that on-line networks can be understood as communities, it is certainly valid to ask whether our understanding of a particular site or a specific network is enhanced by considering its similarity to some forms of off-line communities. Or, to approach the issue from a slightly different direction, one which is probably also more appropriate for examinations of the variety of manifestations of real world communities, we can ask what happens on-line so that some people experience particular sites or networks as community. We can only hope to answer these questions by means of meticulous and conscientious ethnographic research.

Ethnographic research on the internet has investigated on-line social groups primarily with reference to the concept of community. Clearly the potential methodological perspectives for internet ethnography are much broader than this and there are likely to be many instances in which community is not the most appropriate conceptual frame. For example, the output of a discussion group could be interpreted as an exercise in collective story telling, or possibly myth making, rather than in terms of members' interrelationships. Such an approach would clearly draw on theoretical understandings of narrative and would not be concerned with either mapping the social relationships between participants or investigating the nature of community. The burgeoning number of personal blogs that are posted on the internet provides yet another potential area of study in which narrative analysis could be employed, for example to examine the range of individual interpretive strategies for different life cycle events.

Hine's (2000) study of activity on the internet related to the 1997 Louise Woodward trial, a major media event in which a British nanny was accused of murdering an American child in her care, provides an example of internet ethnography that eschews the community metaphor, focuses on a topic rather than a particular site and supplements her on-line participant observation with a specialized methodology looking at discourse. She examined support sites and newsgroups and also contacted site developers in producing this virtual ethnography of 'the status of the Internet as culture and cultural object at the time' (ibid.: 67). In the process of analysing her material, she made extensive use of the techniques of discourse analysis, which enabled her to recognize the ways in which performances, both actively in the discussion groups and statically on the web pages, were organized to promote acceptance of their authenticity (ibid.: 142–6).

The internet in context

Most ethnographic studies of internet sites and activities, even those with no formal off-line component, nevertheless recognize that the internet exists in a broader context and that the effect of this context on research findings needs to be considered. There are two primary ways in which ethnographic research on the internet can be contextualized. In the first place, attention should be given to the off-line context in which internet usage occurs. Thus it is relevant whether a discussion group consists mainly of individuals who log on from their place of work or from an academic institution (e.g. Baym 1998; Kendall 1999), as this will indicate something about the composition of the group, apparent to site visitors as well as of significance to the ethnographer, and may also help explain patterns of usage. The geographic spread of participants may also be relevant, in spite of the internet's much vaunted ability to overcome distance. For example Correll (1995) observed that users of the Lesbian Café retained a real time orientation in their creation of this imagined place: people who logged on in the mornings would order a coffee, not an alcoholic drink; and on-line 'parties' were always held at night. Clearly being able to make such an observation depended on her prior knowledge that all the active participants were from the eastern United States and hence had the same time orientation. In contrast, a study that conducted synchronous on-line focus groups with an internationally recruited set of respondents found that differences in time zones among participants brought practical problems of organizing a mutually convenient time. More seriously, it was essential to be sensitive to how participants could be affected by their real time environment. 'Those starting their day may have responded differently from those who had just finished lunch, or those who were tired after a long day. ... it was clear that many in the group were suffering from a form of virtual jet-lag' (Stewart and Williams 2005: 406).

In addition to paying attention to the off-line contexts of research subjects, ethnographers should cultivate a reflexive awareness of their own internet usage, both how they engage with it and the effect of their off-line circumstances on their usage. Hine (2000) reports being particularly aware of the interface between on-line and off-line environments during the period when she was awaiting the Louise Woodward trial verdict, which was to be announced first on the internet. Thus she was intensely involved in events that were taking place within a time zone hours earlier than her own lived time. Furthermore, she notes the potential for simultaneously being engaged in other activities, not necessarily related to her on-line activity.

> It was thus, when the first news of the judge's ruling appeared on the Internet, that I found myself in my office, feet up on the desk and leaning back in my chair, engaged in a prearranged telephone meeting via the receiver I held in my left hand, following discussion on a topic totally unrelated to Louise, while clicking my mouse with the right hand visiting Louise Woodward web sites, and listening to conversations through the door of my office and trying to work out whether Allegra [her research assistant] had realized that the ruling was out. ... The feeling was one of being multi-present and thoroughly engaged.
>
> (Ibid.: 72)

To some extent this passage can be read as rhetoric, which establishes the ethnographer's authority by demonstrating that she has really 'been there', a similar function to the arrival stories of classical ethnographies. But its significance goes beyond this. Hine is aware of the great difficulty of conducting research both to observe internet culture on-line and to observe internet use, which seems to require being in two settings at once, namely the virtual on-line site and a physical location (ibid.: 40). The only way ethnographers can fully experience this is during their own on-line activities, when they are aware of the simultaneity of on-line and off-line engagement and can observe activities at this interface. Although they cannot claim that all users have similar experiences at this interface, the reflexive awareness of their own observations can increase sensitivity to the existence of these effects and guide enquiries about how the interface may be experienced by their informants.

The second way in which ethnographic research on the internet should be contextualized is by considering the internet as itself a cultural product. Working within the environment of a communications technology that has been heralded as having a revolutionary potential to transform human social relationships, ethnographers need to cultivate a critical awareness of the assumptions and the particular interests that lie behind the way this technology has been developed and promoted. For example, the claims often made for the internet as an egalitarian technology must be viewed in the context of actual internet access worldwide which is heavily concentrated among the economically prosperous in Western societies. It is especially important that ethnographers not treat technology as socially, culturally or politically neutral. 'Technology does not spring, *ab initio*, from some disinterested fount of innovation. Rather, it is born of the social, the economic, and the technical relations that are already in place' (Bijker and Law 1992: 11). From this more sceptical perspective ethnographers are able to challenge some of the assumptions about the nature and significance of this developing technology. As we have seen, this is already being done successfully regarding communitarian claims about the internet by critical ethnographic studies of the nature of community at actual on-line sites.

Ethnographic researchers also need to cultivate their awareness of debates about the broader social context and effects of the internet, especially regarding how it is implicated in processes of globalization. Thus some have argued that the internet is fundamentally a tool of global capitalism 'that is mobilising new information and communications media to create an extraterritorial space of enterprise, in defiance of the cultural and political realities of the actual world most of us are living in' (Robins and Webster 1999: 225). Ignoring such a critique, or failing to recognize its significance for anyone wanting to explore the internet as a site for ethnographic research, bears an uncomfortably close resemblance to anthropology's failure, over decades of ethnographic research in non-Western settings, to recognize the significance for their research, and for the groups they studied, of the colonial and post-colonial environment in which they worked.

Internet research, therefore, is no exception to the expectation that good ethnographic research must be reflexive at all levels of awareness, from individual sensitivity to the effects of their on-line presence on their data and the inclusion of researchers' experiences in the data to the more general level of examining both the internet itself as context and ways the broader social context affects the current uses and developmental direction of this technology.

Ethics on the web

The internet provides a massive new resource for ethnographic research with a range of 'field' sites that are comparatively easy to access. Superficially it may appear that data obtained via internet research are comparable to observations made in any public setting and, as such, while not immune to ethical constraints, are usually not ethically problematic. However, computer-mediated communication occupies an ambiguous position on the public/private spectrum. Even personal e-mail messages are not usually secure (Ess and AoIR 2002: 5) and in any case are notoriously vulnerable to breaches of privacy in that they are so readily copied and forwarded to other users. And the various on-line forums that are the focus of most ethnographic research, while publicly available to an almost unlimited audience, are experienced by many contributors as private, with the anonymity they appear to offer encouraging even greater intimacy and self-revelation than in face-to-face contacts. Thus data consisting of postings to such sites are better treated as comparable to those obtained from other ethnographic methods such as participant observation and interviewing. And researchers using these data sources are subject to similar ethical expectations, in particular the avoidance of covertness, the necessity to obtain informed consent, respect for confidentiality and protection of the anonymity of informants.

However, these ethical expectations often present special considerations or cause difficulties peculiar to internet research (Ess and AoIR 2002). In the first place ethnographers must take account of the variation in the nature of different sites. Clearly a site set up by an organization to provide information to the public can be treated, and analysed like any public document. To some extent this is also the case for sites established by private individuals whose clear intention is to attract an audience and inform or entertain them in some way; such a site is roughly comparable to a published work and a more relevant consideration here is the right of the author to be acknowledged rather than protection of anonymity. But caution needs to be exercised if the author of the site is in some way less accountable or more vulnerable, for example a minor or someone with a mental illness. One difficulty in this respect is that the identity of the site author may not be readily available, so researchers must be alert to internal evidence that might indicate the vulnerable status of such individuals.

Interactive sites vary regarding their provisions for users, with some having a posted site policy that emphasizes its public nature, warns users of the limitations to privacy and sets out the arrangements regarding archiving and accessing of postings. Nevertheless even on a site with clear guidelines about the public character of postings, users are not likely to expect that their interactions may become data for an unknown research project nor that their postings might be quoted in a context of which they are totally unaware. For these reasons – even though 'lurking' may be acceptable in the very early stages of selecting a research site – it is imperative for researchers eventually to identify themselves and explain their purpose in logging on to the site. Furthermore, because of the changing nature of personnel on any given site, this identification and explanation has to be repeated at regular intervals, arguably each and every time the researcher comes on-line.

The task of obtaining informed consent presents a number of difficulties. With an indeterminate number of visitors to any given site, it is not at all straightforward to decide whose consent should be sought. This is somewhat analogous to a village or community study, where it is not normally practicable, nor considered necessary to obtain the consent of all the residents. But consent is required from all the principal informants, certainly from anyone who is quoted or discussed at any length in subsequent publications. This can usually be done via the e-mail addresses in the postings and, if the context in which a posting is being used is explained, it can sometimes generate additional useful commentary from informants (e.g. Sharf 1999: 251). Informed consent often also entails a commitment by researchers to respect confidentiality and protect the anonymity of their informants, a commitment that raises particular problems in the context of internet research. Because of the efficiency of search machines and the potential longevity of postings on the web, the usual ethnographic means of ensuring anonymity through changing names (both site names and user names) will not provide absolute assurance that a quotation cannot be traced back to its originator. In fact, 'complete anonymity is almost impossible to guarantee, as information about the origin of a computer-transmitted message is, for most users, almost impossible to remove' (Stewart and Williams 2005: 411). This inability to provide total anonymity is a function of the internet environment, not a characteristic of the research, but informants should be made aware of this limitation to the researcher's ability to guard their privacy.

It may be that internet research is even more likely than research off-line to concentrate on socially disadvantaged or marginalized populations, a tendency that is problematic in social research more generally. Certainly it is widely acknowledged that there are 'many vulnerable populations – people in acute stages of grief, with sexual dysfunctions, life-threatening diseases, or addictions, ... for whom interchange via computer has become a primary source of information and social support' (Sharf 1999: 246). Any research with such vulnerable groups must be particularly careful about protecting individual privacy and confidentiality. There are sufficient examples of research on more privileged groups (e.g. Baym 1998; Kendall 1999) to illustrate the potential for 'researching up' via the internet but, as with social research in general, the potential of those with political and economic power in society for limiting access by researchers is just as great on the internet as it is off-line.

Conclusions

Rather than engaging in debates about whether internet ethnography can really be classified as ethnography, it is more helpful to consider the similarities and differences in research strategies as they are actually employed. Internet ethnographers make validity claims on grounds similar to those of conventional ethnography, namely, their long-term, in-depth, multidimensional contacts with informants, and they face similar concerns, for example regarding the best balance of observation and participation, the possibility for deliberate deception by informants, as well as concerns about multiple and shifting identities. On the other hand, the disembodied nature of internet interactions, and hence the lack of access to the information that physical presence may convey, cannot be fully compensated even by the most technologically advanced sites, while the pursuit of off-line contacts entails other difficulties both practical and theoretical. In addition, some ethical issues, such as ensuring anonymity for informants while using data from interactive sites, can be particularly problematic.

Certainly the inclusion of internet ethnography in debates about the location of the field and the changing nature of fieldwork gives an informative new perspective to these discussions. Furthermore, several internet-based ethnographies have made a valuable contribution to studies of community and of the conceptualization of community. The potential of internet research to contribute to other methodological approaches used by ethnographers, such as narrative analysis, has yet to be fully realized.

Internet ethnography shares with other forms of ethnographic research the absolute necessity for the reflexive engagement of the ethnographer, from the personal level of reflection on one's own on-line interactions, to the broader consideration of the internet as cultural product and the examination of our culturally conditioned assumptions about the nature and social significance of this technology.

Chapter 8

Structuring research

Surveys, networks, discourse analysis

While more formalized methods of social research, such as social surveys, networks and some of the techniques developed in the area of cognitive anthropology, are not characteristic of ethnographic research, they are frequently supplementary to it. It is certainly desirable that ethnographic researchers be aware of the potential utility of these techniques, and their respective strengths and weaknesses, so as to assess whether and how they may be properly employed in specific research situations. Arguments both for and against their use tend to focus on their so-called objectivity and whether such objectivity is either achievable or desirable for the subject matter of ethnographic research. The discussion in this chapter draws attention to the continuing role of reflexivity often disregarded in such methods and suggests that, while this places knowledge derived from these sources on a less objective footing than is asserted for them by some of their adherents, it makes these methods both more compatible with and more useful for ethnographic researchers.

Social surveys and official statistics

Social surveys are commonly defined in terms of their most prevalent form of data collection, namely, the administration of a highly structured questionnaire, each question usually being provided with a preselected set of possible responses. The questionnaire may be in written form to be completed by the respondents themselves or it may be administered verbally by interviewers who record responses. However, a more useful definition is one that does not link the social survey to any particular form of data collection but rather defines it in terms of a particular method of recording data. Marsh (1982) defines a social survey on the basis of the following characteristics. Fundamentally, the data on which the survey is based must be organized into a rectangular array of numbers, for purposes of analysis. The horizontal rows in this array consist of the individual cases in the survey. These may be individual persons, households, organizations, even countries. The only restriction is that all the rows must represent the same units; thus it is incorrect, for example, for some cases to be individuals and others family groups. The vertical rows represent the variables, queries made and answered about each of the individual cases. The values in the array are numbers that represent the responses to these queries for each of the cases. In some instances the variables will have actual numerical values that can be recorded directly in the array, for example age, income or number of children. More commonly, the numbers recorded are values linked to a numerical code which converts qualitative characteristics into numbered categories. For example the variable 'sex' may be recorded as '0' or '1' representing 'female' or 'male', the variable 'ethnicity' may be given a numerical value linked to one in a list of possible ethnic groups or identities.

Data organized in this fashion can subsequently be analysed very efficiently and thoroughly with two main purposes in mind. First, descriptive material, particularly frequency tables and cross-tabulations, for the entire dataset or specified subsets, can be produced. Thus the distribution of cases for a given variable, for example the numbers in each of the ethnic groups, is readily obtained, as are tables that break this distribution down according to another variable such as sex. The other main purpose of the social survey form of data organization is to search for relationships between variables using various kinds of inferential statistics. Various computer statistical packages are available for analysis of this kind of data (two that are widely used are SAS and SPSS), and they make the production of such results a very easy matter indeed once the data are coded and entered into the correct format.

When this definition of social surveys is adopted, it becomes apparent that, while considerations regarding the suitability of survey research for ethnography must pay attention to its characteristic form of data collection, they must also be concerned in the first instance with issues of quantification and categorization. Thus, Johnson and Johnson (1990) argue that ethnographic field notes can be used as a basis for a survey form of data organization and, furthermore, that 'counting cases from fieldnotes is an improvement over vague, impressionistic generalities that obscure negative cases' (ibid.: 176; also cf. Mitchell 1967). However, they also warn that consideration must be given to whether the precision implied by such quantification is warranted and whether the units being counted and the categories into which they are divided can be supported, in effect raising questions in these two related areas of quantification and categorization.

In a classic critique of the use of survey methods, Leach (1967) discusses examples of misinterpretations, stemming from these two processes of categorization and quantification, in the conclusions of a survey conducted in an area of Ceylon (now Sri Lanka) culturally similar to a small village he had studied previously using ethnographic methods. He notes that the unit of analysis for the survey was the household, defined as being those who cook their rice from the same pot, and that by using this particular unit, the survey determined that over 60 per cent of households were landless. He suggests, based on his intensive experience with a single village, that a proportion of these landless households were likely to be young recently married children living under the same roof as their parents from whom they expect to inherit land, suggesting that such households should not really be regarded as landless. Leach seems to believe that such errors are inevitable because categorization of necessity disregards the ethnographic insight that 'a social field does not consist of units of population but of persons in relation to one another' (ibid.: 80). Another criticism that relates more to the process of quantification than categorization is his objection to the finding that sons inherit from two to eight times more land than their sisters. Although agreeing that there is a bias in favour of males in inheritance practices, he objects that 'the effect of reducing this bias to a precise numerical figure is entirely misleading. It gives a false air of scientific precision to what is, at best, a highly variable "general tendency"' (ibid.: 83). He then points out some observations on the ground that make this reported figure suspect, such as the tendency of male heirs to purchase the land inherited by their married sisters, as well as noting the likelihood of not being given fully honest and straightforward responses to questions about such a culturally sensitive topic as inheritance.

While such criticisms of social surveys are certainly germane to their use in ethnographic research, other considerations argue rather more forcefully that they do have a place when properly employed. The objections to their use deriving from the necessity for categorization can be met, in part, by undertaking preliminary intensive ethnographic investigation in order to assess what can be learned through surveys and to develop appropriate and meaningful categories for the particular research locale (Speckmann 1967: 60; Wallman and Dhooge 1984: 261). Leach's second objection, to quantification per se, seems to stem from his recognition of the relatively greater persuasiveness of an argument bolstered by numbers. The use of statistics as rhetoric is clearly a matter for concern and is discussed more fully below. Nevertheless, ethnographers do use quantifications, such as 'many', 'the majority', 'very few', and these should be used advisedly. That is, ethnographers who assert that the majority of informants report 'x' or a minority of villagers do 'y' should themselves know on precisely what evidence this assertion can be made. And this requires counting. Otherwise they are as prone as anyone else to exaggerate particularly noteworthy comments or occurrences and translate this unconsciously into quantity. If such counting indeed takes place, there is little reason not to share this with the reader, who then knows whether 'the majority' means 85 per cent or just over half, and also knows the size of the group for which this assertion is made.

There are other technical issues that ethnographers who want to employ social surveys must take into account (for detailed information about the use of surveys see, for example, Bryman and Cramer 1997; de Vaus 1991; Robson 1993). Of these, the two most fundamental are sampling and questionnaire construction. Ethnographers working in very small communities over an extended period of time will often be able to complete a simple survey for virtually a 100 per cent sample. However, such circumstances are becoming less and less common in ethnographic research and thus ethnographers need to concern themselves with the details of sampling techniques. For surveys whose main purpose is to assess the range of values for a particular set of variables – for example if the aim is to gauge the extreme opinions and internal variations on a given issue – non-probabilistic sampling of the type employed for ethnographic interviewing may be adopted. However, if the survey results will be used to provide background to the ethnography such as the relative size of various categories within the research population or the frequencies of various opinions among different groupings, then some form of probabilistic sampling must be employed. It should be stressed again that the process of sampling tends to reify the units of analysis which compose the sampling frame and hence to conceal the reflexivity inherent in the surveyor's decisions about how to define these units and how to subcategorize them. In good ethnographic research, ethnographic insights gained through intensive fieldwork will inform these decisions and furthermore they will be considered in the analysis and made visible in writing up.

Although I have stressed that questionnaires are not the only form of data collection for social surveys, they are prevalent enough that some of the problems and issues regarding questionnaire design and administration need to be mentioned here. If the research is being conducted among people who are from a different society and culture to that of the ethnographer, or even from a different subcultural group in the same society, it is unlikely that a mutually intelligible questionnaire can be constructed until some fieldwork has been undertaken. Ethnographic research will almost certainly be required to determine what kinds of questions to ask as well as how to ask them. It is also important to understand how such a formal process of asking questions is likely to be interpreted in the cultural environment in which the research is undertaken and whether there are any local reasons that would cause interviewers to be regarded with suspicion. If the questionnaire has to be translated into a different language for administration, this can also introduce serious misunderstandings between researchers and respondents. The validity of the translation is best tested by 'back' translation, that is, having someone who has not seen the original questionnaire translate back to the original language and compare the two versions. Although the opportunities for misunderstanding are more obvious when there are cultural and linguistic differences between researcher and respondents, surveyors who rely on their own cultural assumptions when working in their home society can easily introduce assumptions that are not shared by their respondents. It is as important to attempt a degree of defamiliarization, of making the everyday seem strange, when designing a survey as it is for more traditional ethnographic research 'at home'. One process that is very important to improve questionnaire construction, no matter where the research is undertaken, is effective use of a pilot. That is, the questionnaire should be administered to a small group, with results analysed for anomalies, and their feedback as to how they interpreted specific questions and what they meant by their responses should be solicited. In other words, in-depth ethnographic interviewing should be undertaken with this pilot sample in order to improve questions and increase the likelihood that researcher and respondents are interpreting questions similarly. Finally, consideration must be given to the social interaction during the administration of the questionnaire and how it may affect responses. In particular, factors such as gender, social class, age and ethnicity must be considered. If interviewers other than the ethnographer are to be employed, they must be chosen with such factors in mind and given adequate training in terms of how responses are to be interpreted and entered on the questionnaire. Furthermore, they should also be given guidance regarding other observations they might be able to make during the interviews and their feedback should be sought in debriefing sessions (Wallman and Dhooge 1984: 266–7). In other words, they should be encouraged and trained to undertake some other forms of ethnographic research in the process of administering the survey.

Considerations such as these make clear that social surveys cannot lay unambiguous claim to objectivity. In fact, their apparent objectivity appears to owe more to the particular way in which they organize data using numbers, and the reporting language and conventions they adopt, than to any properties inherent in them as a form of data organization and analysis. If, by objectivity, is meant the reduction of reflexive input by the researcher to as low a level as possible, as seems to be implied in survey researchers' particular concern with reliability, an ethnographic perspective suggests that this is by its nature not really possible and in any case self-defeating in that it is likely adversely to affect the validity of the survey. From the perspective of ethnographic research, the recognition of the reflexivity of social surveys is to be welcomed in that it is through the use of the reflexive engagement of the ethnographer with other sources of knowledge about a society that social surveys can be made more meaningful and useful for such research. For example, Pugh (1990) criticizes an exercise in collecting statistics on homelessness undertaken by a small voluntary youth advisory service as unenlightening because they hide too much significant variation among the youth counted as homeless. However, on returning to the source of the statistical data, her own recorded information, she argues that it is possible to produce valid and meaningful statistics by using her own experience as a volunteer in the organization and paying attention to the context of their creation. She argues that statistics such as these are acceptable within a feminist, and essentially ethnographic, theoretical framework 'which considers the researcher as central in the research process and which challenges the monopoly by statistics of correct practice' (ibid.: 112).

The most thoroughgoing consideration of the reflexive component of statistical knowledge is put forward by an ethnomethodological perspective which directs attention to three foci in the process of creating statistical arguments: the production of statistics; the use of statistical analysis; and the presentation of statistics in order to convince/support an argument (Gephart 1988: 9–10). This perspective directs attention to the working practices and assumptions of those who produce and analyse statistics, rather than to the ideal of statistical knowledge as derived solely from mathematical first principles and hence seen as fully objective. At this workaday level, 'statistics lack the consistency and finality found in published scientific products' (ibid.: 15), and furthermore their interpretation is negotiable and affected by power relationships within the institutions that employ them. Thus, in a study that looked at the production of statistics within social service institutions where staff were convinced of the factual status of numerical data (Gubrium and Buckholdt 1979), it was found that they routinely made decisions about recording statistics based on their interpretation of behaviour. For example, in a programme to monitor the success of bowel training, patients were recorded as having a 'clean day' if dirtying could be interpreted as a deliberate act to get attention and not as a failure of physical control. Similarly, when required to count instances of teasing, the discourse among staff shows that they actively define such behaviour in the process of counting; thus they decide that '"givin' the finger" [to a teacher] does not count because teasing is understood to be countable only when kids are involved, not kids and teachers' (ibid.: 125). (For an example of the social factors that affect collection and production of mortality statistics, see Prior 1985.) At the level of analysis it is argued, for example, that the widely adopted method of asking respondents to assign numbers to qualitative characteristics, as is done with opinion scales, is assumed to provide a level of reliability which, while usually unquestioned, is probably not warranted and which when analysed by commonly used statistical methods may produce distortions that go completely unrecognized even as possibilities (Gephart 1988: 35–41). Finally, attention is drawn to the persuasive power of statistics, in particular to the way in which a discourse among researchers adopting statistical methods may build up an edifice of objectivity through various rhetorical devices without ever confronting the question of the meaning of their measurements. Thus, through the use of various verbal formulae, the meanings of numbers are reified, so that discussions of general statistical trends often conceal specific numerical findings that do not support the general conclusions. 'The results and conclusions were not products of the inherent properties of numbers nor of the rule bound translation of numeric values into verbal interpretations' (ibid.: 61) but were constructed in an interpretative exercise at least as reflexive as any engaged in by ethnographic researchers and rather less transparent.

With the radical critique by ethnomethodologists of social statistics as background, it is important to consider briefly the use by ethnographers of statistics produced by others – in particular, the official statistics produced by various governmental organizations and other bodies. Such statistics, as with those produced by social researchers, must be seen as social products, and it is often argued that official statistics are particularly suspect in that they, as government products, will necessarily reflect and support the interests of the state that collects, interprets and publicizes them. The production of crime statistics, and especially statistics on juvenile crime (Cicourel 1968), has proven particularly vulnerable to exposures of the ways in which such statistics themselves create various types of crime and criminals (cf. May 1997: 67–78). Another area that has also been a target for political pressure in the production of statistics is that of unemployment figures (Levitas 1996). On the other hand, it is clear that a wholesale rejection of all official statistics cuts us off from a very large and potentially informative database (Bulmer 1984). Official statistics are by no means uniform in their quality or in the political considerations to which they may be responding, and some sources of official statistics are more acceptable than others (Levitas and Guy 1996). Thus it is important to stress that ethnographers not use official statistics uncritically. As with any secondary source, the conditions of their production must be probed. The more open and accessible these are, the greater the likelihood that they can be genuinely informative to research questions that were not a part of their original brief and the greater the confidence that can be placed in their use.

I conclude this section with an example of good practice in the use of statistics in a central role in ethnographic research, namely, a study by Jane and Peter Schneider (1996) of fertility decline in

Sicily. The statistical base for this study was constructed from the municipal records of marriages, births and deaths in a Sicilian town over the period from 1860 to 1980. By employing these official data sources the researchers reconstitute families in marriage cohorts for each decade of their study. The demographic data with which they work include tables such as age at marriage, numbers of children born and numbers surviving, and intervals between births, all differentiated on the basis of social class. The strength of this statistical database owes much to the fact that the researchers, having themselves developed it, are aware of its assumptions and limitations; furthermore, they improve its validity by making use of older people to help them interpret some of the official registers (ibid.: 90–5). Using these data, they are able both to compare them to broader demographic patterns in Europe and also to problematize the internal variation that they reveal. The explanations they develop for the variation between classes draws upon their ethnographic fieldwork in this Sicilian town, including extensive ethnographic interviewing, observations of material culture and collection of sayings and proverbs about family size and relationships. They note that the main theories that deal with such demographic variation – in particular the lag in limiting family size among the lower classes – explain it either in terms of some rational calculus about the economic value of children or by reference to traditional values that are slow to change in the face of modernization. They reject both of these explanations and, based on their ethnographically informed insights, argue that 'deprived of economic resources – in particular property with which to structure their children's marriages – and assigned to roles that enhanced the families of others while sapping their own, landless laborers could hardly generate a new ideal of family as happened among the artisans' (ibid.: 245).

A further strength of the study is its attention to the specific forms of birth control, primarily *coitus interruptus*, rather than simply assimilating the various techniques to the fact of control over reproduction. They are able to assess the meanings that the adoption of this technique has for different classes: they note a similarity across classes in forging a connection between respectability and sexual continence encouraged by this form of birth control; they also recognize substantial differences in interpretations of its meaning for gender relations, with the artisan class basing it in somewhat more cooperative marriage arrangements, whereas the landless peasants when they adopted the technique retained aspects of a much more patriarchal relationship. As all these considerations suggest, this study provides an excellent example of the way in which a creative combination of official statistical sources with ethnographic knowledge can not only provide a more clearly problematized and interpretatively rich local study, but also can be linked to global processes of population change and challenge and inform macro-theoretical analyses of these processes.

Network analysis

Social network analysis was one response to practical methodological difficulties that anthropologists encountered as they began to undertake research in locations that could not be readily treated as relatively isolated social and cultural units, in particular as they moved from village studies to research in urban areas (Mitchell 1966: 54–60). It was also a response to the perceived theoretical inadequacies of the then prevailing paradigm of structural functionalism for these emerging research interests (Noble 1973). Thus, in the first study to apply the concept of social networks to formal analysis, Barnes (1954) argued that the organization of social life in an island parish in western Norway could not be understood solely, or even primarily, in terms of the area's institutional structure, composed of territorial and occupational groups, like the hamlet and the fishing crew. Instead, he examined a myriad of cross-cutting interpersonal ties of kinship, friendship and acquaintance, which he argued made up a class network and was one basis of the social class system. By far the best known example of this analytical approach is Bott's (1957) classic study of conjugal relationships within nuclear families in which she found that things such as the allocation of domestic tasks were more closely linked to the kinds of interpersonal networks that couples were involved in than to structural features such as social class.

Certainly all forms of social research are concerned with various manifestations of social relationships expressed through interpersonal relations – what has been termed a metaphorical use of the concept of social networks (Mitchell 1974). But there are several distinctive features characteristic of social network analysis, in its focus of investigation as well as other methodological implications, that need to be unpacked. In the first place, social network analysis is more concerned with the pattern of relationships among social actors than with the content of these relationships, which may simply be specified as being of a particular type, for example primarily convivial or primarily exchange (Mitchell 1984). In one of the most widely cited examples of social network analysis, Kapferer (1969) is concerned to explain the progress and resolution of a dispute he observed in a work unit responsible for the final step in the purification of zinc being extracted by a mining company in Zambia. Through an examination of the linkages between the 23 men in this unit he assesses 'why specific individuals and not others were initially involved in the dispute, why certain issues and not others achieved prominence, and why this particular dispute should have resulted in a settlement in favour of one disputant and not the other' (ibid.: 183). His formal analysis consists in specifying the linkages between each pair of men in terms of five types of interaction (from conversation and joking to various kinds of material assistance) and then examining, both in tabular and diagrammatic form, the formal pattern of these linkages among this bounded set of individuals. By considering the span, density and degree of multiplicity of types of interaction of the personal networks of the two disputants, as well as the other workers, he provides explanations for the questions he had raised about the conduct of the dispute.

Once interpersonal relationships are formalized in this manner so as to represent them as an abstract pattern of linkages of varying strengths between nodes, the patterns so produced can be treated using the assumptions and analytical tools of mathematical graph theory. Hage and Harary (1983) are among the relatively few who have developed such formal analysis and tried to show that it 'can yield results that could not have been obtained by unassisted common sense' (Barnes 1983: x). For example, they apply formal matrix operations, that compute 'reachability' between actors in two or more steps, to Kapferer's data, reaching the same conclusion as he had done by somewhat less formal means (Hage and Harary 1983: 138). Leaving aside the question of whether the nature of the additional insights produced by the application of such mathematical operations warrants their adoption, it must be stressed that when such systems are used they always come with their own set of assumptions about the formal entities that they manipulate, and ethnographers must both make themselves aware of these assumptions and evaluate their own data carefully as to whether such assumptions can be accepted. In particular, they cannot be accepted as applicable to social relationships generally but must be reevaluated for each potentially new application: for example social relationships among workers in a processing unit in Zambia might be expected to have a very different character to those in other social locations. Furthermore, Kapferer draws on his broader ethnographic knowledge, such as the role of witchcraft outside the workplace and the use of kinship terms to suggest proper relations between generations, to complete his analysis. Thus what Mitchell refers to as a '"quantum leap" from anthropological concepts, which are not necessarily axiomatically arranged, to mathematical operation, which assumes this property' (1974: 297), has not generally been successful nor has such an approach been widely adopted. Nevertheless, as was suggested regarding the utility of quantification, the use of formal techniques for recording interpersonal relationships may often assist the ethnographer to perceive patterns and their transformations more readily and may also be a corrective to over-emphasizing some relationships simply by virtue of their more striking character or ease of observation. That is, formalizing analysis in this way can assist in improving both precision and completeness in observations of this nature. However, as was also found with the use of quantification, it is quite fallacious to ascribe a greater objectivity to such methods. The reflexive input of the ethnographer is evident in such matters as categorizing the content of relationships, deciding on what sets the boundaries of the networks and collecting information about the nature of the linkages (cf. Mitchell 1974: 292-6).

A second feature characteristic of social network analysis has to do with the feasibility of collecting datasets that fulfil the requirements of formal analysis. Mitchell stresses that distortions can arise unless information is provided 'about every link of every actor with every other actor' (1984: 268). In practice this can very quickly get beyond the means of an ethnographic study. For example, Kapferer's (1972) study of relationships among African workers in an Indian-owned clothing factory in Zambia was based on his observations and those of an assistant of the interactions among the 54 members of the shop. If all possible linkages were explored, there would be a total of 54 × 53, or 2,862 potential binary relationships to investigate (or half this number if ties are not directional). Most of these potential linkages will be non-existent or of the most rudimentary and uninformative nature. What was done in practice was to concentrate on those relationships that ethnographic research based on more generalized observation had identified as significant, so that in the end only 173 linkages were used for the analysis (Mitchell 1984: 270).

Clearly, in working even with relatively small sets, if formal analysis requires completeness to be valid, then the collection of data will have to be done on the basis of some form of structured interviewing rather than by ethnographic methods, and careful consideration needs to be given to the way in which information about linkages is elicited. Most of the comments made earlier in the discussion of social surveys stressing the necessity for ethnographically based knowledge in order to improve the validity of questionnaires are equally applicable here. There is a further conceptual difficulty in ensuring the completeness of social network datasets, namely, the assumption that the boundary of the set is for all intents and purposes impermeable. Some social network analyses that have adopted formalized techniques have been based on so-called closed networks – that is, on a set of individuals defined in terms of their relationship to some organization which also sets clear boundaries for who is or is not a member of the set, for example a factory or shop (Kapferer 1969, 1972) or a ship's crew (Bernard and Killworth 1973). However, even in these sets, relationships may be influenced by external linkages that would not necessarily be apparent in either observing or asking about linkages within the closed setting. For example, such superficially insignificant ties as discovering a common acquaintance, or a shared hobby, or even supporting the same football team, can have a latent effect on the content of a relationship. Such an effect might become known to an ethnographic observer but is very unlikely to be revealed in any kind of structured data-collecting procedure. The significance of any such effects for the assumption of closure is also going to be variable, sometimes having virtually no effect on the dynamics of the network and at other times significantly altering the nature of relationships within the network. In other social network studies, particularly studies of family or household networks in urban areas (e.g. Cubitt 1973; Kapferer 1973), expanding or criticizing some of Bott's findings, the individuals or families whose networks are examined are not linked, nor are their networks closed. Rather attention is given to their most significant linkages, usually in terms of frequency of contact, and to the degree of connectivity within individual networks, and the networks are then compared on these bases with attempts made to explain differences on the basis of other social factors. Such observations point to the difficulty of fitting such data to very formalized analytical techniques based in mathematical graph theory and clearly show the ways and stages at which interpretations and decisions by the researcher reflexively influence the content of the data and the process of analysis.

This latter type of more open network is halfway between the closed network based on a set of individuals in a bounded situation or structure and the ego-based networks where focus is on a single individual and his or her network. However, the practical difficulties in achieving completeness are as acute here as in set-based closed networks. Boissevain (1974) worked with two principal informants, both schoolteachers in Malta, asking them to make lists of their acquaintances. One produced a list of 1,751 people, the other 648. Extensive interviewing allowed Boissevain to develop a database containing details about the extent and nature of their relationships as well as linkages among the members of each of their personal networks (ibid.: 245–6). There are a number of particular strengths to be found in the subsequent analysis. In the discussion of these two personal networks, Boissevain not only identifies different kinds of linkages, for example with patrons, and compares the two for the influence of urban and rural social settings, he also is careful to discuss the dynamic character of such personal networks, considering the way in which linkages over time may weaken or disappear, or be strengthened, or change their content. Furthermore, the more detailed and formal analysis of these two personal networks is then used along with other comparative ethnographic materials to provide insight for his subsequent discussion of social brokers and a variety of more organized coalitions from cliques and gangs to goal-oriented factions.

All of these strengths in fact depend on Boissevain going beyond the formalized analysis of networks. In fact, his presentation of the social network material does not depend heavily on technical analyses but does clearly bring into play his other sources of knowledge, drawing upon his more broadly based ethnographic research. In spite of Barnes's criticism that 'much that appears under the banner of network analysis fails to make use of its specific potentialities' (1972: 25), it is apparent that the application of formal mathematically derived analysis has not proven attractive nor particularly fruitful to ethnographers. There seem to be good reasons for this. Both the nature of social networks and the practicalities of ethnographic research are such that they are unlikely to provide data that adequately fulfil the assumptions of the mathematical systems applied to them, in particular requirements of closure or completeness. Furthermore, the sheer size of the networks that most individuals generate means that various decisions must be taken that discriminate among linkages, eliminating some, taking others as highly significant, and these are best taken based on ethnographically developed insights. It is essential that the inherent reflexive component of any such selectivity be made visible in analysis and subsequent presentation. With these considerations in mind, it can be argued that the best use of social network analysis, in spite of Barnes's misgivings, is as an instructive paradigm and a method of working that directs attention to a particular kind of data. When used in this way, it does have the advantage of directing attention to the importance of individual social relationships, as well as broader structural positionings, in both the conduct of individual lives and the development of institutions. It also helps to increase confidence in data by systematizing observations and ensuring that although not all linkages will be taken as of equal significance, the omission of some will be carried out on examined and public considerations, not by default.

Clearly some research questions will be more amenable to this kind of analysis than others, in particular perhaps those that are concerned with the fit of particular individuals or categories into a social system. One example where the use of the concept of social networks has been effective as a research strategy and an analytical perspective is in studies concerned with the policy-related question of providing care in the community for various categories, such as people with disabilities or with mental illnesses, who had previously been placed in institutions. At the level of paradigm, the concept of social network has been used as a corrective to the implicit and unwarranted assumptions contained in the community care programme about the nature of community in urban societies (Davies 1998a). Social networks have also been employed more analytically in this context by Wenger (1991), who examines the personal networks of elderly people as an indication of their relationship to the community and their access to the specific services they require. She then compares the various types of networks found among her informants and by making use of personal histories discusses how they develop networks that make so-called care in the community a reality (or not) for them as individuals.

As the quantity of research on and about the internet increases (see Chapter 7), network analysis is gaining recognition as an effective method to study the social networks that computer-mediated communication may support (Garton *et al.* 1999). For example, ego-centred networks have been used to examine the maintenance of a sense of community among residents widely dispersed across an urban area (Wellman and Wortley 1990). And analyses of closed networks are particularly appropriate for studies of the effects of computers on communication within organizations, considering issues such as how the introduction of e-mail and video-conferencing has affected workplace organization and relationships (Fulk and Steinfield 1990; Wellman *et al.* 1996). The difficulties in handling datasets with the scale and complexity of even comparatively small networks is to some extent being overcome by the development of computer software that represents the data in numerical matrices and can also facilitate generation of network diagrams (cf. Garton *et al.* 1999: 94–100). Interestingly some of the classic findings of network analysis have gained new relevance in its application to computer-assisted social networks. For example, Granovetter's (1973) work on the importance of relatively weak social ties, as opposed to the strong ties of family and close friends, in securing access to new information such as employment opportunities, provides insight into the role of many internet-based relationships. Although there are few examples of social network analysis influencing ethnographic research on the internet, there is clearly great potential for it to do so as this field develops.

Cognitive anthropology and discourse analysis

Another approach to ethnographic research that concentrates its focus and formalizes analysis is the very broad area that is concerned with cognitive processes and their relationship to culture. As this distinctive theoretical orientation developed in the 1960s, it directed the attention of researchers not to material phenomena but rather to the cognitive organization of such phenomena. It was assumed that all people carry a set of rules and assumptions in their heads and that coming to know what these are and how they operate is the way to understand other cultures, indeed that these cognitive systems constitute what is meant by culture. The question that had to be answered by researchers on the ground was how to gain access to these cognitive systems. The answers that they developed relied very heavily on the use of language, both as a metaphor for what they were trying to uncover and as a means of access to cognition (Tyler 1969). Language served as a metaphor based on the recognition that the formal analysis of culture that was proposed was similar to the production of a grammar for a language, in that grammatical rules are related to the production of speech but they do not predict speech nor fully explain it; however, a speaker must know, perhaps without being able to articulate them, the rules of grammar for the language they speak. The other way in which language was important was as the principal means of access to cognition. Thus ethnographers use language as a way of discovering how people perceive and organize their world. A great deal of early work looked at the organization of a particular limited semantic domain through the construction of a taxonomy of terms relevant to that domain – for example American kinship terms (Goodenough 1965) or Ojibwan 'living things' (Black 1969). These examples are highly formalized in their presentation as well as in the methods of elicitation that they use to obtain their data. Another study which also intensively explores a restricted semantic domain, but links the analysis to a broader ethnographic interpretation, is Frake's (1964) 'How to ask for a drink in Subanun', in which the focus is less on terminology, such as kinds of drink, than on understanding the various stages of drinking and how they are linked to different forms and functions of discourse. And Basso (1972) elaborates, not a specific lexical domain, but the meanings of silence in Western Apache culture. This latter study clearly redirects linguistic observation from matters of vocabulary and grammatical structure to a broader interest in communicative behaviour.

In a more wide-ranging study of a particular form of joking behaviour among Western Apache in which they imitate White Americans, Basso (1979) undertakes a detailed analysis of these discourses as a way of enhancing ethnographic understanding. His study uses classical ethnographic methods, observing examples of such jokes himself and collecting other instances from informants with whom he had worked for several years. Thus he is able to propose a set of generalizations about the social context of these joking performances: who usually performs these joking imitations; who are the immediate foils for the joke; and in what context they are performed (ibid.: 32). He also documents occasional exceptions to these generalizations (ibid.: 10). At the same time, his detailed analysis of comparatively small segments of everyday, naturally occurring talk makes this study a good early illustration of the use of discourse analysis in ethnographic research. For example, he takes a very brief scenario in which a man at home in the evening with his wife answers the door to find a clan brother; ushering him into the house, he switches from Apache to English to perform a joking imitation of 'the Whiteman'. Basso records this scene and then analyses it line by line, including the tone of voice in which it is delivered, to expose the opposing assumptions underlying Apache and white social interaction. He then comments about the broader meaning of such behaviour for Western Apaches:

> By presenting the behavior of Anglo-Americans as something laughable and 'wrong,' by displaying with the help of butts how and why it violates the rights of others, they denounce these standards as morally deficient and unworthy of emulation ... On most occasions, perhaps, Apache jokers tell their fellows nothing about themselves and Anglo-Americans that they don't already know or suspect. But they tell them about it in a manner that crisply reminds them of its enduring importance, and they urge them – without really coming out and saying so – never to forget it.
>
> (Ibid.: 64)

In this otherwise very good example of the use of cognitive analysis in ethnography, Basso is not entirely invisible; however, it is not always clear when he is present and no consideration is given to the effects of the presence of a particular, if known and accepted, 'Whiteman' on the nature of the performances. Such a consideration if taken into account could only have further deepened the insights that the study presents.

Subsequent studies in the area of cognitive anthropology continued to focus on language but did not concentrate primarily on lexical domains. Instead, as in the example above, they analysed discourse, not in order to classify, but rather to uncover cultural models in people's heads. This research interest in talk and in the underlying assumptions that talk may reveal is closely related to ethnomethodology, with its concern with discovering the unconscious methods that people use to construct everyday life (cf. Heritage 1984), and to the conversation analysis that this theoretical orientation has inspired (cf. Sacks 1984). Such an approach has been criticized for what is regarded as an excessive concern with what people say, without considering how this may relate to behaviour. However, although cognitive analysts do not assume any simple relationship between talk and behaviour, they argue that the cultural models they are able to infer from analysing what people say, are related to behaviour in complex and powerful ways (Quinn and Holland 1987). They point out that researchers attempting to develop artificial intelligence, in particular those working with computers for translation, discovered early on that the ability to use a language involves a great deal of other cultural knowledge, making translation much more than simply a process of de-coding and re-coding. Similarly, analyses of discourse provide a way of access to shared cognitive systems that make meaningful social interaction possible. Thus they reject a rigid dichotomy between cultural models that underlie talk and those that guide behaviour, suggesting that proposals 'to sort cultural understanding into a kind for thinking and a kind for doing and to associate talking with the former may reflect more about the mind-body duality in our own western cultural model of the person than it does about how cultural knowledge is actually organized' (ibid.: 8–9). Furthermore, talk is itself a form of behaviour, which may be used to legitimize, conceal or influence, to mention only some of the forms of talk that are themselves consequential social acts.

As already discussed, this more recent theoretical basis for cognitive analysis is related to a methodological shift in emphasis from formal elicitation of terminologies to collection of talk in context, often naturally occurring discourse, sometimes semi-structured interviews, but treated as discourse, not isolated responses. And analysis is more likely to seek rules for decision-making or sense-making rather than systems of classification. Thus, for example, a study of terms that Americans use in discussing gender types (Holland and Skinner 1987) rejects the classic approach of delineating a lexical domain, arguing instead that the relationship of lexical items is variable and has to be understood in the context of an underlying taken-for-granted model of gender relationships. They attempt to access and describe this model using semi-structured interviewing that could respond to their informants' tendency to answer queries about terms by describing 'scenarios in which the prototypical male/female relationship is disrupted' (ibid.: 103). In another example, fully naturally occurring discourse in the form of unsolicited illness stories collected in the process of participant observation, provides data to investigate cultural models of causes of illness, as well as models of the family and gender relations, among barrio residents in Ecuador (Price 1987). A methodological reflection of the continuing influence of linguistics in the area of cognitive analysis is the use by a few researchers of their own cultural knowledge as native speakers to develop cognitive models. D'Andrade (1987), in an example of reflexivity in research that is related to but considerably more structured than the use of autobiography discussed in Chapter 10, draws on his own intuitions in exploring a folk model of the mind, as well as on a long Western philosophical tradition of introspection regarding the concept of mind. But he also tests the model with interpretations of mental processes collected in interviews.

When we look at the uses of linguistic analysis in ethnography, we see a progression from a concern with the examination of formal properties of language in order to reveal cognitive processes to an emphasis on naturally occurring discourse and communicative events in order to understand broader social and cultural patterns. For example, Kulick (1992), in his research on Gapun, a Papua New Guinea community, analyses a particular form of speech event, called a *kros*, in which women initiate loud, obscene, public complaints directed at husbands, relatives or other fellow villagers. He discusses the setting, nature and conduct of these events, then analyses one example of this form of conflict talk in detail, arguing that such speech events are a major means by which gender is defined and negotiated in this community.

> In kroses, women lay claim not only to specific female identities, but because the talk is built on opposition and because it is concerned with dissatisfaction (in the case of domestic arguments, with the actions of her spouse), women purposely counterpose those female positions with ones they assert are male. In kroses, women thus effectively define not only femaleness, but maleness as well. Women who have kroses are, in this sense, engaged in a highly consequential political act, ...
>
> (Ibid.: 512–13)

In further research on this community, Kulick (1998) contrasts women's linguistic practices for dealing with anger (the kros) with those of men, who utilize oratories conducted in the men's house. In an analysis of a specific example of this form of discourse, Kulick shows how these oratories, which use formulaic and polite linguistic markers, are designed to expose anger and simultaneously redefine it as not anger, hence avoiding conflict. He then discusses how these differences in dealing with anger, an emotion his informants regard as dangerous and destabilizing, are linked to the devaluing of women's discourse and are consequently leading to the decline of the local language Taiap (spoken by women during their kroses) and its replacement by the more widely spoken creole language Tok Pisin (used by men in their oratories).

I conclude this discussion of the use of discourse analysis in ethnographic research by considering more fully one final example, Goodwin's (1990) *He-Said-She-Said*, in which the analysis of discourse is central to an ethnographic study of the social world of black children in a Philadelphia neighbourhood. Goodwin observed social interactions among the children of Maple Street for 18 months; she had initially thought she would concentrate on their games, but found that all the children, and the girls in particular, spent more time talking than playing and that the data she obtained from her audio tapes were more useful than those from other sources, in particular filming, with which she had experimented. She argues that the discourse analysis on which she models her study is particularly effective in getting at indigenous interpretations, because through such naturally occurring talk, people are themselves interpreting meanings in the process of talking rather than simply reporting on them in interviews. She thus makes use of extensive transcripts in her analysis and includes significant excerpts from them in her discussion. Her primary methodological objective is to 'observe repetitive sequences of talk' (ibid.: 11) without becoming a participant in that talk. Thus she is concerned that the discourse be embedded in its social context, noting that 'the production of talk is doubly contextual' (ibid.: 5) in that each turn is both a response to the existing context and a moulder of the new context. Given this concern with naturally occurring discourse, she tries to be a non-participating observer but nevertheless recognizes that she is not invisible and does not attempt to render herself so to the reader. Instead she notes the particular characteristics that make such a role feasible: in particular, that this relatively self-contained group of children customarily socializes in publicly accessible areas on their street with very little adult interference for several hours each day. She furthermore includes several sections of transcripts to illustrate her relationship to the group and their perceptions of her. For example, when one of the girls, Ruby, appeals for Goodwin's help during a disagreement with Malcolm, he counters by asserting that she 'will not intervene in an argument since, as he puts it, the ethnographer is "just here studying us. Watchin' what we do"' (ibid.: 24).

The findings that emerge from this integration of discourse analysis into ethnography are both interesting and impressive in that they are of much broader application than is often seen in studies using these more restricted and highly focused methods. For example, Goodwin describes a form of dispute unique to the group of girls which is instigated by an accusation by one girl that another has been talking behind her back. Based on an analysis of several of these so-called he-said-she-said disputes, Goodwin challenges the extensive literature that suggests that female speech is characterized by a lack of concern for legalistic debate. In particular, she argues against Gilligan's (1982) contention that the speech and thought patterns of girls and women express an ethic of care and responsibility in contrast to those of boys and men who are primarily concerned with abstract principles of justice and moral right. Instead, she provides examples in which 'preadolescent girls formulate charges that their individual rights have been violated with respect to how they are to be treated in the talk of others. They do so by constructing opening accusation utterances of considerable sophistication that not only state the charge formally but also provide the grounds for it – invoking what is in fact a vernacular legal process' (Goodwin 1990: 219). Furthermore, drawing on her broader ethnographic fieldwork, Goodwin is able to show how each such dispute is related to social action, in expressing other grievances not explicitly mentioned, in involving and shaping alignments of other members of the group besides the two main protagonists and in having subsequent consequences often persisting for months for how individuals relate to and are treated by the group. This particular study is an excellent example of the use of discourse analysis within an ethnographic study in a manner that both strengthens and clarifies the ethnographic analysis without sacrificing the broader vision and sense of connectedness of which ethnography is capable.

Chapter 9

Expanding the ethnographic present

Documents, life history, narrative, longitudinal studies

The concept of an ethnographic present is not a simple one but contains several distinctive interpretations, each giving rise to a particular critique, about both doing and writing ethnography. To a degree the concept of an ethnographic present, much like a strict positivism, is more important for the criticisms it generates than for its actual application. It might be suggested that the concept was really simply an attempt to make a virtue out of practical necessity for anthropologists encountering societies without a written tradition. However, the concept has been influential in the development of ethnographic research and it will be useful to consider some of the meanings and related criticisms attached to it.

The most common interpretation of the ethnographic present is undoubtedly the practice of developing analyses and generalizations from ethnographic research as if they represent a timeless description of the people being studied. Clearly such an approach implicitly denies the historicity of these people. The data on which such analyses are based are acquired in an historically located encounter between an ethnographer and some individuals from among the people so described. Yet, whereas the ethnographer moves on, temporally, spatially and developmentally, the people he or she studied are presented as if suspended in an unchanging and virtually timeless state, as if the ethnographer's description provides all that it is important, or possible, to know about their past and future.

Why was such a patently unsatisfactory approach developed? One reason was doubtless an attempt to signal that such ethnographies were intended as scientific reports; one of the conventional uses of the present tense in English is to discuss something that is true, either by definition or induction (Davis 1992), and this grammatical usage thus bolstered the scientific credentials of ethnography. Such an approach was further encouraged by the theoretical underpinnings in structural functionalism of much ethnography, certainly through the 1950s (Smith 1962; Stocking 1983a: 107). Functionalist analysis with its emphasis on mechanisms that maintained social structure clearly encouraged abstracting self-regulating processes from the specificities of particular events and observations. It tended to absorb change, either past or potential, into fluctuation around some set of stable institutions and to regard individual behaviour as essentially rule-governed and uncreative. Fabian (1983) agrees that the use of the present tense in ethnographies was to signal that the ethnographer intended to provide commentary, or scientific analysis; however, he argues further that when this essentially dialogic tense is combined with the consistent use of the third person, the purpose is to emphasize that the commentary is directed to other ethnographers and explicitly marks an excluded Other, the people being discussed, as outside the dialogue. Thus, the use of the ethnographic present has ethical and political implications in its taking knowledge about other peoples away and using it elsewhere, not for their benefit or enlightenment, analogous to the colonial exploitation of material resources.

Another use of the ethnographic present is in the deliberate attempt to reconstruct a society and culture as it was in some imagined pristine state prior to Western contact. This essentially relocates the ethnographic present in a past that was implicitly seen as unchanging prior to colonial contact. Such so-called salvage ethnography was regarded as extremely important in the early decades of anthropology's establishment as an academic discipline, due in part to its close association with museums (cf. Mead 1972). In American anthropology, with its interest in Native American populations, such a perspective had particular force, so that Boas and many of his students worked primarily with a few older informants trying to reconstruct, through their memories, a society and culture before the massive changes and often severe dislocations brought on by white contact. However, this approach, creating an ethnographic present that was by definition prior to the arrival of the ethnographer, was not restricted to American anthropology. Malinowski consistently wrote about the Trobrianders in the present tense and only came to suggest in an appendix in his final volume that his ignoring the reality of European influence was perhaps a 'serious shortcoming' (Sanjek 1991: 613). Thus, in this approach, the ethnographic present was not even the present of the ethnographer's fieldwork but some prior time which placed people outside the historical experience of colonialism, an experience that had, in fact, enabled the ethnographic encounter to occur. Such an approach has had profound implications for the course of ethnographic research, a point perhaps made most strongly by imagining an alternative.

> Imagine what anthropology would look like today if Boas's texts concerned conversions to Christianity, work histories and the mundane folklore of a multiracial, polyethnic society; if Malinowski had charted the expeditions of pearl buyers, and provided case materials involving resident magistrate, chiefs and their subjects; if Radcliffe-Brown had written 'Three Tribes in Western Australia's Concentration Camps'.
>
> (Sanjek 1991: 613)

Nevertheless the persistence of this approach through subsequent decades of anthropological research can be observed, for example, in ethnographic films. Marshall's *N!ai, The Story of a !Kung Woman, 1952–78,* made in 1980, and Asch and Balikci's *Sons of Haji Omar,* made in 1978, both systematically cut out, from the available footage, images of Western technology such as automobiles and radios (Kuehnast 1992: 189–90).

A third way of viewing the ethnographic present is not so much in terms of ethnographic practice but rather in terms of reporting style. In this interpretation, ethnography is seen as primarily defined in and by the activity of writing (cf. Clifford and Marcus 1986). The ethnographic present is seen as primarily a rhetorical device which attempts to locate the ethnographer among the research subjects and thereby authenticate the text. A fuller discussion of this interpretation of ethnographic research and its written products may be found in Chapter 12.

However, ethnographers have never apparently taken the ethnographic present quite as literally in their practice as they may have done either in their theoretical assumptions or reporting style. They have used a variety of documentary sources including those produced by colonial administrators, missionaries and travellers. They have attempted to gain access to indigenous histories through the memories of their informants and the performances of story-tellers. They have also sought to optimize their own experience of historical process, not only through emphasis on the length of time spent in the field, but also through subsequent return research visits to a research site. This chapter considers these practices, and other ways of expanding the ethnographic present, so as to recognize and incorporate into ethnographic analysis the mutual historicity of ethnographers and the peoples they study. Specifically, it looks at the use of documents, the collection of life histories, the use of narrative, and the nature and importance of ethnographically based longitudinal studies. Since ethnographers share some of these data sources with historians, it is important to consider what distinguishes ethnographic research from historical study. This is not in order to defend disciplinary boundaries, but rather to clarify the particular purposes of ethnographers in using such sources and to understand any differences in their application.

One of the main differences between history and anthropology is different emphases in their respective understandings of the relationship between the past and the present. Whereas historians are more likely to treat the past as behind us and as productive of the present, anthropologists frequently challenge both of these perspectives. First, many adopt what has been called a memorial approach to the past which emphasizes that 'as memory it [the past] remains very much with us: in our bodies, in our dispositions and sensibilities, and in our skills of perception and action' (Ingold 1996: 202). And on the second point, the formal remembering of events that have passed can be seen as a process of making them explicable in terms of the present, virtually the present producing the past (altered by knowledge of what has come since) rather than the reverse (Ingold 1996; Lewis 1968; also cf. Hobsbawm and Ranger 1983 for a similar approach by social historians). These two views of the past can also be linked to the two ways in which power may be said to interact with culture, in external forms that are hegemonic in terms of the first perspective and ideological in terms of the second (cf. Comaroff and Comaroff 1992: 27–31).

What is the significance of these differing perspectives on present and past for ethnographers using some of the same sources and methods as social historians? Ethnographers with a research interest in the past may collect data via the same sort of archival research as historians but will argue that their research is informed by characteristically anthropological theoretical interests (Comaroff and Comaroff 1992: 17–18; Sanjek 1991: 615–17). For example, it may be concerned with interpreting contemporary social processes, such as racism, and have a comparatively broad temporal and spatial perspective; one example is Wolf's (1982) theoretically led study of the relationships over five centuries between Europe and the peoples of what became the colonized world. In fact, this study and others of its kind are quite similar to cultural history and there is little point in disputing disciplinary boundaries. Instead, the relevance of this field of historical study as well as the evidential criteria of social and cultural historians should be accepted and utilized by ethnographers. Another historical approach that, in contrast to the above, is focused on a particular ethnographic setting and hence bears some similarity to the microhistory of many cultural historians (cf. Davis 1990), is the use of the past to inform or criticize current theoretical positions, the debate on the significance of caste in Indian ethnography being a particularly apt example.

Another approach to the role of history in ethnography relies as much on traditional ethnographic methods of participating, observing and interviewing as on documentary resources, but it emphasizes that data obtained in these ways be regarded as 'current history' (Moore 1987: 727). In this perspective it is argued that the ethnographic present must be expanded in two directions, that ethnography must be consciously located with regard to the past, which situates both subjects and ethnographer in time and space, and it must give attention to the likely future that is being produced, a concern which both undermines any structuralist tendency to overlook heterogeneity and change and brings political and moral responsibility to the fore (Sanjek 1991: 616–17). Some of the ways in which this may be accomplished are the subject of the remainder of this chapter; however, the general methodological effects would seem to be to emphasize historically located and hence contingent processes, as opposed to the iterative and self-regenerating processes associated with structuralist accounts, whether structural functionalist, Lévi-Straussian or Marxist. Such an approach does not deny the existence of structure, or its utility for enhancing understanding, but argues that structures themselves must be seen as partial, contingent and changing (Comaroff and Comaroff 1992: 17, 35–8; Moore 1987).

Documents

The variety of documentary sources that may be of interest to ethnographic researchers is potentially immense (cf. Scott 1990). They include: official statistics, such as those generated by a national census or by smaller-scale surveys commissioned by various governmental organizations (see Chapter 8); other official governmental records, from transcripts of parliamentary debates to official reports or committee minutes; records generated by a huge variety of non-governmental organizations, including sports clubs, professional associations, businesses, parent–teacher associations, festival organizers, political parties, and so forth; mass media, from newspaper archives to radio and television recordings to works of fiction, biography and autobiography; and personal documents (cf. Plummer 1983), the most widely recognized being correspondence, personal diaries and a variety of visual records, from family photograph albums to video recordings (cf. Pink 2001: 71–4). Ethnographers must also be alert to the potential of less conventional forms of documentary evidence. For example, referring to their attempt to tease out the processes of colonial domination in southern Africa in the nineteenth century, Comaroff and Comaroff begin with conventional documentary evidence produced by and about Nonconformist missions, but they also pursue other sources, 'traces found in newspapers and official publications as well as in novels, tracts, popular songs, even in drawings and children's games' (1992: 33).

One of the main dangers in using data sources that are conventionally taken as peripheral to the main ethnographic methods is the tendency to be less critical in their application. Certainly, it is important that researchers using specific forms of documentary evidence familiarize themselves with the specialized literature regarding their interpretation. Here I make only a few general comments regarding the critical scrutiny that should be given to documentary sources, some of which are specific to such sources but many of which are based on the same general principles that ethnographers routinely apply to their own characteristic data sources (cf. Platt 1981b). In utilizing any document, researchers should give initial consideration to questions of its authenticity, credibility and representativeness (Scott 1990: 19–35; also cf. Platt 1981a).

Authenticity has to do with whether the document is a genuine example of the evidentiary type which it purports to be. For example, legal documents may be forgeries, letters may have been written by someone other than the signatory, statistics may be altered or eyewitness reports falsified. There are numerous methods for testing documents for authenticity, both based on internal characteristics as well as on tracing the place of origin and subsequent movements of the physical document itself. Such methods are quite specialized and ethnographers will, for the most part, be well advised to seek assistance from those trained to employ them. Authenticity is in fact usually less of a problem for the kinds of documents ethnographers want to employ than are questions of credibility. This criterion has to do with the accuracy and honesty of the record. For example, it is important to know whether reported events are eye-witness accounts or based on hearsay, and, if the latter, at what remove from the actual event. Furthermore, the honesty of the author often has to be assessed as well as the extent to which the special interests of those who produced the document are involved in it and likely to affect its content. This latter need not be a matter of deliberate deception. For example, the diaries and personal notes of a public persona will almost certainly be kept with an eye to future publication and will reflect their particular perspective and attempt to ensure their future best interests, insofar as these can be anticipated, but without necessarily being deliberately untruthful. Similarly in evaluating diaries, life histories and the like produced at the behest of a social researcher, the likely effects of the fact that this material was recorded for a given audience needs to be included in any evaluation of it. The third criterion, that of representativeness, relates to the incompleteness of the historical record. Some documents survive, others disappear, most with no record of their ever having existed. In perhaps one of the clearest examples, and easiest to deal with, one may have only half of a correspondence – letters received without those written, or vice versa. More difficult is to remain sensitive to the partial and fragmentary nature of all documentary sources, particularly in the face of the relatively greater persuasiveness of a documentary evidentiary base, its appearance of solidity and of providing 'hard data'. Thus researchers need to be sensitive to the fact that those with greater social power and cultural capital are also much more likely to create documents and these in turn are more likely to be preserved. This problem is compounded for ethnographers working in societies that have not had a written tradition until the advent of colonialism. Thus Comaroff and Comaroff warn against uncritical acceptance of the 'established canons of documentary evidence, because these are themselves part of the culture of global modernism – as much the subject as the means of inquiry' (1992: 34). However, this question of representativeness is in fact one that ethnographers may be particularly well placed to recognize given that it is essentially the same as the questions they must ask regarding their ability to generalize from their discussions with selected informants and from observations that are of necessity fragmentary.

Thus, without attempting to discuss specific evaluative techniques for particular documentary sources, it can still be stressed that the sorts of questions ethnographic researchers need ask of and about documentary sources are not dissimilar to those they pose when dealing with more familiar and conventional ethnographic data sources such as observation and interviews. So, just as with interview data, ethnographers should examine their documents at the three levels of text, interaction and context (see Chapter 5). Although initial interest in a document, its production and reception, may be at any one of these three levels, consideration needs to be given to the other two. For example, Garfinkel's (1984 [1967]) classic ethnomethodological paper '"Good" organizational reasons for "bad" clinic records' begins with a close consideration of the text of a particular type of document – the clinic records of outpatients at a psychiatric treatment centre. The inadequacy of these records for researchers, even though the clinic was part of a research facility, led him to consider other factors affecting record production, some of which were located in the broader context of organizational structure and others in the ways in which personnel interacted with the records, specifically in their intended and imagined audience. Thus, questions arising about the textual level of documentary data can be interpreted to develop understanding of social relationships and cultural assumptions at individual interactional and social structural levels. Certainly, any documentary sources should be submitted to a critical examination of their internal textual meanings, which considers what is not said as well as what is present. They should also be evaluated in terms of the relationships between their author and intended audiences, as well as the nature of the researcher's relationship with the document. And, finally, the ethnographer should ascertain the context of their production and reception.

The variety of documents that may be useful for ethnographic research is immense, as already noted, and is expanded further by the need for ethnographers to be open to creative uses of documentary sources. For example, the interpretation of secondary historical materials can often provide significant insights into social and cultural processes, as can the productions of the mass media, from hard news to advertisements. Furthermore, the use of visual documentary materials provides a rich source of ethnographic material (Ball and Smith 1992; Scherer 1990). In addition, a wide variety of other forms of expression, architectural and artistic for example, can be treated as documentary. Yoneyama's (1999) study of the incorporation into contemporary Japanese society of particular understandings of the atomic bombing of Hiroshima makes extensive use of the built environment as text. She examines both urban development projects and the significance of three structures that were not completely destroyed by the bomb. The examples which follow of the use of documents in ethnographic research are thus intended to be suggestive of the possibilities and approaches to such data rather than a comprehensive survey.

In her historical ethnography *Scottish Crofters*, Parman (1990) expands the ethnographic present in two ways. In the first place, she summarizes various secondary historical accounts of the Celts in European history and of the development of modern Scotland. This exposition is not simply background to her ethnography but, rather, is central to her discussion of the construction of crofting culture, both by islanders and by those from outside. She is able to illustrate links between these constructions and local economic and social structures, such as the decentralized nature of the local Harris tweed industry, as well as trace their influence on cultural forms like the role of whisky in the crofting community as 'an avenue for cultural resolution' (ibid.: 153). In addition to the use of a particular category of documents to develop a temporally expanded sense of its subject, this ethnography provides an illustration of Moore's (1987) admonition that ethnography be regarded as 'current history' (see above). Thus, for example, Parman is able to document how gossip provided a means of constructing and reworking community history, noting as well her own incorporation into this history and its myths (1990: 101–5, 127–9).

Such use of historic interpretations is important in that it helps to guard against the uncritical acceptance of history as simply and unproblematically an explanatory resource rather than seeing it as also implicated in contemporary social and cultural constructions. In my research on Welsh nationalism (Davies 1989), I found it necessary to consider nationalist uses of the Welsh past in several contexts. In the first place, it was important to see the relationships between the creation of a history of Wales and the development of a self-conscious political nationalist movement. This involved contesting other histories, in particular, an established British (or English) history that was seen to absorb and then disregard a distinctive Welsh past. But it also involved shifts in the focus of Welsh history, from a chronicle of princes to the development of a Welsh working class, as the nature of the nationalist movement altered. It is important to recognize that this is not simply, or even typically, a matter of argument about which history is valid, but rather of disagreement about what is remembered and recorded and how it is interpreted. Such disagreements have real social consequences, as seen in individuals' accounts of how they became active in nationalist politics (ibid.: 31–2), and may inspire social conflict, for example over control of the school curriculum (cf. Phillips and Sanders 2000).

Both of these examples illustrate the application to ethnographic research of one of the commonest means of expanding the ethnographic present, namely, the use of secondary historical materials and analyses. Both emphasize that while these materials are of great utility to ethnographic research, they should be employed critically, not simply as background, but as implicated in the cultural meanings and social actions the ethnographer is studying. Another example, in which Scott's (1990) criteria are of less importance than are ethnographic criteria of meaning based on an analysis of production and reception at the levels of text, interaction and context, is to be found in studies of early photographs of Native Americans. Krouse's (1990) study of the work of Joseph K. Dixon, who photographed Native Americans in the period 1908–26, begins with a discussion of their very fine technical and dramatic quality. This was achieved, for example, by the use of silhouettes or, in another instance, by showing one individual in full headdress riding into the sunset. Krouse's analysis further highlights the strenuous efforts Dixon made to eliminate any trace of White culture. He then links Dixon's photographic work both to the social context, so that he is seen to have been expressing a widely held view of Indians as a vanishing race, and to the form of his interaction with Native Americans, primarily his efforts to assist their assimilation into American society. Albers and James (1990) also discuss the photographic representation of Native Americans in the first two decades of the twentieth century but use picture postcards of Great Basin Indians as their documentary base. They identify two types of postcards, those produced and used locally, which they see as presenting essentially private images, and those bearing public images produced for the developing mass tourist market. The kinds of documents produced for these two audiences are starkly contrasting, with private postcard images showing Great Basin Indians 'engaged in ordinary activities, dressed in everyday attire, and embedded in a commonplace setting' (ibid.: 353–4). Messages on the postcards for the most part either say nothing about the image or refer to it in a way that shows the individuals were personally known to the sender. The images on public postcards, in contrast, show Native Americans in elaborate costumes surrounded by cultural artefacts; they are usually studio photographs with their subjects posed in highly stylized manners. Much as with Dixon's photographs, these public postcard images are both stimulated by and help to develop a romantic stereotype of Native Americans which denies their historicity and undermines the reality of their contemporary existence, turning them instead 'into symbolic objects to be stereotyped and possessed by mediamakers and their audiences' (ibid.: 358). Thus, this study of two forms of a particular visual document, which considers content in the light of both the audiences and the social context of their production and reception, provides an understanding of the processes which create certain cultural stereotypes. It also presents a non-anthropological example of the creation of an ethnographic present and shows how such a process acts effectively to deny people their histories. There are clearly a host of visual documents that may serve as data for ethnographers. Other examples employing more recent technology look at audience responses to television productions by both indigenous and Western mass media (e.g. Gillespie 1995; Hughes-Freeland 1997).

Another example of research based in part on products of the mass media is Martin's (1994) study of what she argues is a major shift in cultural perceptions of immunity in American society between the eras of polio in the 1950s and AIDS in the 1980s. She makes reference to depictions of the immune system, particularly diagrams, in popular journals such as *Time* and *Newsweek* to develop and support her argument that American cultural understandings shifted from a view of the body stressing cleanliness and avoidance as external defences against infection to one relying upon internal flexible response related to mental and physical fitness. Because she is concerned to locate the reasons for this shifting perspective regarding immunity, and to argue a case for its broader cultural effects, Martin also uses a variety of other ethnographic methods as well as other documentary resources. For example, she does participant observation in an immunology research laboratory and makes use of publications in scientific journals.

In fact, an earlier ethnographic study in which the primary concern was with the processes whereby scientific facts are produced (Latour and Woolgar 1986 [1979]) based its argument primarily upon the range of documents produced and used by research scientists. In an extended period of participant observation in a research laboratory, the ethnographer came to focus on the writing and publishing of scientific papers as its central productive activity, a process of transforming other kinds of documents (sheets of figures, diagrams, computer printouts), themselves dependent on various record-keeping inscriptions, into what is presented as scientific fact at various levels of persuasiveness. In the end, the authors argue that the activity and purpose of scientific laboratories is best described as 'the organization of persuasion through literary inscription' (ibid.: 88; also cf. Latour 1990). This research project furnishes an example in which the use of a documentary database arises from ethnographic observation rather than being anticipated at the start of research.

One of the aspects of using documents in ethnographic research, which ethnographers may readily lose sight of, is the continuing relevance of reflexivity. The processes of selection and interpretation in which researchers engage when working with documents are bound to be affected by the social situations and cultural understandings arising out of their individual histories and the broader intellectual and social context in which they work. It is fairly unusual for documentary-based studies to consider or make visible these influences, but the value of research is likely to be enhanced if this is done. Clifton (1990a, 1990b) explains the social and intellectual context that led him to assemble a collection of essays, *The Invented Indian*, which evaluates documentary evidence to challenge elements of what he argues is a complex of cultural fictions about Native Americans and their historical interactions with Euro-Americans.

Life histories

The use of biography, or life histories, has long been a methodological approach available in ethnographic research. Among the most influential applications of this approach, which has been described as 'the first systematically collected sociological life history' (Bulmer 1986: 54), was the life history of Wladek Wiszniewski, which comprised the second volume in the classic study of *The Polish*

Peasant in Europe and America published from 1918 to 1920 by Thomas and Znaniecki. This is a first-person account compiled by a Polish immigrant in Chicago at the behest of the authors and checked against a series of his family letters; it is accompanied by a comparatively brief analysis of the effects of the varying social settings on the formation of Wladek's character. There is an extensive anthropological corpus of life histories (cf. Gottschalk *et al.* 1945), perhaps related in large measure to the tendency of ethnographers to develop one key informant in the course of long-term fieldwork. Among these are Radin's 1926 biography of the Winnebago Crashing Thunder, Ford's *Smoke From Their Fires* (1941) and Spradley's *Guests Never Leave Hungry* (1969). The main exponent of a life history approach in anthropology, judged in terms of output in this genre, has been Oscar Lewis, whose studies of individuals and families in urban slums was the basis for his theorizing about the existence and nature of a culture of poverty (Lewis 1965). The Chicago School also stimulated a number of sociological life histories: Shaw's (1930) study of a delinquent and Sutherland's (1937) of a professional thief being among the better known, with more recent examples in this same intellectual tradition being Bogdan's (1974) study of a transvestite and Strauss and Glaser (1970) on a woman with terminal cancer. Langness (1965) provides a review of the research based on the use of life histories.

As these examples suggest, much of the use of life histories in social research has been either to provide insight into ways of life that were believed to be disappearing, hence the popularity of Native American biographies, or into life ways that are regarded as deviant and hence not generally familiar. However, the use of life history is of much greater significance and applicability in studying social processes than these examples suggest. Before turning to some examples of the use of life histories for theorizing – as well as to the related issue of generalization – I look at data collection methods for collection of life histories.

The most familiar, and possibly the most common, way in which life histories are collected is through interviewing. Usually a single life history is the product of a series of interviews, largely unstructured aside from perhaps suggesting topics or periods that might be covered in a given session. Such a series will normally run over an extended period of time, sometimes over several years, but more typically over a few weeks or months. These interviews are frequently supplemented by personal documents supplied by the interviewee, by other documents such as educational or occupational data, by interviews with family members or friends and by participant observation – that is, simply spending time in the company of the person whose life history is being recorded. This approach is appropriate for research in which the entire study is based on the life history of one, or a very few, individuals. In many ethnographic studies, shorter and more focused life histories are sought from a larger number of individuals; in such studies the same methods may be used but clearly less time is spent with each individual and interviews are more directed towards specific aspects of their lives of particular interest to the study. Finally, life histories may be sought for individuals who are no longer alive through use of documentary sources, as discussed above, as well as interviews with people who knew the subject.

When interviewing individuals about their life histories, it is important to bear in mind that what is being collected are remembered lives. Obviously there will be great individual variation in what is remembered, why certain things are remembered and how the memories are presented. It is essential for the ethnographer to be aware of how the relationship is developing with their informant as, for example, even slight inattention may be interpreted as disinterest and persuade the informant to omit certain memories as unimportant or not to elaborate on them. Thus, a careful review of tape recordings should be made after each session, not just for content, to see what has been discussed, what needs expansion, what areas to pursue next, but also to evaluate the interaction and how it may be affecting content. It is also important to assess the audience for which the informant is producing their life story. Is it primarily addressed to the ethnographer and, if so, how is the ethnographer perceived? Is it directed to some imagined wider public and perhaps rather more self-justifying than reflective? Are informants using the occasion to try to understand their lives themselves? Or are they really talking to a parent or partner? In many cases, individuals will alternate among several imagined audiences depending on topic. And if the ethnographer can come to understand the nature of these audiences, from considering the internal evidence of the interviews, as well as any contextual evidence, this will assist in analysing the material collected.

In addition to these factors of interpretation at the level of individual difference and interaction, ethnographers need to be aware of cultural differences in thinking about and presenting biography.

For example, Llewellyn-Davies in discussing her filming of Maasai women suggests that remembering an individual past is not really an acceptable cultural activity for them (Grimshaw 1995).

Ethnographers collect and study life histories not primarily out of interest in individual stories but in order to improve understanding and knowledge of social and cultural processes more generally. Thomas and Znaniecki maintain that 'the experiences and attitudes of an individual ... are not exclusively limited to this individual's personality, but can be treated as mere instances of more or less general classes of data' (quoted in Plummer 1983: 64). C. Wright Mills (1959) characterizes this as a concern with the intersection of personal troubles and public issues. Thus, the use of life histories raises again the issue of generalization in ethnographic research (see Chapter 4). In considering the kinds of generalization that can be made from life histories, it is important to retain the distinction between empirical generalization to a larger population, which highlights the question of representativeness, and theoretical induction, in which social and cultural processes observed in individual cases are argued to be relevant in other contexts. These two aspects of generalization are not entirely separate, both may be operating in a given study, but it is helpful to consider them individually. Certainly no individual life history can be said to be representative in its entirety, in that each individual set of life experiences is unique to a single person. On the other hand, it may be possible to abstract various themes from the lives of individual members of a given social category that are indeed representative of most of the members of this category and hence provide empirically generalizable knowledge. To this end, it is not necessary to seek out a large number of individuals, so much as to find those with broad experience and in-depth knowledge of a particular social and cultural milieu and the ability to reflect upon and discuss this knowledge (cf. Plummer 1983: 100). However, it is important that if empirical generalization is intended, then the population to which the conclusions apply must be specified. One of the criticisms directed against Lewis's use of life histories in *La Vida* (1965) was that the population his informants represented tended to shift between those living in a culture of poverty, those occupying an intermediate class position and other examples of extreme deviance (cf. Valentine 1968). It can be argued that the more effective use of life histories is not to make generalizations but to challenge them (see discussion of Clifton 1989b below) or to provide material about the processes behind established generalizations. For example, Mac an Ghaill's (1994) study of masculinity begins with an assumption about the dominance of masculine perspectives in English secondary schools and uses life histories to examine the social interactions and cultural understandings that lie behind this generalization.

Now consider two examples to illustrate how life histories contribute to theoretical understandings and generalizable knowledge in some of the ways discussed here. The first is a collection of essays exploring the life histories of people with mild mental retardation (Langness and Levine 1986). This collection explores common themes in the lives of this collectivity and also illustrates the potential for anthropological theorizing on the basis of such life histories. Set against a series of statistically established generalizations about people with mental retardation, such as the skewed representation of social class and ethnic groups in this collectivity, the authors' first intention is to give some depth to this rather flat picture by attempting to provide an emic view of the life experiences of people with mental retardation. But beyond that they argue that this approach helps to overcome the fragmented nature of studies of mental retardation, which are based in different disciplinary perspectives, by attempting 'to isolate an individual's unique perspective on his or her biology and personality, and to tease out the reciprocal relations between these aspects (which define him or her as an individual) and each of those social and cultural contexts in which the individual interacts – family, work, community, and society' (Whittemore *et al.* 1986: 8). The essays in the collection illustrate how to develop theoretical generalizations without losing sight of the unique individual experiences characteristic of life histories. One of the themes that emerges from the essays is the situational nature of official determiners of mental retardation along with descriptions of the ways in which individuals are labelled and de-labelled and the effects of such processes (e.g. Edgerton 1986). Another theme is the socialization of individuals into the role of someone with mental retardation. For example, Koegel's (1986) description of the way in which one young man was introduced to drinking shows how this experience – which consisted of offering him as much as he could consume with the result that he was ill for several days – induced subsequent behaviour of such extreme avoidance that it isolated him socially. The experience contrasted sharply with that of his 'normal' brother who, nevertheless, was considered by all family members to have been introduced to alcohol in exactly the same way. This young man's life history was collected in interviews with him and other family members, and the drinking story emerged as one that was of great significance to all of them. 'Indeed, so vivid was this story in all their minds that each shared it with me more than once' (ibid.: 54). Once the centrality of this incident in their family narrative was recognized, it was clearly important to try to understand its meaning. When it is perceived in terms of a particular kind of socialized incompetence, then this theme can be explored in the lives of other individuals with mental retardation without loss of the richness of detail of the individual life story.

Another example of the use of life histories in ethnographic research is the collection *Being and Becoming Indian* (Clifton 1989b). This set of biographical studies is directed more towards challenging generalizations – both popularly held racial and cultural stereotypes and certain anthropological assumptions about the nature of Indian–White relationships – than it is towards establishing them. These life histories of individuals who moved between Indian and white, as well as black, identities, social settings and communities emphasize the flexibility and situational nature of these identities and the interrelationships of the social groupings. They further illustrate the interplay between external understandings, both popular and academic, and the development of Indian identities and actions. For example, the life history of Dan Raincloud (Black-Rogers 1989), collected in a series of research interviews and participant observation over a 10-year period, traces the development of his commitment to the perpetuation of Ojibwa religious–medical knowledge and also discusses how his authority among the Ojibwa was both bolstered and threatened as a consequence of the growth in white interest in such knowledge beginning in the late 1960s. As already noted, this collection of life histories is primarily engaged in challenging and undermining generalizations, both popular and academic. However, it also seeks to establish, or at least to suggest, others. For example, it contests the idea that individuals who live at the so-called social frontiers between ethnic groups are necessarily marginal; it claims that their life histories argue instead that such people 'master knowledge of both cultures, which is used to organize their behavior as called for and appropriate in different social contexts. Such people become, not diminished, but culturally enlarged' (Clifton 1989a: 29).

Narrative

Research for which ethnographic interviewing is the principal method often asks informants to discuss particular aspects of their life histories. For example, in my research with young people with learning disabilities, I mainly wanted to talk to them about their experiences and understandings of social adulthood. Research of this nature encourages informants to tell their own stories, to develop a narrative, about how they experienced certain life events. This narrative approach to ethnographic research refers both to a form of data collection and to a method of data analysis that searches for narrative themes in informants' accounts (see Chapter 11). The life history approach to data collection aims to develop a valid historical account of an individual's life and nearly always contextualizes interviews with the principal subject with supplementary interviews with their significant others, supporting documentation and participant observation. In contrast, the main aim of a narrative approach is to construct an understanding of informants' perceptions of particular life experiences. For this, the ethnographic interview – normally with a series of individuals, not a single subject – is central, and participant observation, when it is carried out, tends to be more under the direction of informants, who may want the ethnographer to observe particular objects or events in order to illustrate their narrative. Linde (1993) analyses the use of narrative in Western culture to construct coherent life stories; she further illustrates the openness of these constructions by examining how informants reshape their narratives to accommodate altered circumstances (also cf. Roberts 2002: 115–33).

Narrative studies are often used to investigate collectivities who have shared an experience of some traumatic past event. In her research on how Hiroshima is remembered in contemporary Japan – in particular its use in Japanese political culture to project a statist ideology that conceals both past militarism and contemporary economic dominance – Yoneyama (1999) did not initially believe that the testimonies of survivors would be central to her research. However, she found that their narratives, far from simply supporting routinized representations of 'atomic victimization and Hiroshima's call for world peace' (ibid.: 213), challenged these official versions of the past and instead promoted other narrative themes such as the significance and individuality of their pre-war experiences, the relevance of other war-time atrocities and injustices for their stories, and the fallibility and incompleteness of their knowledge.

Skultans's (1998) study of narrative and memory in post-Soviet Latvia was originally conceived as an anthropological investigation of neurasthenia, or nervous exhaustion, a diagnosis common in Latvia that had long since been discarded in contemporary Western medical practice. However, she reports that her informants' stories eventually forced her to change her research focus. '[I] found myself pulled ineludibly by people's memories of the past. The past could not be laid to rest and left people little motivation to talk about the present.... Eventually I let myself be carried by the narrative flow' (ibid.: xi). She argues that the usual sources of narrative unity, in particular the unity of time and space, were not available to her informants who had experienced the rupturing effects of war, imprisonment and exile in their lives. Instead she discusses how they imposed both unity and meaning on their narrated lives by making use of cultural resources, such as familiar Latvian literary themes and archetypal images. Skultans also reflexively explores the significance of links between her own cultural imagery, acquired as a Latvian-born exile who had been raised in London from infancy, and the narrative themes of her informants.

Longitudinal studies

Doing a longitudinal study can simply mean returning on several occasions over an extended period of time, usually a decade or more, to the same research site or the same research population. More formally planned longitudinal studies are problem-oriented in that they follow the effects of some major change over time, for example following migrants from a rural field site to the city (Kemper 1979), or develop a comparison based on observations made at different times (Harris *et al.* 2006). Although the intentional setting up of longitudinal studies is relatively rare in ethnographic research, many anthropologists develop a career-long association with a particular location and eventually accomplish an unplanned de facto form of longitudinal study. Certainly, the extended fieldwork and related expectations of much anthropological research tend to encourage return research visits. For example, the investment in learning a language, and the benefits that accrue from increasing fluency with subsequent visits, positively reward ethnographers who maintain long-term research interests in a given area or people.

Furthermore, the personal ties that often develop in the course of fieldwork not infrequently mean that contact is maintained after the ethnographer's departure and tend to be an incentive to return. Even if this is not the case, the contacts made in an initial period of fieldwork can usually be renewed relatively easily making reentry much easier and shortening the adjustment period at the start of subsequent research visits. And returning after an extended absence gives the ethnographer greater credibility as part of a community, more clearly committed to it, and also allows an adjustment of social roles, permitting the ethnographer to develop different perspectives. This latter is possible both because of the changes that will have occurred in social relationships among research subjects, and also because ethnographers themselves will have changed. Kenna (1992) discusses the changes in her research on the Greek island of Anafi from her first long-term fieldwork in the 1960s as a single postgraduate student to her return visits, first in 1973 as a married woman and a university lecturer and again in 1987 with her husband and young son. Making use of fieldnotes, letters, photographs and her personal diary, she has also written a reflexive ethnography which looks at her year of doctoral research on Anafi from her perspective over 30 years later (Kenna 2001a). This long-term association with her research site has also enabled her to follow island migrants to Athens as well as to discover and analyse a photographic archive depicting the life of political dissidents exiled to the island in the 1930s (Kenna 2001b).

There are examples of more deliberately conceived longitudinal ethnographic studies in which the original research design included one or more restudies. Often these are studies of the social and cultural impact of some major change in an area, for example a study of the effects of the relocation of four Gwembe villages following the construction of the Kariba Dam in Zambia in the late 1950s (Scudder and Colson 1979; Colson 1989). Others have involved a gradual accumulation of funding for researchers and teams of students from a particular academic centre to concentrate research interests in a given area over an extended period of time, as for example the Harvard Chiapas project (Vogt 1979). Most studies of this sort involve more than a single ethnographer which means that some of the other effects stemming from individual development and personal connections mentioned above will be less salient.

The principal strengths of longitudinal studies of all sorts lie in their greater sensitivity to change, the increased likelihood of being able to distinguish between superficial fluctuation and fundamental change, and the greater depth of ethnographic understanding achieved from the multiple perspectives that such research facilitates (cf. Foster *et al.* 1979). On the other hand, there are some considerable practical and theoretical difficulties attendant upon longitudinal studies of all types, and perhaps particularly so those that are planned in advance. One of these is attrition, both in the research population – as people may die, disappear or simply become too busy or disinterested to cooperate in the restudies – and among the researchers. If a study involves a group of researchers, it is virtually certain that personnel will change over time. These changes do not invalidate the study but they must be taken into account in the analysis; that is, consideration needs to be given to the ways in which changes in the personal and social characteristics and intellectual background of members of the research team may have affected the data and analysis. It is almost certainly the case that longitudinal studies using ethnographic methods, in contrast to those that rely on more structured and formalized methods of data collection, are more likely to succeed if there is one individual ethnographer who remains with the project and provides continuity, in terms of maintaining contacts in the field (and hence being able to introduce new members of the team into the field relatively easily) and providing coherence in the developing analysis.

A second difficulty stems from the occurrence of some major alteration in external circumstances that affects the nature or relevance of the research questions over the study period (cf. Davies and Charles 2002). For example, a longitudinal study designed to look at coping strategies for dealing with old age or debilitating accident or illness which spanned years in which a major system of state welfare benefits were introduced would face a significant discontinuity in the external conditions affecting such coping strategies and would have to ask a very different set of questions in a return study. To some degree the original research concerns would be irrelevant and the study would have to be redirected if it were to continue to be meaningful.

A final set of difficulties involves the practical problems contingent on the cost and commitment required for such long-term research. To ensure success, any relatively large-scale longitudinal study requires quite strong institutional backing, including a commitment to fund it through its various projected phases. However, this sort of backing is more likely to be forthcoming for survey research producing quantifiable databases. The ethnographic model of longitudinal research is more likely to be based on the commitment of an individual, usually with institutional backing but without a major funding commitment, for whom the project may involve a major portion of a working lifetime. One of the disadvantages in this model is that a great deal of time and energy is typically expended acquiring funding for each subsequent phase of the research.

Robert Edgerton's *The Cloak of Competence* (1993 [1967]), a study of adults with mild mental retardation, provides a useful example of the way a one-off ethnographic study may evolve into a longitudinal study, illustrating both the advantages in understanding that may accrue from a longer time perspective as well as some of the difficulties. The original research project, undertaken in the 1960s, was a study of some 48 individuals who had recently been released from an institution and were trying to live independently in the community. The principal research method was participant observation as well as extensive unstructured interviewing with them and their associates; the research was carried out by a team of researchers – over 20 individual researchers contributed over all its phases – with Edgerton both actively taking part in the research as well as directing the project and providing continuity over two decades.

The main findings of the initial study concerned the effects of the stigma of the label of mental retardation on the lives of these former inmates and the techniques they developed to manage these spoilt identities. 'Their lives are directed toward the fundamental purpose of denying that they are in fact mentally incompetent' (Edgerton 1993: 132). They accomplished this denial in a variety of ways: they were, for example, very concerned with getting and keeping a job; marriage was a highly valued marker of normalcy, while the fact of their sterilization was regarded as a humiliation and a barrier to the normal lifestyles they sought; the most important conclusion was the universal reliance on benefactors – individuals who gave both practical assistance and help in creating and maintaining their efforts at passing and denial.

There were two restudies (Edgerton and Bercovici 1976; Edgerton *et al.* 1984; also cf. Edgerton and Gaston 1991), one after 12 years, another after 20, neither of which had been anticipated in the original research plan. By the second restudy, the original cohort of 48 had been reduced to 15. Virtually all the major conclusions of the original study were altered: for example the vocational success of the original group was greatly reduced, due in part to age and illness, but also to a much less favourable external economic environment. On the other hand, employment was less a central concern and tended to be seen in a more instrumental light. Most significantly, the role of benefactors was greatly reduced, as was the preoccupation with hiding a stigmatized identity, suggesting that the experience of institutionalization, as many of the original cohort had maintained, was a major reason for their incompetences as well as the main source of stigma. Years away from it both allowed them, unexpectedly, to acquire skills for more independent lifestyles as well as gradually lessening the institutional contribution to their personal histories. What this study argues very strongly is that while the conclusions of a single study are not necessarily invalidated by subsequent restudies, such longitudinal perspectives can often provide insights which alter and deepen the interpretation of the original.

Chapter 10

Researching selves

The uses of autobiography

An interest in reflexivity as a positive aspect of ethnographic research, rather than as an undesirable effect to be minimized, has been growing, particularly so in anthropology, since the 1970s. The open admission of the involvement of ethnographers with the subjects of their research came to be welcomed as an opportunity to liberate the field from a positivist commitment to value-free scientism and to address ethical concerns about the anthropological endeavour and its links to exploitation of Third World peoples (cf. Scholte 1969). This movement was further strengthened by epistemological critiques, particularly feminist and postmodernist, which emphasized the socially situated nature of knowledge and hence the importance of specifying the knower. The perspective of this book is to argue that an informed reflexivity is compatible with, indeed is essential for, both a realist ontology and a commitment to social scientific knowledge in the sense of knowledge that is based in, and can inform us about, a real social world and that is public and open to critical analysis. Even among those committed to the reflexive perspective, some disquiet has been expressed regarding the danger that social enquiry about others could disappear altogether, with ethnography becoming a literary activity mainly concerned with explorations of selves. Thus Rosaldo develops a critique of classic ethnography's objectifying form of reporting and argues that ethnographic understanding often requires the personal involvement of the ethnographer, which must be acknowledged as well in reporting forms. However, he also worries about the dangers of a serious imbalance in the role of reflexivity: 'If classic ethnography's vice was the slippage from the ideal of detachment to actual indifference, that of present-day reflexivity is the tendency for the self-absorbed Self to lose sight altogether of the culturally different Other' (Rosaldo 1993: 7). Such concerns would seem to be even more justified in instances when autobiography becomes an integral part of ethnographic research. Any heavily autobiographical research seems to be vulnerable to two charges: first, that it is self-indulgent and narcissistic, telling us about the ethnographer, not about the social and cultural phenomena that are the proper subject matter of ethnography, essentially Rosaldo's concern; second, that autobiography in any case represents a particular Western literary genre, the Great Man tradition, in which autobiographies are used to describe individual achievements based on a linear and goal-oriented interpretation of what constitutes a meaningful life (Cohen 1992). Certainly, neither of these outcomes is acceptable from the perspective on ethnographic research adopted in this book. In this chapter, I consider some reasons for encouraging the inclusion of autobiography in ethnographic research, and how it can be incorporated without loss of the commitment to developing understanding of a social reality beyond ourselves.

Autobiography is used in ethnography at several levels of involvement. At the most common and widely utilized level, it is simply recognized that ethnographic knowledge is in part a product of the social situation of ethnographers and that this must be acknowledged and its significance addressed during analysis and, perhaps less universally agreed, should be made visible in reporting findings (see Chapter 12). Thus Rosaldo discusses how his interpretation of Ilongot headhunting was transformed in response to his own experience of grief following a tragic personal loss; and he further notes how interpretations of life events will change with age and experience, commenting that 'ethnographic knowledge tends to have the strengths and limitations given by the relative youth of field-workers' (1993 [1989]: 9). Kristmundsdottir (2006) argues that the researcher's autobiography even affects areas where the ethnographer's personal involvement seems fairly remote, such as biographical research on a subject no longer living. In conducting research on the life of Björg C. Thorlaksson, a woman writer from Iceland in the early twentieth century, she had rejected suggestions of her subject's mental instability, assuming this simply reflected the all too common dismissal of strong women. However, she was shocked to learn that her subject's year-long hospital stay, which she had taken to be due to breast cancer, was actually in a mental institution.

> From that moment on my research took a new course. Everything I had done so far had to be rethought in the light of the fact that Björg had been considered mentally deranged by her contemporaries. But most importantly I had to come to terms with myself as location. My feminism had led me to interpret her life according to feminist lights. I, as a location, had influenced the research; it had blinkered my vision and led me to wrong conclusions.
>
> (Ibid.: 171)

Another use of autobiography in ethnography is the consideration of the effects upon the ethnographer of the experience of fieldwork, using others to learn more about and reflect upon oneself. One of the principal products of her fieldwork among the Inuit for Briggs (1970) was an awareness of, and eventual frustration with her tendency to indulge and express her own emotional responses in contrast to her informants' emotional self-control. Okely (1992) discusses the effects of her fieldwork with Gypsies on her physical presentation of self, for example altering her dress and stance. She considers these forms of embodied knowledge to be as informative for her developing understanding as are more conventional direct forms of data gathering. Furthermore, this embodied knowledge is contrasted with the forms of embodiment that Gorgio culture expects of Gypsy women and that she finds being imposed on her during occasional breaks from fieldwork and returns to university culture. In both of these instances the ethnographers use their experience among, and knowledge of, others to expand their knowledge of self. But the selves they explore are of course the products of their own culture and hence this sort of autobiographical exploration in fieldwork also involves greater sensitivity to the way in which cultural realities are constructed. 'Through this vicarious experience of being "the other" to others, I was perforce led back to the stereotypes, which are part of the Gypsies' reality made by Gorgios' (1992:15).

Coming to understand another culture through embodied experiences is also central in Grimshaw's (1992) account of her winter spent in a Himalayan convent of Buddhist nuns. This ethnography, at an initial reading, is heavily autobiographical in that Grimshaw, having decided to discard her anthropological notebooks before her arrival, describes her personal feelings and experiences as a novice member of the convent. Thus, we become acquainted with the lives of the nuns, the hard physical labour, the cold, the inadequate diet and the fleas, as well as their exploitation by the monastery and their own avenues to spirituality, through Grimshaw's relating her own direct experience of their lives with them. Her ethnography is a personal quest, in which she has 'a vision of myself which initially surprised me by its clarity and power; but its source lay in the integrated life I had found at Julichang' (ibid.: 62). On the other hand, it remains ethnography because of the genuine insights the vicarious participation provides of the social factors that shape and restrict the nuns' lives as well as of their resources to resist total submersion. 'Their lives were dominated by unremitting physical labour for the monastery. But I now saw that this was what defined their spiritual persona. The women had both dignity and strength; and they were not unaware of it' (ibid.: 64).

Such uses of autobiography in ethnographic research nevertheless still remain within the conventional ethnographic model of researching others, albeit with close attention to the inherent and informative reflexivity of any such endeavour. In the case of Grimshaw's research, in particular, the focus seems to be on the self, but the self as acted upon and fundamentally altered by contact with others, thus studying such changes becomes a way of providing a view of these others, refracted through this special segment of personal autobiography. Another example of the development of an ethnography of others through living their experiences is Church's (1995) study of the consultative processes within the Canadian social services that were aimed at bringing consumer involvement into the mental health services. Initially working in a standard ethnographic research mode, but from a perspective of commitment to the ideal of consultation and partnership, she eventually suffered a breakdown herself, brought on in part because of the scepticism of one of her key informants about her ability to do such research due to her own stunted personal development. The ethnography that she eventually produces, as both ethnographer and psychiatric survivor herself, draws out the similarity between these personal experiences and the responses of health service professionals whose professional identities are threatened by their admission of consumers to policy processes. 'Ultimately, self-reflection has revealed undeniable connections between reformation of identities and reformation of policies, between subjectivities and large scale social relations' (ibid.: 141–2).

While such examples push to the extreme the use of the ethnographer's self to study and understand others, there are other examples of research in which the ethnographer becomes not simply the collector of data about others, not even data that are primarily the self's response to others, but becomes the other as well as the self of the researcher (cf. Reed-Danahay 1997). This occurs perhaps most commonly in so-called 'native' anthropology, in which 'natives', usually interpreted to be representatives of Third World countries or disadvantaged groups in Western societies, carry out ethnographic research on their own people.

This perspective raises issues about the nature of belonging, or of having an insider's perspective, that often create dilemmas for those undertaking such insider research, or native ethnography (see Chapters 2 and 3 for discussion of some of the ethical and other issues). Thus Lal (1996), who developed a sense of self as a South Asian woman of colour during her postgraduate studies in the United States, found that returning to her native India to do research – while perceived within Western academic circles as native ethnography – presented her with a far more complex reality and precipitated a re-examination of her own identity. She returned to Delhi to do research among women factory workers and found that despite her familiarity with the city, she was seeking out communities she had not known existed and finding them 'often nestled cheek by jowl alongside more affluent communities that were on the map of my familiar. I was a "native" returning to a foreign country' (ibid.: 192). In spite of the advantages of their shared language, gender and Indian identity, she found that her class differences with these factory women were more significant than these other similarities, making her aware of her 'dislocation even within that space that I had thought of as home' (ibid.: 193).

In contrast to Lal's experience of not feeling, or being, an insider in a situation that others less sensitive to internal differences assumed was completely open to her as a native ethnographer, Motzafi-Haller (1997), a member of the Mizrahim, one of the socially disadvantaged groups of Jewish peoples who came to Israel from Asia and Africa, found that her attempts at native ethnography foundered on the difficulties of reconciling her personal concern for political injustices with the feeling that such concern expressed in an academic context might undermine her intellectual credibility. Her awareness of the growing professional discourse in favour of reflexivity, notwithstanding, she first had to work through theoretical questions of power and hegemony in another location, in fieldwork in Botswana, and thereby also establish her credentials in 'the dominant male-Ashkenazi-positivist discourse of Israeli scholarship' (ibid.: 218) before she was able to turn to native ethnography, eventually co-authoring *Birthright,* a historical ethnography of Israel. Although acknowledging that in the process of researching and writing this ethnography, she came more and more to occupy the role of native scholar, she rejects the 'reductive essentializing of identities that it promotes' (ibid.: 215).

> It is too easy, and I would argue historically reductionist, to describe the Mizrahim in Israel as an oppressed Third-World population; to apply preconceived analytical categories and concepts that have little resonance among the people whose life, world, and struggle we try to understand. The historical record we examine in *Birthright* does not lend itself to such reading. The Mizrahi voices we record, *and my own life experiences,* point to great ambivalences and contradictions, and speak of the most powerful urge to belong to the collectivity along with rage and resistance against objectifying, othering dominant discourses.
>
> (Ibid.: 215)

As these experiences make clear, the question of being an insider in any given situation is nearly always problematic. It is difficult to imagine any individuals so unreflective that they consistently feel a complete insider in any situation even within their own family. And certainly anyone with the intention of doing ethnographic research must find themselves feeling detached even from the most familiar and inclusive groups (cf. Narayan 1993). One of the situations in which ethnographers could most readily be assumed to have an insider's perspective is in research not just in their own society but within their own family. An excellent example of this rare occurrence is Panourgia's (1995) study of death and the social organization of dying in the context of modern Athens. In this ethnography she is both self and other as she analyses the social practices, family transformations and cultural meanings surrounding the death of her grandfather, with whom she had a particularly close relationship as a favourite grandchild, an event in which she also participates, being with him for several months before and at the time of his death. Yet she notes that even in this research placement, she cannot simply take her insider's knowledge to be either unquestionably complete or true.

> Although one might be a member of a family – a daughter, let us assume for the sake of this argument – one will not, a priori, be included in all aspects and intimate relationships of that family, whereas a non-family member who has been accorded inclusiveness might ... In other words, simply by being of the country/culture/group/family, one is not automatically guaranteed infinite and interminable self-knowledge.
>
> (Ibid.: 10–11)

In fact, Panourgia, in an attempt to encompass both her family self and her anthropological self, 'to breach the space between experience and analysis' (ibid.: xxii), breaks the central section of her ethnography into two narratives, literally dividing the pages horizontally. In one half she describes her actions and feelings as Myrto, the granddaughter, while below she is Neni, who analyses and contextualizes the occurrences and rituals surrounding the death. But the two dialogues are not mutually exclusive, they intersect in numerous ways as when the anthropological composure at the moment of death temporarily holds back the emotional expression of the family self.

The final step in the direction of researching selves is of course for the self to be not just a central character in the collectivity being researched but the principal character, so that the ethnographer is his or her own key informant. I now want to look at a few examples of such research and consider on what basis they can still be considered social research, distinct from the literary genre of autobiography, in such instances when the researched and researcher are one and the same.

Stanley (1993) draws attention to two sources and justifications of such ethnographic research based in autobiography. The first she refers to as 'sociological autobiography' and notes the origins of the term and the concept behind it in the work of Merton (1988), who argued that autobiographers who utilize theoretical concepts and analytical procedures of social research in constructing their personal history in a broader context are engaging in a form of participant observation where they have privileged access to their own experience. This they interrogate for its broader sociological significance and interpret in terms of the relationship between individual actions and beliefs and macro-level social and cultural structures and processes. This approach to autobiography as social research contrasts with, but is also complemented by, another that developed from feminist practices, both as a political movement and as an academic intellectual current. In this second approach, rather than understanding the social through its influence on the individual, the two levels are seen 'as actually symbiotically linked: the social and the individual, the personal and the political' (Stanley 1993: 44). Thus, in the feminist movement the processes involved in consciousness-raising were seen as a way for individual women initially to understand the effects of patriarchal structures on them and subsequently to reconceptualize their individual responses to these structures so as to effect structural change as well as change in their individual lives.

In social research these same ideas found expression in the placement of reflexivity at the core of methodological principles, not in terms of self-absorption, but rather in order to use the interrelationships between researcher and other to inform and change social knowledge. Thus Stanley (1992) problematizes the dichotomy between biography and autobiography, describing how her biographical research on others' lives is both affected by and ultimately affects her autobiography. The two examples that follow exemplify these two approaches to autobiography as research, the first in which an individual anthropologist considers how his particular experience of disability illuminates broader social and cultural assumptions and processes, and the second in which a group of women collectively research their own early memories to explore processes of gendered embodiment. The two examples also contrast in that the first, in a sense, starts with individual autobiography, recognizes the broader patterns at work in a particular set of experiences and makes connections outward to reveal social structures and processes, whereas the second begins with a general sociological question and moves inward using autobiographical research to address it.

The first example of doing ethnographic research based on the ethnographer's own autobiography is *The Body Silent* (1987) by Robert Murphy, an anthropologist whose previous fieldwork was among Amazonian Indians. In 1972, at the age of 48, Murphy began to develop muscle spasms which within four years were diagnosed as a spinal tumour, the inexorable growth of which meant gradually increasing paralysis. A decade later he had moved through the experience of being in a wheelchair after losing the use of his legs to quadriplegia. These personal experiences are his principal database for this research monograph in which he describes and analyses those experiences using the theoretical and methodological tools of the anthropologist.

> This book was conceived in the realization that my long illness with a disease of the spinal cord has been a kind of extended anthropological field trip, for through it I have sojourned in a social world no less strange to me at first than those of the Amazon forests.
>
> (Ibid.: xi)

He notes that his interest is not in chronicling his personal history but rather in using his experiences as a way of exploring the effect of his disability upon his status as a member of society and his sense of self. Murphy emphasizes the basis on which he wants to generalize his argument when he points out that, whereas the ways in which people become motor disabled vary widely (accidents, strokes, multiple sclerosis and so forth), their social positions and relationships subsequently are essentially the same. He argues that 'disability is defined by society and given meaning by culture; it is a social malady' (ibid.: 4); he thus sets out to interrogate his own experiences, acting as both ethnographer and principal informant, as a way of understanding the social world of people with disabilities and analysing how their experiences also reveal much about broader social structures and processes. From this he is able to address numerous areas of theoretical interest such as the social nature of health and illness, the social world of hospitals and the feedback mechanisms operating to produce and affirm stigmatized identities. One or two specific examples of some of the general and generalizing points made in the study will illustrate the way in which autobiography treated in this manner is an effective form of ethnographic research that cannot be accused of excessive self-absorption. Murphy discusses the nature of embodiment for people with physical disabilities, from considerations of sexuality to the social significance of degrees of disembodiment and its effects on personal identity and interpersonal communication.

> I have also become rather emotionally detached from my body, often referring to one of my limbs as *the* leg or *the* arm. People who help me on a regular basis have also fallen into this pattern ('I'll hold the arms and you grab the legs'), as if this

> depersonalization would compensate for what otherwise would be an intolerable violation of my personal space.
>
> (Ibid.: 100)

He also analyses how relationships with social categories, based on age, class, race and gender, are affected by his marginalized status as someone with a physical disability. For example:

> I found that my relations with most women of all ages have become more relaxed and open; they are at once more solicitous than men and more at ease in my company. I noticed, too, that when I got on the elevator with a woman, she often would greet me or start a conversation; in my walking days, we both would have stared silently at the floor indicator.
>
> (Ibid.: 127)

Such observations as this are placed in the context of the uneven distribution among class and racial groups of certain forms of physical disabilities and the social factors that produce them. It should be noted that Murphy also did research among other people with disabilities and reports that he initially found himself using the fieldworker's role to perpetuate his resistance to accepting his disability as part of his identity, using his ability to continue a productive academic life as a way of bolstering 'a personal myth of almost-normalcy' (ibid.: 126; also cf. Church 1995). Thus even in situations where the identity of self and other are as fully overlapping as possible, where ethnographers as autobiographers become in Merton's phrase 'the ultimate participants in a dual participant–observer role' (1988: 18), even here we find tensions between insider and outsider. Murphy, the ethnographer, is not fully and unproblematically the same as Murphy, the quadriplegic, and, like Panourgia, he sometimes uses one role to stave off the other. In his recognition of this and in the working out of these perspectives to inform his analysis, he clearly shows the effectiveness of a productive and outward-directed reflexivity in a research encounter.

> Research among the motor-handicapped and participation in their organizations forced me to see myself in their lives, and this left me feeling that my own status was insecure and threatened ... I had learned a valuable lesson about the relationship of social standing to disability. I had also learned a great deal about

> myself. All anthropological research involves a process of self-discovery, and my experience among the disabled was often painful.
>
> (Murphy 1987: 126)

In the second example of using autobiography as the primary source of data in ethnographic research, *Female Sexualization* (Haug 1987), a group of women collectively undertake to examine processes of gender socialization by engaging in what they call memory work, that is, 'choosing a theme connected with the body – legs, hair, stomach, height – and calling on members of the group to write down their memories of past events that focus on this physical area' (ibid.: 13). The accounts are then circulated, discussed, analysed and reproduced as a collective account of the production of sexualized female bodies. Again, this is a form of ethnographic research that uses autobiography as its principal database. However, it is not simply autobiography; rather personal memories are directed to understanding specific social relations linked to forms of gender oppression. The women felt that explicit explorations of their early awareness and experience of sexuality were already too far removed from the processes of embodying gender identity to be other than superficial. So they developed this method of recovering early memories of particular parts of the body, often starting with a very specific occurrence or object such as a photograph and recovering as much detail as possible in the remembering of it. They subsequently considered, as a group, how memories such as these were linked to cultural understandings of sexuality, as represented for example in popular literature (books of etiquette or women's magazines).

> We used our own memories to review the ways in which individual parts of the body are linked with sexuality, the way gender is expressed through the body, the routines that have drilled us in a particular relationship to our bodies, and the ways in which all of this is knotted into social structures and social relations between the sexes.
>
> (Ibid.: 34)

Furthermore, in line with Stanley's (1993) second type of autobiographical social research discussed above, they have a feminist political agenda as well as a research agenda, which includes both individual gains in self-awareness and self-confidence (Haug 1987:

26) and social reform through 'extricating the female body from its constricted framework of sexual meanings, and relocating it within more fully "socialized" areas of concern' (ibid.:13).

Thus, in the section on the 'hair project', women recall the importance of highly controlled forms of hairstyles, plaits in particular, in German culture, as a signal of both youth and propriety, and the linking of haircuts with a form of rebellion that was, at the same time, a capitulation to male concepts of sexuality. One woman recalls her main concern on being allowed her first haircut on her fourteenth birthday was her brothers' reactions and her disappointment that they did not confirm her new status as a woman rather than a child. She compares the discourse about hair among women, who talked about its texture and grooming, and with men, who spoke of it in association with sexuality as seductive or boring, and speculates, 'It was within this sexist discourse of masculinity that it was possible for my brothers to manufacture the notions of the wicked woman as sexually attractive, by producing their own sister as a girl who was pure' (ibid.: 105). In another section on the 'legs project', the memories of the women lead them away from the 'obvious' sexual connotations of displaying legs and towards a consideration of the significance of posture and gait, not only in terms of sexualization and gender identities but also as a means of inscribing and perpetuating class difference. 'The notion of the "ladylike" woman capturing a "suitable" husband is a signal of that dual inscription and subordination' (ibid.: 161).

The centrality of feminism for the development of this particular example of the use of autobiography in ethnographic research is not unique. Several of the examples already discussed – in particular Church (1995), less explicitly Grimshaw (1992) and Lal (1996) – were inspired by feminist debates, arguing that research must be politically engaged and, more specifically, that it must be grounded in the experience of gendered oppressions and in the intention to challenge them. In this they are closer to Stanley's (1993) second form of autobiography than some of the others whose political engagement is less apparent. However, Murphy (1987) can arguably be said to be the product of a similar political engagement in his research into another collectivity experiencing social oppression. In any case, the two forms of autobiographical social research she identifies are in fact complementary in that 'both acknowledge that knowledge differs systematically according to social position; therefore both have the capacity to regard "difference" as equally valid epistemologically, rather than seeking to erode such difference' (Stanley 1993: 45). And furthermore, both have the capacity working from individual positions and perspectives to produce general social knowledge, 'the "shared features" of knowledge seen from particular vantage-points' (ibid.: 50).

The uses of autobiography in ethnographic research are various. The most common is the inclusion of autobiography, both in terms of past experiences and experiences during fieldwork, in the analysis of data and reporting of findings. Autobiography may also be more intimately a part of the research process when ethnographers are members of the collectivity they are researching. The nature of such membership and its significance for the research may be no more than a shared collective identity, based on gender, race, class or nationality, or it may increase through varieties of native ethnography to the intimacy of immediate family. The culmination of this increasing closeness is to be found as the ethnographer becomes his or her own principal, or only, informant, when the ethnographer's individual self is also the observed other. The examples of research that I have examined in this chapter assert that the uses of autobiography in research in fact share, with all other forms of research, the methodological problems and epistemological queries of reflexivity in that they cannot disregard the effects of research and the researcher on the overall research process. That is, even in the most autobiographical forms of research the ethnographer does not have unconditional and unhindered access to knowledge: the question of insider status is still problematic. Thus ethnographers, even when they are their own key informants, commonly find their ethnographic self engaged in a process of othering their social self, so that Church (1995), Murphy (1987) and Panourgia (1995) all explicitly report how, in different guises, they were using their professional selves to deny or isolate their other selves. However, it is precisely in this process of interaction between ethnographer-as-self and ethnographer-as-other that social knowledge of general interest and significance is produced. The interaction of the ethnographer-as-researcher, informed by the theoretical positions of other social research and in a dialogue with a social scientific community, with the ethnographer-as-informant, with access to the knowledge and experience of an insider, differs in degree but not in kind to other manifestations of the research relationship through which generalizable knowledge about social and cultural realities is produced.

Part III
Mediations

Chapter 11

Formalizing analysis

The process of analysis is intrinsic to all stages of ethnographic research, and not something that begins once data collection is complete. Thus, discussions of methods in preceding chapters include much material on analysis. However, virtually all research projects eventually reach a stage of withdrawal from the field when analysis becomes more formalized. This chapter considers some of the implications of this withdrawal and the directions analysis may subsequently take. Withdrawal from the field is not simply a matter of physical distancing; it also involves a degree of intellectual distancing from the minutiae of ethnographic observations in order to discern structures and develop theories. However, too great an intellectual distance carries the danger of producing theoretical structures that are irrelevant to the lived experiences of people on the ground and neither grounded in nor answerable to ethnographic data. One commentator on Bhaskar's critical realism sees this dilemma as an intrinsic part of the nature of the human sciences, specifically their 'concrete-boundness':

> We can only directly study concrete entities, not the diverse mechanisms and tendencies which make them what they are. We can study the latter only through the former, not by isolating them in closed systems. The further our theory gets away from the concrete towards the abstract (*which it must nevertheless do*) the more prone to error it is.
>
> (Collier 1994: 255, emphasis mine)

Thus the process of ethnographic analysis involves a constant and hopefully creative tension between the necessary, if risky, processes of generalizing and explaining, and ethnographic knowledge of real people, their actions and interactions gleaned through the experiences of field research. An anthropological perspective on this same sort of tension describes it using other theoretical concepts such as the interplay between agency and structure.

> In order to construe the gestures of others, their words and winks and more besides, we have to situate them within the systems of signs and relations, of power and meaning, that animate them. Our concern ultimately is with the interplay of such systems – often relatively open systems – with the persons and events they spawn; a process that need privilege neither the sovereign self nor stifling structures.
>
> (Comaroff and Comaroff 1992: 10–11)

Wolcott (1994) depicts this tension between data and analysis in terms of different ways of transforming data – what I would call different levels of analysis. Description stays closest to the original data, yet still entails selectivity, organization and focus; that is, it does transform the data into a form of original analysis, by presenting them in a theoretically determined format. It is 'creating something that has never existed before' (ibid.: 15), not simply re-creating experiences and observations in the field. But the transformation of data usually goes beyond this descriptive stage, with general inferences being drawn from them. Basically, this simply means taking the process of abstraction, in the sense of a reasoned selectivity, beyond what is done in structuring descriptions. This further analysis is necessary in part because 'field data themselves, contradictory, subjective, unruly, partial as they invariably are, provide little basis for knowing with certainty. Subjecting them to rigorous analysis offers a way to achieve credibility' (ibid.: 26). Yet such analysis must be tied to ethnographic data and establishing these links is one of the most important aspects of transforming data into theory. Finally, Wolcott suggests that such analysis may move a bit further from description into somewhat broader and more speculative interpretation, so long as the specific nature and strength of the link with the data remains clear. 'When the claim is made that an interpretation derives from qualitative/descriptive inquiry, the link should be relevant and clear' (ibid.: 37).

I turn now to an examination of the ways in which analysis of ethnographic data proceeds, looking first at the nature of such data, then how they may be organized and employed in theory construction, keeping in mind the necessity to retain a creative tension or continual feedback between data and theorizing. Finally, I discuss the uses, pros and cons of computer software for qualitative data analysis.

Organizing and analysing ethnographic data

As the previous chapters on the range of research methods suggest, ethnographic research produces a wide variety of data. The most typical data produced by ethnographers are their field notes, and virtually every form of data collection involves writing field notes, whatever other kinds of data it may generate. The other most common type of data is undoubtedly interview transcripts. In addition, ethnographic databases may contain documents of all kinds, for example: government publications; newspaper cuttings; personal documents like diaries and letters; and various kinds of records, from menus to autobiographical sketches, some written at the request of the ethnographer, others created for another purpose but made available to the research. They may also contain visual and audio records, such as photographs, films and musical recordings; usually these non-textual materials will be accompanied by extensive field notes which help to elucidate and contextualize them.

In spite of the immense variety of types of data, a few general observations can be made about ethnographic databases. In the first place, the quantity of data produced, even by a single fieldworker, is usually immense. Just as an illustration, consider that a single semi-structured or unstructured interview lasting an hour will typically require six to eight hours to transcribe and produce a transcript of approximately 50 pages. In addition, a good fieldworker will also have field notes of the encounter, describing the interviewee, the setting, assessing how the interaction proceeded, noting any points in the interview that are of particular interest or require further investigation and, perhaps, beginning to develop some theoretical speculations; these notes may be brief but they can clearly run to several pages. Thus most ethnographic research generates a vast amount of text.

A second characteristic of ethnographic databases is their relative lack of organization. Of course the data are organized: field notes are, at a minimum, organized as a journal, with dates of entries, and sometimes separate journals are maintained for different activities, such as personal reflections versus observations; interviews may be identified by the respondent, date and time of interview with related field notes attached to each interview; visual or audio materials will usually be catalogued with an identifying number, source and date of acquisition. But the open research design commonly adopted by ethnographers means that there is little, if any, organization based on analytical considerations, and when this is attempted, it is tentative and often altered during the research. Okely (1994) reports that under the influence of the policy-oriented centre sponsoring her research on Gypsies, she initially tried to organize her field notes around the themes that were deemed important for evaluating certain policy initiatives. However, within a short time, 'I jettisoned my earlier, increasingly unsatisfactory attempts at writing notes under prescribed headings. I had been prematurely deciding what was relevant and in the process omitting other details, possibly for ever. My notes took the form of a chronological journal. The only marker was the date on each page' (ibid.: 23; but cf. Sanjek 1990: 386–9 for some examples in which data indexing systems were successfully taken into the field or developed early in fieldwork). Certainly, given that ethnographers are often at pains to observe broadly and eclectically and not to focus on particular theoretical concerns too quickly in their fieldwork, their databases will necessarily reflect this. Ethnographic data collection is sometimes characterized as having a funnel shape, with very broad and fairly indiscriminate interests in its early phases but becoming narrower and more focused on specific kinds of data as the inquiry proceeds (Agar 1980: 13; Hammersley and Atkinson 1995: 206). Nevertheless, the first major analytical task, that may well begin in the field but intensifies and is systematized as analysis proceeds, is to organize a large and unwieldy dataset so that emerging theories may be tested and refined, others may be discerned, and the relevant data are known and accessible for supporting arguments and interpretations. I now consider some of the ways in which ethnographic data are organized to facilitate analysis.

Essentially, the first step in analysis, which may begin even before going into the field and is certainly a part of thinking about if not actually organizing data, is to develop a set of categories for labelling chunks of data. These categories are basically low-level theoretical concepts for classifying and thinking about the data. There will be a number of sources of such categories and it is often helpful to distinguish between them. In particular, some categories are likely to be in your mind prior to beginning research, drawn from your theoretical orientation and the kinds of questions you see the research as designed to address. Thus, in my study of the transition to adulthood of people with learning disabilities, I was already oriented to problematize this transition and hence to look for the presence or absence of various markers of adulthood, both social and cultural. What I was unprepared for was the degree to which the discourse among social service practitioners about adulthood had been adopted by young people with learning disabilities and their parents. Thus, while I continued to ask questions in interviews and record observations in my field notes about what I took to be indications of adult patterns of socializing and forms of entertainment, I was increasingly aware that the professional discourse about such things was deeply implicated in much of what I was recording and would eventually have to be disentangled so as to show the relationship between them.

At the same time, another category which had been relatively unproblematic within the context of the research design – that of people with learning disabilities – came increasingly to the fore as a research question, or, more correctly, series of questions. As I came to realize the degree to which an adult identity was a self-conscious and cultivated part of their personal identity, I also was made aware that the social identity of someone with learning disabilities was not always, or even usually, incorporated into their personal identity. I therefore began to pay more attention to determining the meanings they attached to these categories (Davies and Jenkins 1997). But I was also forced to pay more attention to the category (people with learning disabilities) that provided the basis for the research, and eventually, with further analysis long after completing fieldwork, concluded that it does not cohere in conventional definitional terms but that it does relate to Western understandings of self and personhood (Davies 1998b). In the next section I will look at how some of these ideas were reflected in or grew from a coding system developed for the computer analysis of this dataset. At present it suffices to say that there are always various overlapping categories from different sources. These may be previously developed theoretical categories, categories intended to reflect the subjective understandings of research subjects or categories constructed primarily by the ethnographer during or after fieldwork, to name a few. While such types of categories are not discrete, it is useful to be conscious of the main source of any such system of categorization, in particular whether the system is supposed to represent primarily informants' categories or ethnographer-imposed categories.

The best known way of formalizing this process of category construction and theory building for ethnographic research is that proposed by Glaser and Strauss (1967), which they refer to as grounded theory (also cf. Strauss 1988). Their very influential book had two main aims: to argue for the generation of theory from qualitative data and for the validity of such theory; and to provide a set of procedures which the authors felt constituted a general method of comparative analysis to produce such grounded theory. Of these two aims, the first has been by far the most influential, being taken on the one hand as an argued assertion that the comparatively unstructured techniques of qualitative research are compatible with the development of social theory, and interpreted on the other hand as a plea to ensure that social theory avoids its more speculative formats and is drawn from and hence firmly supported by observations grounded in research practice. The method that they propose for producing such theory, while certainly too mechanical to allow for general application to ethnographic research, is nevertheless consistent with the widespread practice of developing concepts through a process of continually moving back and forth between the data and a gradually refined set of theoretical categories. On the other hand, the method can be criticized for its naive assumption that data can initially be interrogated from a theoretically neutral position, as well as for not allowing sufficient development of more interpretative forms of analysis, that is for keeping the emphasis on substantive as opposed to formal theory (Bryman 1988: 83–7).

It is generally maintained that grounded theory is more often cited to support the use of non-positivist qualitative research methods as a basis for theory than it is actually employed as a detailed model of research (Bryman and Burgess 1994: 5–6). However, even if the suggested ideal of theory-neutral examination of the data is unattainable, it is certainly important to seek a critical reflexive perspective on the theoretical concepts which are guiding the early development of categories. Overing (1987) has warned about the power of technical vocabulary to shape interpretation, maintaining that much of anthropological terminology – headman, shaman, magic, kinship-based society – has nineteenth-century origins and tends to denigrate other, non-Western societies. I have already discussed, in Chapter 3, the feminist argument that most theoretical categories reflect and maintain the domination of social theorizing from a male perspective that reinforces patriarchal relationships. Adopting such a critical reflexive perspective helps to problematize the theoretical categories that initially orient research in ways that inform and advance analysis. Thus Okely (1994) reports that 'I had the opportunity to challenge classical concepts and typologies in both economics and kinship. For example, the classical typology of nomads in economic anthropology includes only hunter-gatherers and pastoralists. There was nothing on the specific nomadic formation found among Gypsies' (1994: 28). At the same time her awareness of the non-Gypsy stereotypes that distinguished between 'real' and 'counterfeit' Gypsies itself suggested other theoretical concepts that her research was able to develop in her analysis of the uses of these stereotypes by both Gorgios and Gypsies.

Thus, the relatively formal analysis of ethnographic data nearly always begins with the consideration and development of concepts to establish and explain categories within those data and then proceeds to explore relationships between these concepts. Such concepts may then be refined, modified, extended, challenged, rejected, but it is essential that the evidence and the reasons for so doing are sought in the data and clearly specified. This process supports the claims of anthropological research, based in ethnographic fieldwork, to provide knowledge through theoretical inference and generalization of a social reality that is neither accessible directly through native understandings nor simply a reflection of the individual anthropologist's psyche. In order to present this view of social reality, anthropologists must be prepared to make their arguments from grounded ethnographic data accessible to a critical scholarly community for evaluation. Both good and bad research are possible, and some criteria – although clearly not in the form of rigid rules – must pertain to recognize the difference and thus to provide a basis for anthropological authority.

Such criteria must fully incorporate the reflexivity that is part and parcel of ethnographic research, while avoiding sinking into a self-absorption that negates the possibility of any knowledge other than self-knowledge. This I suggest can be done by promoting standards of ethnographic enquiry and reporting that accept that ethnographers' data are about something other than themselves of which they are nevertheless a part. It thus requires candour regarding the theoretical influences that structured the research process as well as the variety of ways in which the ethnographer is implicated in the research findings.

Sanjek suggests that a major element in this reflexivity is 'a portrayal of the ethnographer's path in conducting fieldwork' (1990: 621). At the same time, the relationship between actual ethnographic data – in their multitudinous forms, but especially including field notes, interview transcripts, audio-visual recordings and documents – and theoretical influences needs to be made explicit in the analysis. This goes well beyond any rhetorical devices of the 'being there' variety to persuade readers of the validity of the ethnography (Geertz 1988; see also Chapter 12) and bases persuasion in observational accuracy and reasoned selectivity in presentation of evidence. Of course, it is possible to falsify the ethnographic record, although this may not be any more readily accomplished than falsifying evidence in the physical or natural sciences. Nevertheless, the presentation of data that are as correct as you can make them and as honestly evaluated as possible is a matter of professional ethics. But when this is done, it opens the findings of ethnographic research to informed scrutiny, questioning and subsequent modification in ways that enhance their authority, utility and validity.

I want now to consider several examples that illustrate the ways in which validity is supported, through a consideration of the ethnographer's path through the fieldwork experience, as well as through the use that is made of field notes in the analysis. In his study of a village in north Wales in the mid-1950s, Frankenberg (1990 [1957]) examines how community relationships reflect its changing position in a broader economic order in which men no longer were able to find employment locally but left daily to work in scattered locations, often across the border in England. He sees various local institutions, from the parish council to the football club, as attempts to depict and recreate village unity – attempts which founder due to various internal divisions that cannot be overcome for long because the community no longer has a real material basis for social unity. He is further able to document the way in which strangers – or outsiders – are manipulated in these various organizations to make the suggestions that cause conflict and then to take the blame for their eventual failures, failures which really reflect internal village tensions and conflicts. Such research then clearly had to be based on extensive knowledge of the operations of these various councils, and Frankenberg provides detailed descriptions of them, making his own involvement and the reasons for his conclusions transparent. For example, 'The parish council gives an annual report to the public at an annual general meeting at which the other types of councillor also report. I attended two of these meetings, which were both conducted in the English language' (ibid.: 70). He is also explicit about situations where observation was not possible and explains his reasons for some extrapolation of other experiences to these occasions.

> I could not attend any of the private meetings of the parish council, so I cannot say how and with what difficulty they reach decisions. I have, however, no reason to suppose that they differ greatly from other Pentre committees. Evidence in this direction is that the three chairmen who officiated at meetings during the year were all, in some senses, strangers to the rest of the council.
>
> (Ibid.: 71)

Certainly a central pillar of Frankenberg's analysis, and one of the most compelling sections of the book, is his account of his own experience as a member of the organizing committee of the village football club. He was elected on the stated grounds that 'I always attended matches and had been keen enough to attend the annual general meeting' (ibid.: 119). In this capacity he gives a very detailed account of the various conflicts and difficulties, and his own part in them, that eventually led to the demise of the football club and its functional replacement by a village carnival. He is, for example, able to report the way in which he, as an outsider, was manipulated into taking the chair at a meeting in which a controversial motion was being introduced, with the result that he was given responsibility for the conflict and criticism that developed over it within the village.

> I gathered in the village that I ... [was] being blamed for the whole affair. It was asserted, probably with truth, that the proposal would not have been accepted if Percy ... had stayed on to chair the meeting until its close.
>
> Thus once more unpopularity incurred by making a decision which divided villagers was passed onto those it would least harm, and whose unpopularity had least effect on normal social relations within the village.
>
> (Ibid.: 142)

This ethnography provides an excellent illustration of how tracing the path of the ethnographer validates the theoretical conclusions.

It also shows how a thoroughly reflexive approach to fieldwork can still produce an analysis of a social reality that is outside the ethnographer who was nevertheless a part of it.

Myerhoff's (1978) ethnographic study of the people who attended the Aliyah Senior Citizens' Centre lies more towards the descriptive end of the analytical spectrum. Nevertheless, various theoretical conclusions are drawn from this sensitive and carefully observed study. For example, she asserts that the women in the centre were better able to cope with old age than the men and suggests how this is related to the form of patriarchal culture of the Eastern European Jewish ghetto they had experienced, in which they were expected to develop different roles for home and marketplace (ibid.: 241–52); and she discusses the old people's alternative perspective on ageing which they viewed as a career rather than a series of losses: 'a serious commitment to surviving, complete with standards of excellence, clear, public, longterm goals whose attainment yielded community recognition and inner satisfaction' (ibid.: 251). Myerhoff accomplishes this description and analysis through her use of extensive quotations from interviews and from the sessions of the Living History classes that she had organized for people to share their memories, relying particularly upon what one of her principal informants called 'bobbe-myseh', grandmothers' tales. She also derives her findings from observations drawn from what were clearly detailed and extensive field notes. She does not use the device of quoting directly from her field notes, yet the text is clearly based heavily upon them. For example, she describes the occasion of the celebration in the centre to mark the ninety-fifth birthday of one of its central characters, Jacob Koved, a ritual occasion disturbed by his being taken ill immediately after delivering his speech. Although the ceremony goes on, the centre director eventually announces what everyone suspected, that Jacob was dead:

> The ceremony was now unmistakably over, but no one left the hall. People shuffled forward toward the stage, talking quietly in Yiddish. Many crossed the room to embrace friends.
>
> ... Olga reached down and pulled out the hem of her dress, honoring the custom of rending one's garments on news of a death. Someone had draped her scarf over the mirror in the women's room, as tradition requires. Moshe poured his glass of tea into a saucer ...

> Over and over, people discussed the goodness of Jacob's death and its appropriateness. Many insisted that they had known beforehand he would die that day. 'So why else do you think I had my yarmulke with me at a birthday party?' asked Itzak ... Sofie's words were, 'He left us a lot. Now the final chapter is written. Nu? What more is there to say? The book is closed. When a good man dies, his soul becomes a word in God's book.' It was a good death, it was agreed. Jacob was a lucky man. 'Zu mir gezugt [it should happen to me],' said several of the old people that afternoon.
>
> (Ibid.: 213–14)

Several points can be made about this excerpt. In the first place the quality of the field notes on which it is based is transparent. That is, the field notes had to have provided not simply a summary of the event and main happenings, but a detailed record with emphasis on concreteness, in the sense that myriad small events (pulling out a hem, a mirror hidden by a scarf) are noted precisely and in many cases exact speech is recorded. This is not to pretend that any record can ever be complete, obviously selectivity was employed at both the stage of noting and later writing up, but the report shows attentiveness to detail and openness to what constitutes data. Such field notes provide a strong and effective basis for Myerhoff's subsequent discussion of the significance of the event as 'an extraordinarily successful example of ritual' (ibid.: 227). She suggests that what could have been debilitating and disintegrating to the community because it occurred in the middle of a ritual – which 'after all is supposed to provide reassurance, a sense of order and predictability, yet here were awesome intrusions, disruptions suggesting the very opposite of pattern and form' (ibid.: 226) – was transformed by the actions and interactions of the old people into a celebration that gave a sense of continuity and predictability even in death, 'the underlying, unstated goal of all rituals' (ibid.: 227). It is also important to note that in a study which is highly reflexive, the presence of the ethnographer is directed to helping her understand the old people, not primarily exploring her responses to them. She notes that in the chapter devoted entirely to her principal informant, the tailor and philosopher Schmuel, 'I have included my own voice ... for it proved impossible to expunge. His statements and retorts did not make sense without that, for he was directing his commentary to me' (ibid.: 29–30). The reflexivity in this study shows a very different relationship between ethnographer and research subjects than that experienced by Frankenberg, yet in both instances it has been utilized so as to situate and clarify reported actions and words, and to provide a trace of the intellectual and social paths that led to the two studies' different sorts of conclusions. It is this kind of honesty in recording and transparency in reporting ethnographic data that gives credibility to ethnographic analysis and allows for open and informed evaluation of research findings.

Both of the examples above showing how ethnographers develop their analysis and support their findings – by making visible their intellectual pathways through their data – are based on research in 'traditional' field sites, a village and an old people's day centre, 'traditional' in the sense of being single spatially delimited locations, although neither produces what could be called a 'traditional' ethnography. The final example I want to look at is a study that is non-traditional in virtually every aspect of its design. Martin's *Flexible Bodies* (1994) has, as its primary research aim, an investigation of the changing perceptions of health, disease and the immune system in American culture since the 1950s. To this end, she carries out research using a variety of methods – documentary, interviews, participant observation – in a multi-sited ethnographic study, in which there are no obvious linkages between sites. Her analytical pathway begins with a consideration of the ways in which the media portray the immune system and continues with an analysis of interviews with non-scientists occupying diverse socioeconomic positions about their views on 'health, illness, the body, and the society' (ibid.: 10). She then discusses findings from interviews and observations with 12 different practitioners of alternative medicine and from participant observation in an immunology laboratory. In all of this, findings are contextualized in the research process so as to show how they emerged, that is, the experiential and intellectual pathway that led to them is visible, rather than the reader just being presented with conclusions and an array of supporting evidence. One of the best illustrations of this process is her discussion of being led from an interest in how health concerns were handled in a business environment to participation in a training course, with employees of a large corporation, 'in which workers and management would climb sheer walls and tall, slender poles, cross high wires, and jump off cliffs on zip wires' (ibid.: 212). She discusses how this experiential training challenged gender stereotypes and hierarchical relations and relates, based on her own embodied experience, how specific activities promoted a necessity for flexibility and tolerance of instability.

> The experience models physically the nature of the new workers that corporations desire: individuals – men and women – able to risk the unknown and tolerate fear, willing to explore unknown territories, but simultaneously able to accept their dependence on the help and support of their coworkers. In a word, *flexibility*. The isomorphism between the bodily experience of this training and the results desired is entirely deliberate: as trainers would often say, we were there to 'experience the metaphor.'
>
> (Ibid.: 214)

Martin contends that these changing expectations in the world of business represent the same cultural shift as the one she was discovering in ideas of health and illness in lay society, as well as in scientific ideas about the nature of the immune system. Her argument is made more persuasive by the revelation of how she arrived at these conclusions: 'When I was participating in these events, I had little idea at first whether they would shed any light at all on other parts of my research concerning the immune system' (ibid.: 214). She reports being astonished, in a subsequent interview with the head of the company providing the training course, 'that trainers elect to use the image of the immune system to convey the kind of flexible, innovative change they desire' (ibid.: 214).

Martin's study illustrates the effective application of ethnographic analysis, both empirically grounded and analytically transparent, to data obtained from research which, while recognizably ethnographic, adopts a non-traditional approach to the nature of the field and fieldwork. In reflecting on this research subsequently, Martin (1997) argues that ethnographers should be more open to alternative metaphors to guide their research when they are investigating the theoretical links between many unconnected field sites. She suggests that such multi-sited 'fields' may be conceived of as having the properties of rhizomes, subterranean stems that appear in different locations and, although they are interconnected, are unaffected by having their connections severed; or alternatively, they can be seen as similar to string figures, made of the same material, yet with the ability to be transformed, 'to shift suddenly from one form like "cup and saucer" to another like "cat's whiskers"' (ibid.: 145).

Using computers

The use of computers in qualitative research is usually promoted as a way of increasing the efficiency with which researchers can handle the vast amount of comparatively disorganized data that such research normally generates. Various software applications allow researchers to set up their database so that they can access rapidly all the sections relevant to a particular topic or theoretical concept. Clearly, such an automated indexing system can mean significantly greater efficiency, whether measured in terms of saving time in searching through data or ensuring thoroughness of the search and completeness of the data thereby produced. However, such efficiency in analysis is won at a cost of considerable time spent in preparing data for use by such software (Davis 1984: 308–9). On the other hand, if computers are used at all stages of fieldwork, rather than just during formal analysis, much of this additional cost in time and labour can be alleviated. In particular, the development of laptop computers has meant that most data entries can be put directly into some computer readable format; at a minimum, field notes can be written and audio tapes transcribed directly into a word-processing package. Software is available to allow other forms of data, in particular materials such as photographs, video and audio tapes and diagrams, to be recorded, indexed and accessed interactively (Fischer 1994, 1995), and digital photography has further enhanced the ease with which visual materials can be stored and accessed electronically.

The principal area for computers in qualitative research to date is in the use of various software applications that allow for coding a large text-based dataset and subsequently searching it quickly and efficiently to assist in analysis. I want to concentrate on this form of computer use and consider briefly what is involved and some of the implications, both positive and negative, for ethnographic research employing this technology for analysis. The advocates of the use of computers in qualitative research often argue that they should do more than simply increase the efficiency of ethnographic research, that the goal should be to use computers to do better ethnography. Fischer asserts that 'greater benefits will come when computers are used to do things we could not do before' (1995: 111). However, this enthusiasm should also alert us to the potential of computer technology to transform the nature of ethnographic research. That is, as with everything else in ethnographic research, the application of computers should be undertaken with systematic reflexivity that evaluates their effect on both the particular research project and on the nature of ethnographic research more broadly.

Pfaffenberger (1988) argues that the social implications of new technologies tend to be ignored, both by those who see technology simply as a tool to be used, having no social or cultural effects other than improving the activities to which it is applied, and by those who see it as deterministic, essentially as an autonomous force which individuals cannot readily resist. However, 'technology is loaded with preunderstandings ... To use a microcomputer in qualitative research, then, is to use a form of social behavior whose most remarkable characteristic is its built-in denial that it is a form of social behavior' (ibid.: 17; also cf. Robins and Webster 1999). Thus in considering the use of the various software applications that allow for the coding and subsequent rapid searching of ethnographic textual databases, I want to look both at the technical aspects of how they are applied and their effects on what sort of analysis is possible as well as at the ways in which they may affect individual projects and ethnographic analysis more broadly.

The most widely used software applications for ethnographic data analysis, packages such as Atlas ti, ETHNOGRAPH and NVivo, essentially build on the well-established ethnographic analytical practice of creating categories (or codes) and linking them to an index of the textual material that makes up the database of field notes, interview transcripts and so forth. In these systems the codes, and usually the databases themselves, are on-line, that is, can be accessed directly by the computer so that all the sections having a particular code, or a specified combination of codes linked by operators such as AND, OR, NOT, can be accessed very rapidly and with great accuracy; they can normally be displayed on the screen, printed out or moved into another file for subsequent reference. The first point to be stressed is that the codes themselves are developed by the ethnographer and hence both the relevance of the materials produced by a given code and the completeness and accuracy of the computerized search of the database are entirely dependent on the researcher's thought and care in doing the initial coding of the data. Many such programmes provide a facility to search the dataset for keywords and to code sections around those keywords. This facility, in spite of its apparent labour-saving potential, in fact has quite severe limitations and if relied upon too heavily can produce a very shallow understanding of the data. For example, if you are interested in retrieving your own theoretical musings about a concept such as nationalism from a dataset, then doing a search for a few keywords such as 'nationalism', 'nationalist', 'nation' will indeed probably locate most instances in your field notes. On the other hand, if you are analysing the ways in which the experience of learning disabilities is embodied, then you may be concerned with experiences as different as speculations about pregnancy, discussions of food and perceptions of the nature of handicap. It is very unlikely that a set of keywords could be devised to seek out relevant references to this topic and if attempted it would be likely to produce only quite trivial references which included specific reference to the body or words for specific body parts. Thus the most important part of the analysis takes place gradually during fieldwork and later in reading through the data to construct codes and occurs in the ethnographer's head, not in the computer. The advantage of the computer-based coding is to allow the ethnographer to find, and hence compare, all these instances which were felt to relate to the embodiment of learning disabilities quickly and accurately, and also to be able to relate them readily to other factors such as gender or social class.

One of the major expectations of ethnographic analysis is that theory is grounded in the data, emerging from a constant moving back and forth between developing theoretical generalizations and the detailed ethnographic record. Thus, while observations and discussions must be isolated and compared to other instances, whether similar or contrasting, the context of these observations and discussions which in ethnographic research may fundamentally affect how they are interpreted needs also to be retained. One of the criteria on which computer software should be evaluated, then, is the ease with which it promotes the retention of such context. There are various ways to accomplish this retention of context. Most packages allow for additional notes to be inserted in the original document. These can be used to contextualize a section of dialogue or field notes, or to serve as a reminder of some theoretical musing that the particular section stimulated. Such notes are flagged when that section is one of the hits from a search. In addition, it is usually possible to record notes that delimit the meanings ascribed to particular codes, a facility that is of especial importance when more than one researcher is working on the same dataset. And background information, for example data about each interviewee, can be recorded with individual records. Of course, any such software should provide information to enable the researcher to return to the original off-line document, if there is one. However, there tends to be some resistance to moving from computer searches back to hard copies, which in any case may not be immediately at hand, so it is preferable if the software also allows access to the full document for on-line browsing.

The application of this kind of software for analysis can provide ethnographic research with a stronger defence against one of the criticisms most commonly levelled against it, namely, that the evidence provided for its theoretical conclusions is basically anecdotal, being a result primarily of the incidents and comments that were particularly salient for the ethnographer and hence dependent on the idiosyncrasies of human memory. Certainly, such criticisms can be countered through the application of any careful and systematic analysis whether computers are used or not. However, the counter argument is strengthened when software applications are employed in that, given a carefully and conscientiously indexed computerized database, the ethnographer can examine all instances of a given phenomenon, select the most appropriate supporting evidence and take account of any exceptions or variations. Thus, this software may also make much more feasible a rather more formalized process of theory testing, in addition to the usual ethnographic strength for theory generation. It also allows for greater accuracy and confidence in the kinds of quantitative statements that ethnographic reports normally contain, such as, 'a majority of informants said', 'most instances', 'few examples', and so forth (Richards and Richards 1991).

On the other hand, there are some disadvantages that can accrue as a result of too great an emphasis on the potential for completeness that such computer-based searches offer. Because the thoroughness with which the database is searched depends not only on the characteristics of the computer but also on the care and completeness with which the data have been coded, the researcher may be tempted into taking inordinate amounts of time over coding, developing very thorough and complex coding systems and, in the process, postponing analysis until coding is complete. This way of proceeding is much closer to the paradigm for analysis of highly structured survey data than for ethnographic analysis and it tends to undercut one of the main strengths of ethnographic research. It is possible to avoid this trap if you are aware of it. For example, you can begin with a minimal indexing system which could be coded relatively quickly and then refine it, perhaps adding other levels of codes to respond to and further inform developing theories. You can also create 'theoretically "innocent" index categories' (Richards and Richards 1991: 51) which may suggest new interpretations when the eventual contents are examined and compared. In my research on young people with learning disabilities, I found this a particularly useful technique, for example building in categories which I called FOOD, simply because this was a topic which was a useful conversation starter but one that I came to see was of more basic theoretical importance, and INITIATE, which contained all instances in which I felt the young people I interviewed were asserting control over our social interaction.

Another way to alleviate this tendency to postpone theorizing is initially to index only a proportion of the dataset. This allows you to refine and modify the indexing categories as you develop theories and to move back and forth between the data and the emerging set of categories without feeling that changes in the indexing system will mean an excessive amount of time has to be spent in re-coding the data. Once the theoretical directions become clearer from working with this subset of the data, then it is feasible to code the remaining data without expectations that major alterations in categories will have to be undertaken. It is also possible to code for one theoretical area and work on that analysis without having to index the entire dataset on all the categories that may eventually be of interest prior to starting analysis. It is nevertheless important to remain aware that the further indexing proceeds, the more the ethnographer has invested in a given set of categories, and the less likely it is that he or she will see new and totally different ways of viewing the data. This is also true of non-computerized analysis, but the inertia is probably greater for a system that is fully coded and accessible on-line.

Before turning to a consideration of some of the broader concerns linked to the use of such software applications in ethnographic research, I want to describe some of my experiences in using ETHNOGRAPH for analysis of a large dataset. Research which I undertook on the transition to adulthood of people with learning disabilities produced an extensive database consisting of transcribed interviews, most of several hours in length, with 60 young people as well as separate interviews with the parents or carers of 57 of them. It also contained field notes related to the interviews and to participant observation carried out in several different day centres involving extensive contact with most of the young people in the study. Thus this research produced an extremely large, varied and complex dataset which seemed ideal for computer-assisted analysis. On the other hand, the very size and complexity of the database meant that preparing it for such analysis was a time-consuming operation. The interviews with the young people were very unstructured whereas those with parents, for the most part, could be more readily related to the set of topics on the interview schedule that had been used as a guide. Thus it proved fairly effective and more practical in terms of time to use a set of only 15 categories in coding interviews with parents which basically located the general topics that had been discussed. With the young people, however, I developed a much finer grained set of categories, eventually comprising some 75 different codes, some of which were related to the general areas of questioning I tried to follow with them, others to theoretical categories that emerged in the process of working with the data and others to more open topics that were less immediately related to theorizing but seemed to present the potential for theoretical development. Table 11.1 is a list of a subsection of the codes organized so as to provide an aide mémoire for use in coding. I originally developed the codes working with a subset of 12 interviews; this initial categorization was carried out while fieldwork was still in progress, so some of the theoretical directions that emerged from the exercise did feed back into subsequent interviews. By the time the remainder of the dataset was coded, some analysis resulting in conference papers had already taken place. Even so, a few new categories were introduced as the remaining interviews were coded and early ones had to be read again for any instances of the new categories. In retrospect, I clearly did succumb to the trap of over-concern about completeness of coding in this second stage and would have been well advised only to undertake some of the coding, for the particular theoretical

Table 11.1 Subsection of coding system

(⇔)	COMPETENCE (Assessments of)
IDENTITY	
	LEARNING DISABILITY (Self-perception)
	LEARNING DISABILITY GEN (General understanding)
	ADULT (Self-perception)
	ADULT GEN (General understanding)
	ADULT OTHER (Others' treatment of)
	NEGATIVE (Includes bullying, name calling)

categories I was then developing, and return for successive rounds of coding and analysis. Nevertheless, this dense and careful coding has meant that I was able to get back into the dataset very quickly after periods of working on other projects in order to develop some of the theoretical directions that were built into the original system of codes. Certainly, the greater the likelihood of accessing a dataset over a period of years, as is commonly the case for ethnographic studies, the better the case for expending considerable time and effort in developing a dense and extensive coding system in the early stages of analysis while the contact with the field and the data is still fresh.

A few comments about this particular coding system will help to emphasize several other general points about such coding. First, this is not a very hierarchical system, having only two levels, a general category and anywhere from two to eight subcategories. In general, it is impractical to attempt to keep deep hierarchies in your head while coding; more complex hierarchies of categories can be developed if the system you are using allows operations such as creating a new code from a combination of several others. For example, NVivo tends to encourage operations with the indexing system itself, without immediate reference to the data and this may be used to develop more complex hierarchies of categories. Of the more general categories, some were related to the topics I had determined ahead of time to discuss, areas like WORK, MONEY, SELF HISTORY; others were areas that the policy and practice interests of the research sensitized me to notice, such as SERVICES and DAY CENTRES; and others, in particular IDENTITY, were analytical areas pointing to emerging theoretical interpretations. In addition, there was a set of categories that were thought likely to be of theoretical significance but were still quite unfocused – INITIATE (discussed above), FOOD, CONTROL (by others), FANTASY – and these were not subdivided; I tended to be quite tolerant about what might be included in these exploratory categories. A closer examination of the category IDENTITY will give some insights into how the development of categories and theorizing were interrelated. Since the research as originally proposed was concerned with transition to adulthood, the question of social identity as an adult was clearly central. But it gradually emerged that this social identity was related not just to various markers in terms of forms of socializing (SOCIAL) and living arrangements (LIVING), but also intimately connected to personal identity and various bases of self-perception.

Thus, interviews could be interpreted as discussing two bases of identity, as adults and as people with learning disabilities, in two ways, self-perception and understanding of the meaning of the general category. Two sets of sub-categories were therefore created: LEARNING DISABILITY and ADULT for discourse related to perception of self as a member of these categories; and LEARNING DISABILITY GEN and ADULT GEN for discussion of the meanings of these two categories. Reports of others' reactions to these aspects of their social identities were coded as ADULT OTHER and NEGATIVE (a code which suggests the overwhelmingly undesirable nature of these reports). I decided to go back and code references to gender identity after gradually becoming aware of the apparently reduced salience of gender identity for these young people. Assessments of COMPETENCE were initially felt always to be related to identity, but as coding proceeded, I came across examples which did not seem to warrant its continuance as a subcategory of IDENTITY and this is indicated on the aide mémoire with a double-headed arrow, a symbol also used for a handful of other subcategories. This general category and its various subcategories has proved to be quite useful, in large part no doubt because it was developed as theorizing about the relationship between these social identities proceeded.

In retrospect, I think more could have been done with other social identities, particularly gender and class. Given the flexibility to move categories around that virtually all such systems now provide but that was not available in the version of ETHNOGRAPH I used, I might move two of the unfocused categories, GENDER DIFFERENCE and CLASS, into this general IDENTITY category and consider more systematically the degree to which the social identity of learning disabilities affects their expression. Some of the other unfocused categories, in particular CONFLICT and CONTROL, are relevant for some aspects of identity but are better employed in combination with it rather than being subsumed under it, an operation which has implied theoretical implications. Others, such as FOOD and FANTASY, were available for further analysis and while suggestive of the topic are not determinative of the direction of such analysis.

To conclude this chapter, I want to consider some of the other effects that the adoption of computer-based analysis may have on ethnographic research – what one of the developers of this software has himself called 'the dark side of this technological advance' (Seidel 1991: 107). These are of two main forms: one is the tendency to do things and adopt techniques simply because they are available and trendy, thus fitting the ethnography to the software (Agar 1991); the other is to encourage misperceptions and missed perceptions due to the pervasiveness of the software and its closure of other forms of analysis. Because these software applications have the ability to handle such large amounts of data so efficiently, they can promote an excessive concern with the volume of data. It has already been noted how the desire for completeness may lead to a counter-productive postponement of analysis until coding is accomplished for the entire dataset. This can also lead, for instance, to a multiplication of supporting examples for a particular theoretical position rather than a self-conscious searching for variation and complexity that is a strength of ethnographic analysis. This also can inhibit theoretical generalization, both by a sort of descriptive overkill to support low-level and comparatively trivial generalization and by making it too easy to find exceptions when theories are still being formulated, thus rejecting rather than modifying them. As the newer versions of such software appear, they seem to put greater emphasis on model-building once codes are in place, which, if anything, moves ethnographic analysis rather further towards a formalistic analysis (Mangabeira 1995) that does not retain the necessary tension between abstraction and concreteness, but rather treats analysis as a unidirectional process away from the concrete instead of requiring a constant circling back.

The second area of concern in the use of computers in ethnographic analysis is what I have called misperceptions and missed perceptions. The developer of ETHNOGRAPH has expressed concern about the tendency to reify the codes that are created for the datasets (Seidel 1991). Obviously this is not a problem that is unique to computing technology, but the form in which a manually created system appears is a constant reminder of its constructed character. The coding systems developed for these software applications may be particularly prone to such hidden assumptions, and the better the system, the more likely this error in interpretation will creep in, given the combination of consistency in the results and professional looking format of the data output. There is a subtle power to a well-designed and carefully coded indexing system to appear as if it represents things actually found in the data, rather than the interpreting and labelling of fairly untidy and nearly always contentious observations.

Another concern is the way in which the unexamined use of such software may mean missed opportunities for different forms of analysis. At the least, researchers can be so absorbed in adaptation of the research for computer analysis that insufficient attention is given to broader questions about research design, thus developing research that gives 'the right answer to the wrong question' (Agar 1991: 181; also cf. Mangabeira 1995). Thus for certain kinds of questions what may be needed is only a very small dataset intensively analysed, and hence suggesting a research design for which computer applications may be superfluous at best and seriously misleading in a worse scenario. Another consideration is the way in which data are physically present for examination. Computer presentations are restricted to relatively small amounts of data being actually in front of you on the screen at any one time; and although some simultaneous presentations are feasible with a split screen, this is obviously going to be quite limited in scope. Some forms of analysis, especially when close comparison is important, may be facilitated by having a layout of data in which the researcher can physically move between cases and around the dataset – this seems very likely with visual data but may also be the case for text (cf. Agar 1991). Hence the use of computer technology should never be simply assumed to be desirable for any given research project. Rather the likely effects on the specific project as well as on the kind of ethnographic analysis it encourages and supports should be critically assessed before a decision of whether, at what stage and to what ends such software applications should be adopted.

Chapter 12

Writing up, concluding

Writing up involves ethnographers in two kinds of questions: what is the final product of research and how is it to be accomplished? The first of these questions asks what is the nature of the final product – whether classic monograph, research article or ethnographic film – what is its relationship to those aspects of social reality that inspired the research in the first place. The critical realist perspective I have adopted in this book contends that there is a social reality out there, separate from our knowledge of it, which is nevertheless accessible to investigation and understanding. Such understanding while necessarily partial is still open to critical evaluation; there is both good and bad research and criteria to recognize the difference. We can know this social reality because we are, or can become through our actions, a part of it. Clearly, in so doing we both attain insight into this social reality and alter it through our presence. This essential reflexivity is a part of all research, but probably more characteristic of ethnographic research than of any other form. Such fundamental reflexivity must be acknowledged and employed at all stages of the research process. Thus, a critical self-consciousness must be developed and incorporated into the research from the initial stage of selecting research topics through the interactions with others in the field to the final analytical and compositional processes. Such critical self-awareness is not simply about the individual ethnographer's social identities and personal perspectives; it also needs to encompass disciplinary perspectives and broader cultural background. At the same time, this critical reflexivity is not an end in itself – the research is not about the ethnographer; rather it is a means – in fact, the only means – of coming to know, however imperfectly, other aspects of social reality.

From this perspective, social research involves a series of mediations between different constructions of reality to increase understanding of these various constructions and of the social world behind them. These mediations occur throughout the research process. In preparing for research, ethnographers mediate between various previous textual products on their research topic, usually several theoretical perspectives and their own less formalized preconceptions and perceptions about the research topic. In the field, the mediations often take on the form of interaction within a social field in which research subjects and researchers strive to work out acceptable forms of accommodation. In analysis and writing, ethnographers move between their interpretations of others' constructions of reality, their own creation of new constructions, and their expression of these evolving understandings in yet another, usually written, form. This final written product is a mediation that is itself a conduit for further mediations, in particular between author and various possible audiences.

Given the clearly constructed nature of the final product of ethnographic research and the reflexive involvement of the ethnographer in its creation, it is obvious that this product cannot be taken as a straightforward mimetic representation, or imitation, of another aspect of social reality. Thus, the question of how this presentation of the ethnographer's understanding of another social world is accomplished is also raised. Postmodernist critics have argued that ethnography is essentially a literary activity with no possible relationship to a social world outside itself. The perspective of this book rejects this argument (see below) while still appreciating its directing attention to the way in which literary forms and conventions have meanings and promote particular perspectives in and of themselves. Certainly, critical consideration needs to be given, by writer and reader alike, to the textual or rhetorical devices that are employed and their suitability for the ethnographic purpose at hand. On the other hand we do not have to reject the ability of ethnographic research and its products to reveal much about the social world simply because these products are deliberately crafted. This final chapter looks at various aspects of the process of creating and interpreting the end product of ethnographic research, in particular in its most common written format. It thus considers the process of textualization and the role of rhetoric; the question of authority and the postmodernist critique; and the nature and role of audiences for ethnographic reports.

Textualization and rhetoric

Textualization – that is, trying to express experience, observation, reflection, analysis in written form – is a process that is intrinsic to research in all its stages. Yet it is only fairly recently and due in large measure to the postmodernist critique of a naive representation that 'writing has emerged as central to what anthropologists do both in the field and thereafter' (Clifford 1986a: 2). In particular, the central ethnographic method of participant observation is accomplished not simply by doing but also by recording. The writing of field notes is fundamental to doing fieldwork and these field notes become one of the most important data sources for subsequent analysis. Field notes – along with every other way of recording social realities, including visual and audio recordings – are necessarily partial and reflect the ethnographer's perceptions. Thus, although there are criteria for producing good field notes (see Chapter 11), the data on which ethnographers rely in writing up their results are themselves interpreted material and will be read and reinterpreted on multiple occasions in the process of writing up. They have been called liminal texts (Jackson 1990) in the sense that they are themselves undetermined but in the process of becoming something else, a completed analysis or ethnography. The final written ethnography is not only based on field notes but may refer directly to them, even quote from them. It will also almost certainly refer to previous ethnographies themselves based on field notes as well as to other kinds of texts, for example the words of informants, perhaps recorded and transcribed, less frequently written by them. In this bringing together of various written sources, the final written product of research is intertextual (Atkinson 1992: 18–20). And this intertextuality is extended as it becomes a source for comment and criticism within a professional dialogue and, increasingly frequently, among research subjects and other user groups. This textuality and interpreted quality of ethnographic data is as unavoidable as is its reflexivity; in fact, the two are intimately related. It cannot, for example, be avoided by the use only of the words of informants recorded by mechanical means. Leaving aside for a moment the question of the ethnographer's exercise of selectivity in both recording and preparation of a text based entirely on informants' statements, the process of transcription itself is one that is loaded with theoretical assumptions, as was discussed in Chapter 5, and produces a text that is the product of interpretation in a manner analogous to field notes.

Given this intrinsically intertextual nature of ethnographic reporting, it is important that researchers consider their use of particular written forms and styles and the meanings that these convey. Clearly ethnographic writing is at one level rhetorical in the sense that it seeks to persuade through the use of a variety of linguistic strategies. Thus, it is essential that ethnographers be reflexive about the way in which they construct their ethnographic texts as well as the way in which they read those of others. Geertz (1988) has argued that the principal way in which ethnographers have established the validity of their written ethnographies, which he sees as essentially the same as establishing their own authority, is through a variety of literary or rhetorical forms that demonstrate 'their having actually penetrated (or, if you prefer, been penetrated by) another form of life, of having, one way or another, truly "been there"' (ibid.: 4–5). This feat, which Geertz depicts as a resolution of what he calls the signature dilemma – that is, the question of how the author is to be present in the text – is not accomplished in the same way by all ethnographers. Perhaps the most commonly recognized approach is the arrival story, with the subsequent near disappearance of any further personal references from the text. This subsequent adoption of a 'distanced normalizing mode' (Rosaldo 1993 [1989]: 47) – of writing what has elsewhere been typified as a realist tale (Van Maanen 1988) – is regarded as a way of establishing the ethnography as a primarily scientific rather than a literary work. I return below to the question of literary forms and the authority or validity of the text. For the moment, I simply want to emphasize that the choice of style carries messages about the intended nature of the text and its basis of authority.

In addition to general style, numerous specific rhetorical devices and literary conventions are employed in ethnographic writing which help to situate the study, methodologically, theoretically and epistemologically, and contribute to its argument. Even the choice of title is stylized, with a common device being to signal the dual nature of ethnography as both literary creations and social scientific reports through use of a subtitle that contrasts in genre to the title; one such is *Festival of the Poor: Fertility Decline and the Ideology of Class in Sicily, 1860–1980* (Schneider and Schneider 1996; also cf. Atkinson 1990: 75–81). Other messages external to the text itself are present in the list of references, which are as much to locate a work in a particular tradition as to provide either supplementary information or support for its argument. Even the acknowledgements may be read as significant in being the only place in the work not focused primarily on the research, but which explicitly 'bring out how anthropologists are enmeshed in webs of relations, belong to a variety of collectivities, and are subject to a range of duties and obligations, not only in the field, but throughout the development of their ethnographic projects' (Ben-Ari 1987: 65).

In the text itself, rhetorical devices will be employed to render the argument more interesting, compelling and convincing. Furthermore, such devices are shared with other forms of writing that make no claims to represent a reality external to itself. This sharing of literary conventions does not, however, make ethnographic writing a form of literature. In fact, all forms of writing make use of such literary conventions. Even scientific papers in the natural sciences are constructed as persuasive arguments in ongoing disciplinary debates (Atkinson 1990: 43–9). It is not feasible here to review all the various literary conventions employed by ethnographers in constructing their texts (cf. Atkinson 1990; Jacobson 1991; Van Maanen 1988), but I will look briefly at the issues surrounding some of the most widely employed, specifically metaphor, narrative and the presence of other voices in the text.

Metaphor is probably most visible when we examine the functions of the vivid descriptive passages that are to be found in many ethnographies. Such passages, as has already been remarked, are noteworthy in even the most stylistically objectivist ethnographies for locating the ethnographer in the field site. But they often serve another function as metaphor for the ethnographic work that contains them in order to prepare the reader for the intellectual argument that is to follow (cf. Atkinson 1990: 71–5). Consider, for example, Fox's (1995 [1978]) description of arrival at the Irish island of Tory:

> As the little boat rides the waves, one begins to pick out the houses, first at the harbor where the boat is aiming – An Camus Mor (Camusmore Bay). One sees the fabulous tower of Colmcille's monastery, standing out above the cluster of roofs. Then, to the east, a few scattered houses can be glimpsed against the backdrop of the towers of rock. One sees that the island, two-and-a-half miles long running west to east, in fact slopes backward toward the great sea like a wedge of cheese.

> And this is its secret. Had it been flat, it would not have been, in its totally exposed position, habitable.
>
> (Ibid.: 11–13)

In spite of its impersonal narrative form, this passage develops a description that powerfully places the ethnographer in this location and allows the reader imaginatively to experience it. But in addition it introduces into this 'relatively sober anthropological account of the social structure of Tory' (ibid.: 10) an encompassing image of survival in the face of hostile elements, a perspective which provides the broader purpose of the narrative: 'I mean it to be, in some small way, a memorial to this unique and remarkable people who may not be able to survive the worst devastation of all: progress. Soon, for their own good of course, they may be removed forever' (ibid.: 10). In this sense, the arrival story provides a metaphor for the people and society being studied, suggesting to the reader how the subsequent analysis is to be framed.

However, metaphor is used more broadly in ethnographic writing, in ways intrinsic to the analysis. Many of the theoretical constructs employed in ethnographic research may be seen as analytical metaphors, not dissimilar to Weberian ideal types, that provide 'conceptual apparatus and imagery through which we grasp generalities and make comparisons between one setting and another' (Atkinson 1992: 12). One such is Goffman's (1961) concept of the 'total institution'; another is Anderson's (1991) description of nations as 'imagined communities'. Such analytic metaphors are more transparently present in the text than are the metaphors inscribed in more literary descriptive passages. That is, the bases in other texts of these analytic metaphors are known and open to critical evaluation as to suitability in the proposed context to a professional readership defined by their disciplinary concerns, although they will not necessarily be known to other audiences. Descriptive personal metaphors unique to the individual ethnographer are more subtly persuasive, but should not escape critical attention and commentary on evidentiary bases other than their literary appropriateness.

Another textual device that has been much discussed is that of the use of narrative forms; that is, the use of literary forms that in some sense tell a story – whether recounting an incident, interpreting a ritual, reflecting on social relationships or countless other forms. Because the collection of narratives is such an intrinsic part of most forms of ethnographic fieldwork, the process of writing an ethnography can be seen as a sort of meta-narrative, an organizing of these narratives to tell yet another story. Certainly the use of narrative seems to be embedded in human communication, and thus its appearance and reappearance as both data and product of ethnographic research is both appropriate and unavoidable. However, it is important to be sensitive to the variety of ways in which narrative may be organized. Thus, although Western literary conventions have tended to use time and motivation as bases for organizing life history narratives, these are not the only ways of structuring such a narrative, and ethnographers in the field need to be cautious about overly directive enquiry that may impose a particular narrative form and lead to misunderstandings and a failure to develop a mutually satisfactory story (see Chapter 9).

At the same time, it is important to be aware of the narrative conventions that are used in constructing the ethnography from field narratives, both the fieldworker's and those of others. These conventions are suggested by the title and can usually be more clearly discerned in the listing of contents. Thus the study of community social structure undertaken by Fox (1995 [1978]) is in a classical ethnographic tradition organized around social institutions with chapters, for example on 'Kinship and naming' and 'The boats: recruitment of crews'. On the other hand, both the title (*Anthropology Through the Looking-Glass*) and the chapter headings – from 'Romanticism and Hellenism: burdens of otherness' to 'Etymologies of a discipline' – of Herzfeld's (1987) comparative study of Greek ethnography and anthropological theory signal a narrative organized by a critical questioning of the relationship between these two, rather than a focus on either.

Another narrative form that became more prevalent with the growth of post-colonial, postmodernist and feminist critiques of ethnographic relationships is that which is organized explicitly around the encounter between ethnographer and subjects, for example Dumont's *The Headman and I* (1978), with its subtitle *Ambiguity and Ambivalence in the Fieldworking Experience* giving additional clues to its narrative focus. Indeed, although the narrative does encompass traditional topics, such as kinship, it does so in terms of how their understanding is conditioned by specific relationships in the field; thus Dumont depicts anthropological interpretations of other cultures as akin to psychological projections, but maintains that he is in any case 'more interested in the process of production than in the product of anthropology' (ibid.: 96).

In contrast, the narrative form of ethnography that would appear to be closest to the narratives of informants in the field, in a sense appearing to hand the narrative over to them, is that of the life history or portrait of a single individual. One of the earliest experiments with this narrative form is to be found in the work of Oscar Lewis. His study of a Puerto Rican family, *La Vida* (1965), is primarily presented through the first-person narratives of different individual family members. Yet clearly these narratives are collected, edited and organized to address Lewis's theoretical concerns with the culture of poverty. In general, the use of informants' voices in the text, while it does provide an intimacy in the reader's contact with the research subjects and appears to relinquish to a degree the ethnographer's control over the narrative, does not mitigate the constructed nature of the ethnographic meta-narrative. Certainly, the virtually universal use of tape recorders in the field subsequent to Lewis's work has tended to encourage greater use of informants' narratives, presented in their own words, in the resulting ethnographies. Research based primarily on ethnographic interviewing usually makes extensive use of these direct quotations (see Chapter 5), whereas participant observation is more likely to produce accounts based on extensive use of field notes with smaller amounts of direct speech. However, there are several well-known ethnographies that take the form of a life history or portrait of a single key informant based almost entirely on extended conversations with a key informant (e.g., Crapanzano 1985; Dwyer 1987 [1982]; Shostak 1990). Both Crapanzano and Dwyer use an explicitly dialogical format with the ethnographer's questions appearing in the text, which contains extensive quoted material from these conversations, as in the following example:

> On another occasion Tuhami describes how he had to fend for himself:
>
> - I stayed with them [his mother and stepfather] for a month, and then it was finished ... Then I ran off without saying a word.
> - What happened the day you ran away?
> - Nothing. (*Tuhami was very evasive.*) I saw that my stepfather didn't want to feed me. (*He paused.*)
> - Do you remember the first night away from home?
> - I was just walking. I didn't know where I was going. Suddenly I met someone who asked me where I was going. I told him I didn't know. He asked if I wanted to be a shepherd. I said I

> did. I spent seven nights at his house. I wasn't going to work for him but for someone else. He called a neighbor, and he told her I could be her shepherd.
>
> What is most striking about this recitation is that, despite its attestation of independence, it has the autonomous quality of a dream. Tuhami is passive before the forces of fate.
>
> (Crapanzano 1985: 41)

What is especially noteworthy here is the way the ethnographer uses several devices to retain control of both the internal narrative – by inserting parenthetical comments describing Tuhami's non-verbal behaviour and interpreting his demeanour – and the meta-narrative – through framing the sections of dialogue with interpretive commentary.

A narrative convention that foregrounds the ethnographer's experience has produced some experimental work that turns ethnographic writing into fiction. Angrosino's (1998) book on the experiences of men diagnosed with both learning disabilities and psychiatric disorders is based on his long-term fieldwork as a volunteer with an agency that assists their transition into mainstream society. However, he chooses to convey his understanding of his subjects' lives by writing a series of short stories, avowing that 'my personal intention ... is to write creative fiction' (ibid.: 98). To this end, he uses fictional devices such as creating composite characters, shifting scenes, compressing action, and reporting both imagined conversations and his characters' interior monologues. He states that his only appeal for the reality of these stories is that 'things *like these* happened to people *like these*' (ibid.: 101). This is a very dangerous direction for ethnographic research. In the first place, it abandons standards of ethnographic reporting based on evidence and argument that are open to critical evaluation by others. And secondly, as Angrosino himself admits, it carries the highly probable risk that any applied dimension will be 'dismissed as frivolous' (ibid.: 94) by practitioners and that the authority of ethnographic research more generally will be substantially undermined.

While the use of fiction in ethnographic reporting has not been widely accepted, some ethnographers have adopted other forms of experimental writing in which composite events and characters are created from the ethnographic record. In her study of Hutu refugees in Tanzania, Malkki (1995) is concerned with how to represent the intertwining of their personal narratives with constructions of their collective history. 'To be told and retold such similar, almost formulaic historical accounts, and to see stories of people's own lives melt into the general themes of a collective narrative, was a compelling experience. But how can such a powerful sense be conveyed in the retelling?' (ibid.: 56). Her solution was to create a series of panels, 'extended narrative passages clearly demarcated and set apart from the rest of the text' (ibid.: 56), which contain composite accounts sometimes of a single person, sometimes of several individuals on a single theme. Given that these panels are clearly marked in the text and that the way in which each account was composed is clarified in a footnote, this strategy does seem to be acceptable in this particular context. However, the ethnography can usefully be contrasted with Skultans (1998), who dealt with a similar dilemma without resorting to this kind of device (see Chapter 9). In general, ethnographers will be well advised to use such fictional conventions in their writing only with great caution and circumspection. In his ethnography of street vendors in New York, Duneier (1999) advocates great care be taken to ensure both the accuracy of quotations from informants and that the ethnographer's voice be distinguishable from those of informants.

> I have come to believe that this is perhaps especially necessary when a scholar is writing about people who occupy race and class positions widely divergent from his or her own, for the inner meanings and logics embodied in language that is distinctive to those positions can easily be misunderstood and misrepresented if not accurately reproduced.
>
> (Ibid.: 13)

He further eschews the practice of creating composite characters and of combining events and quotations from different times.

Postmodernist critiques and ethnographic authority

In all ethnographies, therefore, there are a variety of voices in the text: some of them the voices of informants, others the different voices of the ethnographer, who may speak for example as interlocutor, social actor or analyst. These different voices in Shostak's (1990 [1981]) account of *Nisa,* a !Kung woman, have been depicted by one of the main figures in the postmodernist critique of ethnographic representation as allegory. Clifford (1986b) disentangles three levels of meaning in the ethnography, 'three registers [which] are in crucial respects discrepant' (ibid.: 104): the constructed life story of a !Kung woman; a story about a woman, and about women's experiences, that has resonances for Western feminism; and a story of an intercultural encounter between the ethnographer and her key informant. The important point about this text for Clifford is this polyvocality and what he regards as Shostak's inability or unwillingness to reconcile them in order to produce a traditional holistic ethnography with a unified perspective, which he takes as indicative of anthropology's 'impossible attempt to fuse objective and subjective practices' (ibid.: 109). Thus the different registers – what I called different voices – in this text are to Clifford an indication of the impossibility of producing a true story about the social world; instead, ethnographers can only produce different stories. Furthermore, Clifford and the postmodernist critics more generally argue with varying degrees of clarity that their use of the term 'stories' is indeed intended to discredit the ability of ethnography to tell us about a separate social reality, apart from the ethnographer's personal and fragmented experiences of it. 'Ethnographic writing can properly be called fictions in the sense of "something made or fashioned," ... But it is important to preserve the meaning not merely of making, but also of making up, of inventing things not actually real' (Clifford 1986a: 6). In a similar if somewhat more fanciful vein, another critic describes the purpose of postmodern ethnography as 'to evoke in the minds of both reader and writer an emergent fantasy of a possible world of commonsense reality' (Tyler 1986: 125); it is poetry, in intent if not form, whose effect is that 'of a vision quest or religious parable' (ibid.: 126).

What this critique primarily tries to accomplish is to redirect attention in the pursuit of ethnographic research from the doing of research to the writing about it. Ethnographies are therefore to be judged not on the basis of evidence and argument but on literary criteria (Jacobson 1991: 114); the postmodernist emphasis on texts is to be distinguished from that of Geertz and other interpretativists. They developed the analogy of social life as like a text and their interpretations of it as a kind of true fiction. But they retain a strong link to fieldwork in their analyses. Even Geertz's (1988) argument for the basis of authority in ethnographic texts, while certainly rhetorical, still depends on the ability to convince the reader of research grounded in practice that requires real and meaningful contact with other social and cultural forms. For postmodern ethnographies the link with, or the necessity of, field research quickly becomes problematic given the assertion that all that can be produced is a fiction. That is, the importance of contact with other peoples and cultures in other societies, from a postmodernist perspective, can be perceived in terms of enriching personal experience to add depth to one's writing. 'Anthropology is potentially reduced to an identity ritual for the anthropologist' (Mascia-Lees *et al.* 1989: 32). But with the concentration on writing stories about this experience, there is no incentive to pursue systematic field research or deliberately to set out to investigate specific questions. In this respect, it rapidly becomes necessary to ask why do ethnographic research in any case.

Although the elements of postmodern ethnography are not clear (cf. Tyler 1986: 137), most advocates emphasize, in their chosen examples that are said to approximate to postmodern writing, the characteristics of reflexivity, dialogic forms and polyvocality. As has been argued throughout this book, reflexivity is inherent to social research at all stages and of all forms. But this reflexivity is not the end purpose of the research; it is the means through which knowledge of a social reality outside ourselves can be approached. This knowledge is always partial and contingent, and its contingent nature can be explored and presented in various formats. Among these formats are the research practices of engaging in open and critical dialogue with our research subjects – dialogues that may be acted out as well as spoken – and in seeking out varying perspectives. Such knowledge also can be presented through the use of dialogue in ethnographic texts and the inclusion of many voices, often enough different registers of the ethnographer's own voice. But reflexivity in the text is not the same as a thoroughgoing reflexivity that informs the research process at each stage. Nor is the use of dialogue or the textual construction of polyvocality any guarantee that another social world, or the varieties of social knowledge in this other world, have been experienced by the ethnographer and may be accessed by the reader through their text. In fact, such literary devices can be used just as effectively and much more subtly to control the overall import of a text or to promote a particular perspective, as do the more transparently structured classic narrative forms.

A brief consideration of some feminist responses to the postmodernist critiques (Mascia-Lees *et al.* 1989; Wolf 1992; also cf. Strathern 1987a) will clarify both the insights that can be gained from them as well as their ultimate failure as a basis or direction for ethnographic research. Many feminists have recognized that their analyses share some convergences with postmodernist positions (Farganis 1994), in particular their rejection of the meta-narrative, the unifying perspective, as disguising the particular perspective of white Western males. Thus feminist researchers had for long emphasized reflexivity, not only in terms of personal experience but also in the recognition of the situatedness of the observer and its effect on social interactions and theoretical perceptions. Furthermore, with the challenge from women of colour and lesbian women to the feminist movement of its own assumptions of a unified women's perspective, feminist social research came to search for ways of accommodating difference and to emphasize dialogue and polyvocality. On the other hand, 'feminist theory differs from postmodernism in that it acknowledges its grounding in polities' (Mascia-Lees *et al.* 1989: 20). In spite of frequent postmodernist references to the political dimension of ethnographic writing, not least in the subtitle of one of the earliest and most influential texts in the postmodernist critique – *Writing Culture: The Poetics and Politics of Ethnography* – postmodernists have been notably unreflexive regarding the politics of their own main (academic) field of endeavour. Thus 'even though the content of the critique may call for the questioning of *textually* constituted authority, the endeavor necessarily constitutes a play for *socially* constituted authority' (Sangren 1988: 406; also cf. Rabinow 1986). From a feminist perspective this has been seen as a way of excluding feminism from the academic mainstream. That is, more than one feminist scholar has remarked on the irony of the postmodernist refusal to privilege any voice at the historical moment when the voices of others – women, former colonized peoples, non-white peoples – were beginning to be empowered. The postmodernist insistence on decentring and multiple perspectives denies material and historical differences in power and perpetuates in reality the dominance of Western white male discourse (Mascia-Lees *et al.* 1989: 29–30). This very process of undermining ethnographic authority has left, in effect, the same social collectivity in control of ethnographic products – products which, it has been suggested, are so obscure that they are clearly 'written for a small elite made up primarily of first-world academics with literary inclinations' (Wolf 1992: 138). For example, Clifford's (1988) study of the federal court case in which the Mashpee, a group of Native Americans, sued for possession of a large tract of what they claimed were tribal lands, a case in which questions of the historical validity of cultural identity was central, was primarily an exploration of multivocality and the contingency of cultural identity.

> However, Mascia-Lees, as someone who has worked with and for the Mashpee in their federal recognition appeal, would argue that it is highly doubtful whether Clifford's insights provide the Mashpee with explanations of social phenomena that they either want or need.
>
> We must question whether the appearance of multiple voices in Clifford's text can act to counter the hegemonic forces that continue to deny the Mashpee access to their tribal lands. Who is the intended audience for this analysis: the Mashpee or other scholars in institutions under Western control? And whose interests does it serve?
>
> (Mascia-Lees *et al.* 1989: 24–5)

Thus, because feminist research insists on its grounding in the political realities of gendered forms of oppression and on the feminist movement's commitment to challenge this oppression, in the end, it diverges sharply from postmodernist perspectives. And this means that feminist research is grounded in and inspired by the experiences of women and concerned with how these can be known, analysed and presented. Rather than experiments with literary forms to undermine textual authority, therefore, they are ultimately concerned with confronting hierarchical social and cultural authority through both textual and interactional practices.

In a similar vein in ethnographic research, it is vital to retain the primacy of the doing of research over the writing of or about it; in other words, ethnography must retain its grounding in practice, so that its relevance is both for other professionals and for those who are its subjects. This means that ethnographic research sets up and maintains a set of analogous tensions that move in various guises through all phases of the research, and its authority is based, to a major extent, on the ethnographer's success in balancing these tensions. They have been considered in various guises in this book. One such is the fundamental challenge of reflexivity, of researching that of which you are necessarily a part, so that knowledge of self does not become self-absorption but remains an instrument for knowing others. The tension between insider and outsider statuses in participant observation is carried over to the tension between description and analysis. Finally, in the process of writing up, ethnographers need to balance tensions in writing for two audiences: the audience of other professional anthropologists and that of the research subjects. It is to considerations of these two audiences and their relationship to ethnographic authority that I now turn.

Audiences and ethnographic authority

Although ethnographers, as with all those involved in investigating areas of potential interest to a broader non-specialized public, may write for a wide variety of audiences, there are two audiences which are of very great importance for evaluating ethnographic research and hence for establishing the validity of their findings. These two primary audiences are: others who have professional training and involvement in their field of research or their discipline – other anthropologists or ethnographic researchers from other social science disciplines – and those who in their everyday activities are involved in the topic of the research, whether as its subjects (and this can be either directly as informants or more broadly as members of the collectivity on which the research focuses) or as practitioners whose activities could potentially be informed by the ethnographic findings. The relationships with these two audiences have great implications for the authority of the ethnographic findings – that is, for evaluating their significance and establishing their validity. Thus the ethnographer should keep these two audiences, with their often conflicting perspectives and expectations, in mind in constructing the ethnography. Insofar as is feasible, ethnographers should also seek input from both audiences at various stages of the writing process. This is fairly routinely done with colleagues, asking them to read drafts of manuscripts in preparation. It may be more difficult to accomplish, but it is becoming increasingly expected with research subjects and so-called user groups. It may be that asking these audiences to read drafts of academic productions is not always appropriate. In my research with people with learning disabilities, I was able to organize a series of seminars with people with learning disabilities, including some of the young people I had worked with, parents and carers, and social service practitioners, to discuss the early research findings and obtain their responses. Even when such an audience is not readily accessible, it is important to keep them and their likely responses in mind as you write. This is both a useful intellectual tool to retain the tension between experience and analysis and a practical response to the changing nature of our world. 'A barefoot village kid who used to trail along after you *will* one day show up on your doorstep with an Oxford degree and your book in hand' (Wolf 1992: 137). Myerhoff (1978) even extended this approach to imagining how her principal informant would have responded to her analyses of situations that occurred after his death. I will therefore consider the critical contributions of each of these audiences to the process of writing up.

I have considered in this chapter the importance of various literary forms, how rhetorical forms may be deployed to increase the persuasiveness of an argument and also how textual devices often form an intrinsic part of the analysis, being not just the medium but carrying much of the message. It is highly desirable that ethnographers cultivate a self-consciousness about the use of these literary forms, both in their own work and in that of others. This is because the evaluation of ethnographic findings should not depend entirely, or even primarily, on the persuasiveness of the writing. Because description and evocation of intellectual perceptions and emotional experiences are such important aspects of ethnographic writing, it is perhaps too easy to accept a set of ethnographic findings due to the literary skills of the ethnographer. However, ethnography is rooted in particular kinds of research practice, and these practices are the basis of its authority; in other words, its validity depends on the effectiveness with which research is carried out and transformed into a formal written argument. The ethnography, then, is evaluated in the sense that its authority ultimately rests on its evidentiary base and its argument – that is, on 'the relationships between claims and evidence' (Jacobson 1991: 114; also cf. Hammersley 1990: 54–72). In order for this to be possible the ethnography must contain indications of how the research was conducted and how findings were reached. This may be done formally in a section devoted to methodology. But it is more frequently the case with ethnographic research that the how of research is incorporated and intermingled with the description of findings. In previous chapters I discuss the bases for good research findings using various ethnographic methods and argue that all of the methods available to ethnographers require an awareness and positive use of the reflexivity which is inherent in such research. Furthermore, as was discussed in Chapter 11, the steps of the analysis should be visible, with an interweaving of supporting ethnographic evidence and theoretical argument.

Finally, ethnographic findings will be evaluated by a professional audience in the context of other ethnographies and theories that constitute the knowledge base of the discipline. Often, in the first instance, this will be within a tradition based in specialization in a particular geographic region (cf. Fardon 1990). But it may also be based in primarily theoretically located interests rather than regionally defined ones. In any case, the authority of any ethnography will be evaluated as well on its linkages and relevance to broader debates within the discipline. Because of the clear centrality of experience and description to ethnography, virtually all forms of writing that present experience are arguably kinds of ethnography, or at least kinds of ethnographic data (e.g. Ellis and Bochner 1996). Some of this experimental ethnographic writing, in which the development of an argument and location within disciplinary debates is minimal, does sometimes stretch the notion of ethnography beyond meaningful limits. Nevertheless, much of this experimental writing when incorporated in ethnographic analysis can be both informative and evocative. Such writing is often autobiographical and the criteria for the uses of autobiography in ethnography were discussed in Chapter 10.

The other audience for which ethnographers should write is that of research subjects and collectivities, often referred to as user groups. These groups will not be judging the ethnography primarily in terms of its internal presentation of evidence and argument, but rather against their own experience and immediate knowledge of the field. Thus, in a study of a mental health system which she came to perceive as a study of psychiatric survivors of that system, Church describes her key informant's response to an early draft of her report:

> She pointed out several places where I highlight the 'outrageous' behavior of survivors without drawing out the 'outrageous' situation (created by professionals) which they were outraged about. Listening to her I suddenly realized that she was reading not just what I had written but also what I had left out. The white spaces: the history of consumer/survivor pain and abuse within the mental health system.
>
> (Church 1995: 126)

This second audience perspective – or in most instances and more realistically, these perspectives – are extremely important and should be conscientiously sought and considered. Clearly, they are more likely to contribute to the analysis and thus influence the final written ethnography if such consultation takes place regularly and begins relatively early in the analytical process. On the other hand, they do not constitute ultimate authority and any agreement to give individuals or constituencies a publication veto should be undertaken with great caution (cf. Punch 1986; Stacey 1988). Indeed, if informants or practitioners were the only basis of ethnographic authority, there would be no need for research. Most of them recognize this and, in fact, look to such research to enlarge their own understanding and provide them with another perspective on issues that are of interest and concern.

The defamiliarization that ethnographers working in their own cultures try to create for themselves can sometimes prove equally revealing for informants who hear or read about their own cultural practices in another unfamiliar idiom. For example, even Rosaldo's ethnographic parody of the family breakfast ritual of his future in-laws, while the cause of great hilarity, was not completely rejected. 'Without taking my narrative literally, they said they learned from it because its objectifications made certain patterns of behavior stand out in stark relief – the better to change them' (1993 [1989]: 48). Thus the involvement of research subjects and user groups in research, while certainly desirable, is not a replacement for other bases of ethnographic authority. In fact, the involvement of this second audience is best treated as an extension of the fieldwork relationships and practices into the processes of analysis and writing. This is likely to increase the validity of the final product; but it does not alter the fact that ultimate responsibility for it lies with the ethnographer, who remains throughout the research at the centre of a series of tensions and mediations and attempts to bring coherence to the experience.

Conclusions

In this discussion of doing ethnographic research, I have emphasized throughout the unavoidable and essentially desirable reflexivity of such research. This reflexivity is to be found at all levels, from the reactions of informants to the presence of an ethnographer to the influences of Western intellectual traditions on ethnographers' theoretical orientations. It is also present in all stages of the research, from selection of topic through fieldwork to analysis and writing up. And it is to be found in all kinds of research methods, whether the open research design of participant observation or the more structured techniques of social surveys or network analysis. I argue that it is possible to make comprehensive and positive use of this reflexivity while still avoiding the inward-looking radical reflexivity, associated with postmodernist critiques, which undermines our capacity to do research intended to produce valid and generalizable knowledge about our own or other societies and cultures. The philosophical foundation for such an endeavour is to be found in Bhaskar's critical realism. This philosophical position begins with an exploration of the nature of the social world, as transcendentally real, which provides a basis for us to gain knowledge about it. Such knowledge must build on the recognition of the separate yet interdependent levels of social reality, those of structure and of the individual. Thus critical realism advocates a form of analysis that is built upon the creative tension between abstract explanation and grounded description.

Throughout the discussions of various research methods, analysis and writing, I have maintained that the ethnographer's task is to recognize, encourage and make creative use of the tensions that this critical realist perspective sets up. Because these tensions are an intrinsic part of the reflexivity of ethnographic research, they occur in a variety of forms and locations within the research process. They may be expressed, for example, in terms of insider–outsider statuses, of description versus analysis, or of the expectations of different audiences for the products of research. Much of the work of ethnographic research involves mediating between these various tensions representing different frames of reference. The success with which ethnographers are able to carry forward these tensions – making informed selections of the most appropriate emphasis for their research within contested sites, mediating without over-balancing in one direction or another – will provide the basis for the overall authority of their findings.

Bibliography

Abberley, P. (1996) 'Disabled by numbers', in R. Levitas and W. Guy (eds) *Interpreting Official Statistics*, London: Routledge.

Abu-Lughod, L. (1991) 'Writing against culture', in R. G. Fox (ed.) *Recapturing Anthropology: Working in the Present,* Santa Fe, NM: School of American Research Press.

Adler, P. A. and Adler, P. (1991) 'Stability and flexibility: maintaining relations within organized and unorganized groups', in W. B. Shaffir and R. A. Stebbins (eds) *Experiencing Fieldwork: An Inside View of Qualitative Research*, Newbury Park, CA: Sage.

Agar, M. (1980) *The Professional Stranger*, London: Academic Press.

—— (1991) 'The right brain strikes back', in N. G. Fielding and R. M. Lee (eds) *Using Computers in Qualitative Research*, London: Routledge.

Ahmed, A. S. and Shore, C. N. (1995) 'Introduction: is anthropology relevant to the contemporary world?', in A. S. Ahmed and C. N. Shore (eds) *The Future of Anthropology*, London: Athlone.

Albers, P. C. and James, W. R. (1990) 'Private and public images: a study of photographic contrasts in postcard pictures of Great Basin Indians, 1898–1919', *Visual Anthropology* 3: 343–66.

Albrecht, T. L., Johnson, G. M. and Walther, J. B. (1993) 'Understanding communication processes in focus groups', in D. L. Morgan (ed.) *Successful Focus Groups: Advancing the State of the Art*, Newbury Park, CA: Sage.

Alderson, P. (1998) 'Confidentiality and consent in qualitative research', *BSA Network* 69: 6–7.

Anderson, B. (1991) *Imagined Communities* (rev. edn), London: Verso.

Anderson, N. (1923) *The Hobo: The Sociology of Homeless Men*, Chicago, IL: University of Chicago Press.

Angrosino, M. V. (1998) *Opportunity House: Ethnographic Stories of Mental Retardation*, Walnut Creek, CA: AltaMira Press.

Appadurai, A. (1990) 'Disjuncture and difference in the global cultural economy', in M. Featherstone (ed.) *Global Culture: Nationalism, Globalization and Modernity*, London: Sage.

—— (1991) 'Global ethnoscapes: notes and queries for a transnational anthropology', in R. G. Fox (ed.) *Recapturing Anthropology: Working in the Present*, Santa Fe, NM: School of American Research Press.

Archer, M. (1995) *Realist Social Theory: The Morphogenetic Approach*, Cambridge: Cambridge University Press.

—— (1998) 'Introduction: realism in the social sciences' in Archer, M., Bhaskar, R., Collier, A., Lawson, T. and Norrie, A. (eds) *Critical Realism: Essential Readings*, London: Routledge.

—— (2003) *Structure, Agency and the Internal Conversation*, Cambridge: Cambridge University Press.

Archer, M., Bhaskar, R., Collier, A., Lawson, T. and Norrie, A. (1998) *Critical Realism: Essential Readings*, London: Routledge.

Arensberg, C. M. and Kimball, S. T. (1940) *Family and Community in Ireland*, Cambridge, MA: Harvard University Press.

Asad, T. (ed.) (1973a) *Anthropology and the Colonial Encounter*, London: Ithaca Press.

—— (1973b) 'Introduction', in T. Asad (ed.) *Anthropology and the Colonial Encounter*, London: Ithaca Press.

—— (1991) 'Afterword: from the history of colonial anthropology to the anthropology of Western hegemony', in G. W. Stocking, Jr. (ed.) *Colonial Situations: Essays on the Contextualization of Ethnographic Knowledge*, Madison, WI: University of Wisconsin Press.

Asch, T. (1992) 'The ethics of ethnographic film-making', in P. I. Crawford and D. Turton (eds) *Film as Ethnography*, Manchester: Manchester University Press.

Ashmore, M. (1989) *The Reflexive Thesis: Wrighting Sociology of Scientific Knowledge*, Chicago, IL: University of Chicago Press.

Association of Social Anthropologists (ASA) (1987) *Ethical Guidelines for Good Practice*, London: Association of Social Anthropologists.

Atkinson, P. (1990) *The Ethnographic Imagination: Textual Constructions of Reality*, London: Routledge.

—— (1992) *Understanding Ethnographic Texts*, Newbury Park, CA: Sage.

Babcock, B. A. (1980) 'Reflexivity: definitions and discriminations', *Semiotica* 30(1/2): 1–14.

Baldwin, J. D. (1986) *George Herbert Mead: A Unifying Theory for Sociology*, London: Sage.

Ball, M. S. and Smith, G. W. H. (1992) *Analyzing Visual Data*, Newbury Park, CA: Sage.

Barnes, J. A. (1954) 'Class and committees in a Norwegian island parish', *Human Relations* 7(1): 39–58.

—— (1972) *Social Networks*, Reading, MA: Addison-Wesley.

—— (1977) *The Ethics of Inquiry in Social Science*, Oxford: Oxford University Press.

—— (1979) *Who Should Know What? Social Science, Privacy and Ethics*, Harmondsworth: Penguin.

—— (1983) 'Foreword', in P. Hage and F. Harary (eds) *Structural Models in Anthropology*, Cambridge: Cambridge University Press.

Basso, K. H. (1972) '"To give up on words": silence in Western Apache culture', in P. P. Giglioli (ed.) *Language and Social Context*, Harmondsworth: Penguin.

—— (1979) *Portraits of 'the Whiteman': Linguistic Play and Cultural Symbols among the Western Apache*, Cambridge: Cambridge University Press.

Baszanger, I. and Dodier, N. (1997) 'Ethnography: relating the part to the whole', in D. Silverman (ed.) *Qualitative Research: Theory, Method and Practice*, London: Sage.

Bateson, G. and Mead, M. (1942) *Balinese Character: A Photographic Analysis*, New York: New York Academy of Sciences.

Baym, N. K. (1998) 'The emergence of on-line community', in S. G. Jones (ed.) *Cybersociety 2.0: Revisiting Computer-mediated Communication and Community*, Thousand Oaks, CA: Sage.

Becker, A. L. (1991) 'A short essay on languaging', in F. Steier (ed.) *Research and Reflexivity*, London: Sage.

Becker, H. S. (1963 [1953]) 'Becoming a marihuana user', in H. S. Becker, *Outsiders: Studies in the Sociology of Deviance*, New York: Free Press.

Bell, B. and Newby, H. W. (eds) (1977) *Doing Sociological Research*, London: Allen and Unwin.

Bell, D. (1983) *Daughters of the Dreaming*, Melbourne and Sydney: McPhee Gribble/Allen and Unwin.

Bell, D., Caplan, P. and Karim, W. J. (1993) *Gendered Fields: Women, Men and Ethnography*, London: Routledge.

Ben-Ari, E. (1987) 'On acknowledgements in ethnographies', *Journal of Anthropological Research* 43(1): 63–84.

Benedict, R. (1934) *Patterns of Culture*, Boston, MA: Houghton Mifflin.

—— (1967 [1945]) *The Chrysanthemum and the Sword: Patterns of Japanese Culture*, London: Routledge and Kegan Paul.

Benney, M. and Hughes, E. C. (1984) 'Of sociology and the interview', in M. Bulmer (ed.) *Sociological Research Methods* (2nd edn), Basingstoke: Macmillan.

Benthall, J. (1995) 'Foreword: from self-applause through self-criticism to self-confidence', in A. S. Ahmed and C. N. Shore (eds) *The Future of Anthropology*, London: Athlone.

Bernal, V. (2005) 'Eritrea on-line: diaspora, cyberspace, and the public sphere', *American Ethnologist* 32(4): 660–75.

Bernard, H. R. and Killworth, P. D. (1973) 'On the social structure of an ocean-going research vessel and other important things', *Social Science Research* 2: 145–84.

Berreman, G. D. (1962) *Behind Many Masks*, Ithaca, NY: Cornell University Press.
—— (1969) '"Bringing it all back home": malaise in anthropology', in D. Hymes (ed.) *Reinventing Anthropology*, New York: Random House.
Bhaskar, R. (1997 [1975]) *A Realist Theory of Science*, London: Verso.
—— (1998) *The Possibility of Naturalism: A Philosophical Critique of the Contemporary Human Sciences* (3rd edn), New York: Harvester Wheatsheaf.
Bijker, W. E. and Law, J. (1992) 'General introduction', in W. E. Bijker and J. Law (eds) *Shaping Technology/Building Society: Studies in Sociotechnical Change*, Cambridge, MA: MIT Press.
Black, M. B. (1969) 'Eliciting folk taxonomies in Ojibwa', in S. A. Tyler (ed.) *Cognitive Anthropology*, New York: Holt, Rinehart and Winston.
Black-Rogers, M. (1989) 'Dan Raincloud: "Keeping our Indian way"', in J. A. Clifton (ed.) *Being and Becoming Indian: Biographical Studies of North American Frontiers*, Chicago, IL: Dorsey Press.
Blauner, B. (1987) 'Problems of editing "first-person" sociology', *Qualitative Sociology* 10: 46–64.
Bloch, M. (1988) 'Interview with G. Houtman', *Anthropology Today* 4(1): 18–21.
Blumer, H. (1969) *Symbolic Interactionism: Perspective and Method*, Englewood Cliffs, NJ: Prentice-Hall.
Bogdan, R. (1974) *Being Different: The Autobiography of Jane Fry*, London: Wiley.
Boissevain, J. (1974) *Friends of Friends: Networks, Manipulators and Coalitions*, Oxford: Basil Blackwell.
Boonzajer Flaes, R. (1993) 'Video elicitation in music research – the world behind the notes', in P. I. Crawford (ed.) *The Nordic Eye*, Hojbjerg, Denmark: Intervention Press.
Bott, E. (1957) *Family and Social Network*, London: Tavistock.
Briggs, C. L. (1986) *Learning How To Ask: A Sociolinguistic Appraisal of the Role of the Interview in Social Science Research*, Cambridge: Cambridge University Press.
Briggs, J. L. (1970) *Never in Anger: Portrait of an Eskimo Family*, Cambridge, MA: Harvard University Press.
British Sociological Association (1996) *Guidance Notes: Statement of Ethical Practice*, Durham: British Sociological Association.
Bryman, A. (1988) *Quantity and Quality in Social Research*, London: Unwin Hyman.
Bryman, A. and Burgess, R. G. (1994) 'Development in qualitative data analysis: an introduction', in A. Bryman and R. G. Burgess (eds) *Analyzing Qualitative Data*, London: Routledge.
Bryman, A. and Cramer, D. (1997) *Quantitative Data Analysis with SPSS for Windows: A Guide for Social Scientists*, London: Routledge.

Bulmer, M. (1982a) 'The merits and demerits of covert participant observation', in M. Bulmer (ed.) *Social Research Ethics: An Examination of the Merits of Covert Participant Observation*, London: Macmillan.
—— (1982b) *The Uses of Social Research*, London: Allen and Unwin.
—— (1984) 'Social survey research: introduction and further reading', in M. Bulmer (ed.) *Sociological Research Methods* (2nd edn), Basingstoke: Macmillan.
—— (1986) *The Chicago School of Sociology: Institutionalization, Diversity, and the Rise of Sociological Research*, Chicago, IL: University of Chicago Press.
Casagrande, J. B. (ed.) (1960) *In the Company of Man: Twenty Portraits of Anthropological Informants*, New York: Harper.
Cassell, J. and Jacobs, S. (eds) (1987) *Handbook on Ethical Issues in Anthropology*, Washington, DC: American Anthropological Association.
Chagnon, N. A. (1992 [1968]) *Yanomamo* (4th edn), Fort Worth, TX: Harcourt, Brace, Jovanovich.
Chalfen, R. (1989) 'Native participation in visual studies: from Pine Springs to Philadelphia', in R. M. Boonzajer Flaes (ed.) *Eyes Across the Water*, Amsterdam: Het Spinhuis.
—— (1992) 'Picturing culture through indigenous imagery: a telling story', in P. I. Crawford and D. Turton (eds) *Film as Ethnography*, Manchester: Manchester University Press.
Charles, N. and Davies, C. A. (1997) 'Contested communities: the refuge movement and cultural identities in Wales', *Sociological Review* 45(3): 416–36.
Charles, N. and Kerr, M. (1988) *Women, Food and Families*, Manchester: Manchester University Press.
Chirban, J. T. (1996) *Interviewing in Depth: The Interactive-Relational Approach*, Thousand Oaks, CA: Sage.
Church, K. (1995) *Forbidden Narratives: Critical Autobiography as Social Science*, Amsterdam: Gordon and Breach.
Cicourel, A. V. (1968) *The Social Organization of Juvenile Justice*, New York: Wiley.
Clifford, J. (1986a) 'Introduction: partial truths', in J. Clifford and G. E. Marcus (eds) *Writing Culture: The Poetics and Politics of Ethnography*, Berkeley, CA: University of California Press.
—— (1986b) 'On ethnographic allegory', in J. Clifford and G. E. Marcus (eds) *Writing Culture: The Poetics and Politics of Ethnography*, Berkeley, CA: University of California Press.
—— (1988) *The Predicament of Culture: Twentieth-Century Ethnography, Literature, and Art*, Cambridge, MA: Harvard University Press.
Clifford, J. and Marcus, G. E. (eds) (1986) *Writing Culture: The Poetics and Politics of Ethnography*, Berkeley, CA: University of California Press.

Clifton, J. A. (1989a) 'Alternate identities and cultural frontiers', in J. A. Clifton (ed.) *Being and Becoming Indian: Biographical Studies of North American Frontiers*, Chicago, IL: Dorsey Press.

—— (ed.) (1989b) *Being and Becoming Indian: Biographical Studies of North American Frontiers*, Chicago, IL: Dorsey Press.

—— (1990a) 'Introduction: memoir, exegesis', in J. A. Clifton (ed.) *The Invented Indian: Cultural Fictions and Government Policies*, New Brunswick, NJ: Transaction Publishers.

—— (1990b) 'The Indian story: a cultural fiction', in J. A. Clifton (ed.) *The Invented Indian: Cultural Fictions and Government Policies*, New Brunswick, NJ: Transaction Publishers.

Cockburn, C. (1991) *In the Way of Women: Men's Resistance to Sex Equality in Organizations*, Basingstoke: Macmillan.

Code, L. (1993) 'Taking subjectivity into account', in L. Alcoff and E. Potter (eds) *Feminist Epistemologies*, New York: Routledge.

Cohen, A. P. (1992) 'Self-conscious anthropology', in J. Okely and H. Callaway (eds) *Anthropology and Autobiography*, London: Routledge.

Coleman, S. and Collins, P. (2006) 'Introduction: "Being...where?" Performing fields on shifting grounds', in S. Coleman and P. Collins (eds) *Locating the Field: Space, Place and Context in Anthropology*, Oxford: Berg.

Collier, A. (1994) *Critical Realism: An Introduction to Roy Bhaskar's Philosophy*, London: Verso.

Colson, E. (1989) 'Overview', *Annual Review of Anthropology* 18: 1–16.

Comaroff, J. and Comaroff, J. (1992) *Ethnography and the Historical Imagination*, Boulder, CO: Westview Press.

Correll, S. (1995) 'The ethnography of an electronic bar: the lesbian café', *Journal of Contemporary Ethnography* 24(3): 270–98.

Cowan, J. K. (1996) 'Being a feminist in contemporary Greece: similarity and difference reconsidered', in N. Charles and F. Hughes-Freeland (eds) *Practising Feminism: Identity, Difference, Power*, London: Routledge.

Crapanzano, V. (1985) *Tuhami: Portrait of a Moroccan*, Chicago, IL: University of Chicago Press.

Crawford, P. I. (1992) 'Film as discourse: the invention of anthropological realities', in P. I. Crawford and D. Turton (eds) *Film as Ethnography*, Manchester: Manchester University Press.

Crick, M. (1982a) 'Anthropological field research, meaning creation and knowledge construction', in D. Parkin (ed.) *Semantic Anthropology*, London: Academic Press.

—— (1982b) 'Anthropology of knowledge', *Annual Review of Anthropology* 11: 287–313.

—— (1992) 'Ali and me: an essay in street-corner anthropology', in J. Okely and H. Callaway (eds) *Anthropology and Autobiography*, London: Routledge.

Crook, S., Pakulski, J. and Waters, M. (1992) *Postmodernization: Change in Advanced Society*, London: Sage.
Cubitt, T. (1973) 'Network density among urban families', in J. Boissevain and J. C. Mitchell (eds) *Network Analysis: Studies in Human Interaction*, The Hague: Mouton.
D'Andrade, R. (1987) 'A folk model of the mind', in D. Holland and N. Quinn (eds) *Cultural Models in Language and Thought*, Cambridge: Cambridge University Press.
Davis, A. and Horobin, G. (eds) (1977) *Medical Encounters: The Experience of Illness and Treatment*, London: Croom Helm.
Davies, C. A. (1989) *Welsh Nationalism in the Twentieth Century: The Ethnic Option and the Modern State*, New York: Praeger.
—— (1998a) 'Caring communities or effective networks? Community care and people with learning disabilities in South Wales', in I. R. Edgar and A. Russell (eds) *The Anthropology of Welfare*, London: Routledge.
—— (1998b) 'Constructing other selves: (in)competences and the category of learning difficulties', in R. Jenkins (ed.) *Questions of Competence: Culture, Classification and Intellectual Disability*, Cambridge: Cambridge University Press.
—— (2002) 'The dictionary, the reader and the handbook: approaches to qualitative research', *Qualitative Research* 2(3): 417–21.
—— (2007) 'Food and the social identities of people with learning disabilities', *Disability Studies Quarterly* 27(3).
Davies, C. A. and Charles, N. (2002) 'The piano in the parlour: methodological issues in the conduct of a restudy', *Sociological Research Online* 7(2): http://www.socresonline.org.uk/7/2/davies.html.
Davies, C. A. and Jenkins, R. (1993a) 'When I get a job I want to be ...', *Llais* 29: 3–5.
—— (1993b) 'Leaving home', *Llais* 30: 12–14.
—— (1994a) 'Socialising', *Llais* 31: 8–9 (reprinted in *Mencap News* 46: 6–7).
—— (1994b) 'Negotiating adult status', *Llais* 32: 18–19.
—— (1997) '"She has different fits to me": how people with learning difficulties see themselves', *Disability and Society* 12(1): 95–109.
Davies, C. A. and Jones, S. (2003) *Welsh Communities: New Ethnographic Perspectives*, Cardiff: University of Wales Press.
Davis, J. (1984) 'Data into text', in R. F. Ellen (ed.) *Ethnographic Research: A Guide to General Conduct*, London: Academic Press.
—— (1992) 'Tense in ethnography: some practical considerations', in J. Okely and H. Callaway (eds) *Anthropology and Autobiography*, London: Routledge.
Davis, N. Z. (1990) 'The shapes of social history', *Storia Delta Storiografia* 17: 28–34.

Deacon, A. B. (1934) *Malekula: A Vanishing People in the New Hebrides*, London: Routledge and Kegan Paul.
Delphy, C. (1981) 'Women in stratification studies', in H. Roberts (ed./trans.) *Doing Feminist Research*, London: Routledge.
Deutscher, I. (1984) 'Asking questions (and listening to answers)', in M. Bulmer (ed.) *Sociological Research Methods* (2nd edn), Basingstoke: Macmillan.
DeVault, M. L. (1990) 'Talking and listening from women's standpoint: feminist strategies for interviewing and analysis', *Social Problems* 37(1): 96–116.
De Vaus, D. A. (1991) *Surveys in Social Research* (3rd edn), London: UCL Press.
Doheny-Farina, S. (1996) *The Wired Neighborhood*, New Haven, CT: Yale University Press.
Donath, J. S. (1999) 'Identity and deception in the virtual community', in M. A. Smith and P. Kollock (eds) *Communities in Cyberspace*, London: Routledge.
Douglas, J. D. (1985) *Creative Interviewing*, Beverly Hills, CA: Sage.
Dumont, J.-P. (1978) *The Headman and I: Ambiguity and Ambivalence in the Fieldworking Experience*, Austin, TX: University of Texas Press.
Duneier, M. (1992) *Slim's Table: Race, Respectability, and Masculinity*, Chicago, IL: University of Chicago Press.
—— (1999) *Sidewalk*, New York: Farrar, Straus and Giroux.
Dwyer, K. (1987 [1982]) *Moroccan Dialogues: Anthropology in Question*, Prospect Heights, IL: Waveland Press.
Edgerton, R. B. (1986) 'A case of delabeling: some practical and theoretical implications', in L. L. Langness and H. G. Levine (eds) *Culture and Retardation*, Dordrecht: D. Reidel.
—— (1993 [1967]) *The Cloak of Competence* (rev. edn), Berkeley, CA: University of California Press.
Edgerton, R. B. and Bercovici, S. (1976) 'The cloak of competence: years later', *American Journal of Mental Deficiency* 80: 485–97.
Edgerton, R. B., Bollinger, M. and Herr, B. (1984) 'The cloak of competence: after two decades', *American Journal of Mental Deficiency* 88: 345–51.
Edgerton, R. B. and Gaston, M. A. (eds) (1991) *'I've Seen It All!' Lives of Older Persons with Mental Retardation in the Community*, Baltimore, MD: P. H. Brookes.
Eidheim, H. (1993) 'Making and watching anthropological film: some armchair reflections', in P. I. Crawford (ed.) *The Nordic Eye*, Hojbjerg, Denmark: Intervention Press.
Ellen, R. F. (1984) 'Introduction', in R. F. Ellen (ed.) *Ethnographic Research: A Guide to General Conduct*, London: Academic Press.
Ellis, C. and Bochner, A. P. (eds) (1996) *Composing Ethnography: Alternative Forms of Qualitative Writing*, Walnut Creek, CA: AltaMira Press.

Ess, C. and AoIR (Association of Internet Researchers) (2002) *Ethical Decision-making and Internet Research: Recommendations from the AoIR Ethics Working Committee*, URL (consulted 14 December 2005): http://www.aoir.org/reports/ethics.pdf.

Evans-Pritchard, E. E. (1940) *The Nuer*, New York: Oxford University Press.

Fabian, J. (1983) *Time and the Other: How Anthropology Makes Its Object*, New York: Columbia University Press.

Fairclough, N. (1989) *Language and Power*, London: Longman.

Fardon, R. (1990) 'Localizing strategies: the regionalization of ethnographic accounts', in R. Fardon (ed.) *Localising Strategies: Regional Traditions of Ethnographic Writing*, Edinburgh: Scottish Academic Press.

Farganis, S. (1994) 'Postmodernism and feminism', in D. R. Dickens and A. Fontana (eds) *Postmodernism and Social Inquiry*, London: UCL Press.

Ferguson, J. (1997) 'Anthropology and its evil twin: "development" in the constitution of a discipline', in F. Cooper and R. Packard (eds) *International Development and the Social Sciences: Essays on the History and Politics of Knowledge*, Berkeley and Los Angeles, CA: University of California Press.

Festinger, L., Riecken, H. W. and Schachter, S. (1956) *When Prophecy Fails*, New York: Harper and Row.

Finan, T. J. (1996) 'Anthropological research methods in a changing world', in E. F. Moran (ed.) *Transforming Societies, Transforming Anthropology*, Ann Arbor, MI: University of Michigan Press.

Finch, J. (1984) '"It's great to have someone to talk to": the ethics and politics of interviewing women', in C. Bell and H. Roberts (eds) *Social Researching: Politics, Problems, Practice*, London: Routledge and Kegan Paul.

Finnegan, R. (1992) *Oral Traditions and the Verbal Arts: A Guide to Research Practices*, London: Routledge.

Firth, R. (1936) *We, The Tikopia*, London: George Allen and Unwin.

Fischer, M. D. (1994) *Applications in Computing for Social Anthropologists*, London: Routledge.

—— (1995) 'Using computers in ethnographic fieldwork', in R. M. Lee (ed.) *Information Technology for the Social Scientist*, London: UCL Press.

Fiske, S. J. and Chambers, E. (1997) 'Status and trends: practice and anthropology in the United States', in M. L. Baba and C. E. Hill (eds) *The Global Practice of Anthropology*, Williamsburg, VA: Department of Anthropology, College of William and Mary.

Fontana, A. (1994) 'Ethnographic trends in the postmodern era', in D. R. Dickens and A. Fontana (eds) *Postmodernism and Social Inquiry*, London: UCL Press.

Ford, C. S. (1941) *Smoke From Their Fires: The Life of a Kwakiutl Chief*, New Haven, CT: Yale University Press.

Foster, G. M., Scudder, T., Colson, E. and Kemper, R. V. (1979) 'Conclusion: the long-term study in perspective', in G. M. Foster, T. Scudder, E. Colson and R. V. Kemper (eds) *Long-term Field Research in Social Anthropology*, New York: Academic Press.

Fox, Richard G. (1991a) 'For a nearly new culture history', in R. G. Fox (ed.) *Recapturing Anthropology: Working in the Present*, Santa Fe, NM: School of American Research Press.

—— (1991b) 'Introduction', in R. G. Fox (ed.) *Recapturing Anthropology: Working in the Present*, Santa Fe, NM: School of American Research Press.

Fox, Richard G. and Field, L. (eds) (2007) *Anthropology Put to Work*, Oxford: Berg.

Fox, Robin (1995 [1978]) *The Tory Islanders: A People of the Celtic Fringe*, Notre Dame, IN: University of Notre Dame Press.

Frake, C. O. (1964) 'How to ask for a drink in Subanun', *American Anthropologist* 66(6): 127–32.

Frankenberg, R. (1990 [1957]) *Village on the Border: A Social Study of Religion, Politics and Football in a North Wales Community*, Prospect Heights, IL: Waveland.

Freeman, D. (1983) *Margaret Mead and Samoa: The Making and Unmaking of an Anthropological Myth*, Cambridge, MA: Harvard University Press.

Friedl, E. (1962) *Vasilika: A Village in Modern Greece*, New York: Holt, Rinehart and Winston.

Fulk, J. and Steinfield, C. W. (eds) (1990) *Organizations and Communication Technology*, Newbury Park, CA: Sage.

Gans, H. J. (1962) *The Urban Villagers: Group and Class in the Life of Italian-Americans*, New York: Free Press.

Garfinkel, H. (1984 [1967]) *Studies in Ethnomethodology*, Cambridge: Polity Press.

Garton, L., Haythornthwaite, C. and Wellman, B. (1999) 'Studying on-line social networks', in S. Jones (ed.) *Doing Internet Research: Critical Issues and Methods for Examining the Net*, Thousand Oaks, CA: Sage.

Geertz, C. (1968) 'Thinking as a moral act: ethical dimensions of anthropological field work in the new states', *Antioch Review* 28(2): 139–58.

—— (1973) 'Deep play: notes on the Balinese cockfight', in C. Geertz, *The Interpretation of Cultures*, New York: Basic Books.

—— (1988) *Works and Lives: The Anthropologist as Author*, Stanford, CA: Stanford University Press.

Gephart, R. P., Jr. (1988) *Ethnostatistics: Qualitative Foundations for Quantitative Research,* Newbury Park, CA: Sage.

Gergen, K. J. and Gergen, M. M. (1991) 'Toward reflexive methodologies', in F. Steier (ed.) *Research and Reflexivity*, London: Sage.

Giddens, A. (1990) *The Consequences of Modernity*, Cambridge: Polity Press.
Gillespie, M. (1995) *Television, Ethnicity and Cultural Change*, London: Routledge.
Gilligan, C. (1982) *In a Different Voice: Psychological Theory and Women's Development*, Cambridge, MA: Harvard University Press.
Glaser, B. G. and Strauss, A. L. (1967) *The Discovery of Grounded Theory: Strategies for Qualitative Research*, New York: Aldine de Gruyter.
—— (1968) *Time for Dying*, Chicago, IL: Aldine.
Gleason, J. (1989) *Special Education in Context: An Ethnographic Study of Persons with Developmental Disabilities*, Cambridge: Cambridge University Press.
Goffman, E. (1961) *Asylums*, New York: Doubleday.
Gold, R. L. (1958) 'Roles in sociological field observations', *Social Forces* 36: 217–23.
Goodenough, W. H. (1965) 'Yankee kinship terminology: a problem in componential analysis', *American Anthropologist* 67(5): 259–87.
Goodwin, M. H. (1990) *He-Said-She-Said: Talk as Social Organization Among Black Children*, Bloomington, IN: Indiana University Press.
Gottschalk, L., Kluckhohn, C. and Angell, R. (1945) *The Use of Personal Documents in History, Anthropology, and Sociology*, New York: Social Science Research Council.
Granovetter, M. (1973) 'The strength of weak ties', *American Journal of Sociology* 78: 1360–80.
Grillo, R. and Rew, A. (eds) (1985) *Social Anthropology and Development Policy*, London: Tavistock.
Grimshaw, A. (1992) *Servants of the Buddha: Winter in a Himalayan Convent*, London: Open Letters.
—— (1995) *Conversations with Anthropological Film-makers: Melissa Llewellyn-Davies*, Cambridge: Prickly Pear Press.
—— (2001) *The Ethnographer's Eye: Ways of Seeing in Anthropology*, Cambridge: Cambridge University Press.
Grimshaw, A. and Hart, K. (1995) 'The rise and fall of scientific ethnography', in A. S. Ahmed and C. N. Shore (eds) *The Future of Anthropology*, London: Athlone.
Grimshaw, A. and Papastergiadis, N. (1995) *Conversations with Anthropological Film-makers: David MacDougall*, Cambridge: Prickly Pear Press.
Gubrium, J. F. and Buckholdt, D. R. (1979) 'Production of hard data in human services institutions', *Pacific Sociological Review* 22 (1): 115–36.
Gubrium, J. F. and Holstein, J. A. (1994) 'Analyzing talk and interaction', in J. F. Gubrium and A. Sanker (eds) *Qualitative Methods in Ageing Research*, Thousand Oaks, CA: Sage.

Gudeman, S. and Penn, M. (1982) 'Models, meanings and reflexivity', in D. Parkin (ed.) *Semantic Anthropology*, London: Academic Press.

Gupta, A. and Ferguson, J. (1997) 'Discipline and practice: "the field" as site, method, and location in anthropology', in A. Gupta and J. Ferguson (eds) *Anthropological Locations: Boundaries and Grounds of a Field Science*, Berkeley, CA: University of California Press.

Habermas, J. (1971) *Knowledge and Human Interests*, trans. J. J. Shapiro, Boston, MA: Beacon.

Hage, P. and Harary, F. (1983) *Structural Models in Anthropology*, Cambridge: Cambridge University Press.

Hakim, C. (1987) *Research Design: Strategies and Choices in the Design of Social Research*, London: Routledge.

Hammersley, M. (1990) *Reading Ethnographic Research: A Critical Guide*, London: Longman.

—— (1992) *What's Wrong with Ethnography? Methodological Explorations*, London: Routledge.

Hammersley, M. and Atkinson, P. (1995) *Ethnography: Principles in Practice* (2nd edn), London: Routledge.

Hannerz, U. (1969) *Soulside: Inquiries into Ghetto Culture and Community*, New York: Columbia University Press.

—— (1990) 'Cosmopolitans and locals in world culture', in M. Featherstone (ed.) *Global Culture: Nationalism, Glabalization and Modernity*, London: Sage.

Harding, S. (1987) 'Conclusion: epistemological questions', in S. Harding (ed.) *Feminism and Methodology: Social Science Issues*, Bloomington, IN: Indiana University Press.

Harper, D. (1987) *Working Knowledge: Skill and Community in a Small Shop*, Chicago, IL: University of Chicago Press.

—— (1989) 'Interpretive ethnography: from "authentic voice" to "interpretive eye"', in R. M. Boonzajer Flaes (ed.) *Eyes Across the Water*, Amsterdam: Het Spinhuis.

—— (1998) 'An argument for visual sociology', in J. Prosser (ed.) *Image-based Research: A Sourcebook for Qualitative Researchers*, London: Falmer Press.

Harris, C., Charles, N. and Davies, C. (2006) 'Social change and the family', *Sociological Research Online* 11(2): http://www.socresonline.org.uk/11/2/harris.html.

Harris, M. (1983) 'The sleep-crawling question', *Psychology Today* May: 24–7.

Hasan, H. (1999) 'Afterword', in M. Duneier, *Sidewalk*, New York: Farrar, Straus and Giroux.

Haug, F. (1987) *Female Sexualization: A Collective Work of Memory*, trans. E. Carter, London: Verso.

Heider, K. G. (1976) *Ethnographic Film*, Austin, TX: University of Texas Press.

Hendry, J. (1992) 'The paradox of friendship in the field: analysis of a longterm Anglo-Japanese relationship', in J. Okely and H. Callaway (eds) *Anthropology and Autobiography*, London: Routledge.

Heritage, J. (1984) *Garfinkel and Ethnomethodology*, Cambridge: Polity Press.

Herzfeld, M. (1987) *Anthropology Through the Looking-Glass: Critical Ethnography in the Margins of Europe*, Cambridge: Cambridge University Press.

Hine, C. (2000) *Virtual Ethnography*, London: Sage.

Hobbs, D. (1988) *Doing the Business*, Oxford: Oxford University Press.

—— (1993) 'Peers, careers, and academic fears', in D. Hobbs and T. May (eds) *Interpreting the Field: Accounts of Ethnography*, Oxford: Oxford University Press.

Hobbs, D. and May, T. (eds) (1993) *Interpreting the Field: Accounts of Ethnography*, Oxford: Oxford University Press.

Hobsbawm, E. and Ranger, T. (eds) (1983) *The Invention of Tradition*, Cambridge: Cambridge University Press.

Holland, D. and Skinner, D. (1987) 'Prestige and intimacy: the cultural models behind Americans' talk about gender types', in D. Holland and N. Quinn (eds) *Cultural Models in Language and Thought*, Cambridge: Cambridge University Press.

Holmes, L. D. and Holmes, E. R. (1992) *Samoan Village Then and Now* (2nd edn), Fort Worth, TX: Harcourt Brace.

Holstein, J. A. and Gubrium, J. F. (1995) *The Active Interview*, Thousand Oaks, CA: Sage.

Homan, R. (1986) 'Observations on the management of mood in a neurological hospital', *British Medical Journal* 293: 1417–19.

—— (1991) *The Ethics of Social Research*, London: Longman.

Horowitz, I. L. (ed.) (1967) *The Rise and Fall of Project Camelot: Studies in the Relationship between Social Science and Practical Politics*, Cambridge, MA: MIT Press.

Hughes, D. (1988) 'When nurse knows best: some aspects of nurse/doctor interaction in a casualty department', *Sociology of Health and Illness* 10(1): 1–22.

Hughes, J. (1990) *The Philosophy of Social Research* (2nd edn), London: Longman.

Hughes-Freeland, F. (1997) 'Balinese on television: representation and response', in M. Banks and H. Morphy (eds) *Rethinking Visual Anthropology*, New Haven, CT: Yale University Press.

Humphreys, L. (1975) *Tearoom Trade: Impersonal Sex in Public Places*, New York: Aldine de Gruyter.

Hymes, D. (ed.) (1969) *Reinventing Anthropology*, New York: Random House.

Illingworth, N. (2001) 'The internet matters: exploring the use of the internet as a research tool', *Sociological Research Online* 6(2): http://www.socresonline.org.uk/6/2/illingworth.html.

Ingold, T. (ed.) (1989) *Social Anthropology is a Generalizing Science or It is Nothing*, Manchester: Groups for Debates in Anthropological Theory.

—— (1996) 'Introduction to 1992 debate: the past is a foreign country', in T. Ingold (ed.) *Key Debates in Anthropology*, London: Routledge.

Jacknis, I. (1990) 'James Mooney as an ethnographic photographer', *Visual Anthropology* 3(2/3): 179–212.

Jackson, A. (1987) 'Reflections on anthropology and the ASA', in A. Jackson (ed.) *Anthropology at Home*, London: Tavistock.

Jackson, J. E. (1990) 'Déjà entendu: the liminal qualities of anthropological fieldnotes', *Journal of Contemporary Ethnography* 19: 8–43.

Jacobson, D. (1991) *Reading Ethnography*, Albany, NY: State University of New York Press.

Jarrett, R. L. (1994) 'Living poor: family life among single-parent, African-American women', *Social Problems* 41: 30–49.

Jay, R. (1969) 'Personal and extrapersonal vision in anthropology', in D. Hymes (ed.) *Reinventing Anthropology*, New York: Random House.

Jayaratne, T. E. (1993 [1983]) 'The value of quantitative methodology for feminist research', in M. Hammersley (ed.) *Social Research: Philosophy, Politics and Practice*, London: Sage.

Johnson, A. and Johnson, O. R. (1990) 'Quality into quantity: on the measurement potential of ethnographic fieldnotes', in R. Sanjek (ed.) *Fieldnotes: The Makings of Anthropology*, Ithaca, NY: Cornell University Press.

Johnson, J. C. (1990) *Selecting Ethnographic Informants*, Newbury Park, CA: Sage.

Jones, S. G. (ed.) (1998) *Cybersociety 2.0: Revisiting Computer-mediated Communication and Community*, Thousand Oaks, CA: Sage.

Jones, S. P. (1997) '"Still a Mining Community": Gender and Change in the Upper Dulais Valley', PhD thesis, University of Wales Swansea.

—— (2003) 'Supporting the team, sustaining the community: gender and rugby in a former mining village', in C. A. Davies and S. Jones (eds) *Welsh Communities: New Ethnographic Perspectives*, Cardiff: University of Wales Press.

Jorgenson, J. (1991) 'Co-constructing the interviewer/co-constructing "family"', in F. Steier (ed.) *Research and Reflexivity*, London: Sage.

Kapferer, B. (1969) 'Norms and the manipulation of relationships in a work context', in J. C. Mitchell (ed.) *Social Networks in Urban Situations*, Manchester: Manchester University Press.

—— (1972) *Strategy and Transaction in an African Factory*, Manchester: Manchester University Press.

—— (1973) 'Social network and conjugal role in urban Zambia: towards a reformulation of the Bott hypothesis', in J. Boissevain and J. C. Mitchell (eds) *Network Analysis: Studies in Human Interaction*, The Hague: Mouton.

Kemper, R. V. (1979) 'Fieldwork among Tzintzuntzan migrants in Mexico City: retrospect and prospect', in G. M. Foster, T. Scudder, E. Colson and R. V. Kemper (eds) *Long-term Field Research in Social Anthropology*, New York: Academic Press.

Kendall, L. (1999) 'Recontextualizing "cyberspace": methodological considerations for on-line research', in S. Jones (ed.) *Doing Internet Research: Critical Issues and Methods for Examining the Net*, Thousand Oaks, CA: Sage.

Kenna, M. E. (1992) 'Changing places and altered perspectives: research on a Greek island in the 1960s and in the 1980s', in J. Okely and H. Callaway (eds) *Anthropology and Autobiography*, London: Routledge.

—— (2001a) *Greek Island Life: Fieldwork on Anafi*, Amsterdam: Harwood Academic Publishers.

—— (2001b) *The Social Organisation of Exile: Greek Political Detainees in the Nineteen-thirties*, Amsterdam: Harwood Academic Publishers.

Kirk, J. and Miller, M. L. (1986) *Reliability and Validity in Qualitative Research*, Beverley Hills, CA: Sage.

Kitzinger, J. (1994) 'The methodology of focus groups: the importance of interaction between research participants', *Sociology of Health and Illness* 16: 103–21.

Knodel, J., Havanon, N. and Pramualratana, A. (1984) 'Fertility transition in Thailand: a qualitative analysis', *Population and Development Review* 10: 297–328.

Koegel, P. (1986) 'You are what you drink: evidence of socialized incompetence in the life of a mildly retarded adult', in L. L. Langness and H. G. Levine (eds) *Culture and Retardation*, Dordrecht: Reidel.

Kondo, D. K. (1990) *Crafting Selves: Power, Gender, and Discourses of Identity in a Japanese Workplace*, Chicago, IL: University of Chicago Press.

Kristmundsdottir, S. D. (2006) 'Far from the Trobriands? Biography as field', in S. Coleman and P. Collins (eds) *Locating the Field: Space, Place and Context in Anthropology*, Oxford: Berg.

Krouse, S. A. (1990) 'Photographing the vanishing race', *Visual Anthropology* 3: 213–33.

Kuehnast, K. (1992) 'Visual imperialism and the export of prejudice: an exploration of ethnographic film', in P. I. Crawford and D. Turton (eds) *Film as Ethnography*, Manchester: Manchester University Press.

Kuhn, T. S. (1962) *The Structure of Scientific Revolutions*, Chicago, IL: University of Chicago Press.

Kulick, D. (1992) 'Speaking as a woman: structure and gender in domestic arguments in a New Guinea village', *Cultural Anthropology* 8(4): 510–41.

—— (1998) 'Anger, gender, language shift, and the politics of revelation in a Papua New Guinean village', in B. B. Schieffelin, K. A. Wollard, P. V. Kroskrity (eds) *Language Ideologies: Practice and Theory*, Oxford: Oxford University Press.

Kuper, A. (1988) *The Invention of Primitive Societies: Transformations of an Illusion*, London: Routledge.

Lal, J. (1996) 'Situating locations: the politics of self, identity, and "other" in living and writing the text', in D. L. Wolf (ed.) *Feminist Dilemmas in Fieldwork*, Boulder, CO: Westview Press.

Lamphere, L. (2003) 'The perils and prospects for an engaged anthropology: a view from the United States', *Social Anthropology* 11(2): 153–68.

Langness, L. L. (1965) *The Life History in Anthropological Science*, New York: Holt, Rinehart and Winston.

Langness, L. L. and Levine, H. G. (1986) 'Introduction', in L. L. Langness and H. G. Levine (eds) *Culture and Retardation*, Dordrecht: Reidel.

Larcom, J. (1983) 'Following Deacon: the problem of ethnographic reanalysis, 1926–1981', in G. W. Stocking, Jr. (ed.) *Observers Observed: Essays on Ethnographic Fieldwork*, Madison, WI: University of Wisconsin Press.

Lash, S. (1990) *Sociology of Postmodernism*, London: Routledge.

Latour, B. (1990) 'Drawing things together', in M. Lynch and S. Woolgar (eds) *Representation in Scientific Practice*, Cambridge, MA: MIT Press.

Latour, B. and Woolgar, S. (1986 [1979]), *Laboratory Life: The Construction of Scientific Facts*, Princeton, NJ: Princeton University Press.

Laws, S. (1990) *Issues of Blood: The Politics of Menstruation*, Basingstoke: Macmillan.

Leach, E. R. (1954) *Political Systems of Highland Burma*, Boston, MA: Beacon Press.

—— (1967) 'An anthropologist's reflections on a social survey', in D. G. Jongmans and P. C. W. Gutkind (eds) *Anthropologists in the Field*, Assen, Netherlands: Van Gorcum.

Levitas, R. (1996) 'Fiddling while Britain burns? the "measurement" of unemployment', in R. Levitas and W. Guy (eds) *Interpreting Official Statistics*, London: Routledge.

Levitas, R. and Guy, W. (1996) 'Introduction', in R. Levitas and W. Guy (eds) *Interpreting Official Statistics*, London: Routledge.

Lewis, I. M. (1968) 'Introduction', in I. M. Lewis (ed.) *History and Social Anthropology*, London: Tavistock.

Lewis, O. (1970 [1953]) 'Tepoztlan restudied: a critique of the folk-urban conceptualization of social change', *Rural Sociology* 18(2): 121–36.

—— (1965) *La Vida: A Puerto Rican Family in the Culture of Poverty – San Juan and New York*, New York: Vintage Books.

Liebow, E. (1967) *Tally's Corner: A Study of Negro Streetcorner Men*, Boston, MA: Little, Brown.

Linde, C. (1993) *Life Stories: The Creation of Coherence*, Oxford: Oxford University Press.

Llewellyn, C. (1981) 'Occupational mobility and the use of the comparative method', in H. Roberts (ed.) *Doing Feminist Research*, London: Routledge.

Loizos, P. (1993) *Innovation in Ethnographic Film: From Innocence to Self-consciousness, 1955–85*, Manchester: Manchester University Press.

—— (1997) 'First exits from observational realism: narrative experiments in recent ethnographic films', in M. Banks and H. Morphy (eds) *Rethinking Visual Anthropology*, New Haven, CT: Yale University Press.

Lupton, D. and Seymour, W. (2003) '"I am normal on the net": disability, computerised communication technologies and the embodied self', in J. Coupland and R. Gwyn (eds), *Discourse, the Body, and Identity*, Basingstoke: Palgrave Macmillan.

Lyman, C. M. (1982) *The Vanishing Race and Other Illusions: Photographs of Indians by Edward S. Curtis*, Washington, DC: Smithsonian Institution Press.

Lysloff, R. T. A. (2003) 'Musical community on the internet: an on-line ethnography', *Cultural Anthropology* 18(2): 233–63.

Mac an Ghaill, M. (1994) *The Making of Men: Masculinities, Sexualities and Schooling*, Buckingham: Open University Press.

McDonald, M. (1989) *'We Are Not French!' Language, Culture and Identity in Brittany*, London: Routledge.

MacDougall, D. (1995 [1974]) 'Beyond observational cinema', in P. Hockings (ed.) *Principles of Visual Anthropology* (2nd edn), Berlin: Mouton de Gruyter.

Malinowski, B. (1922) *Argonauts of the Western Pacific*, London: Routledge and Kegan Paul.

—— (1929) *The Sexual Life of Savages in North-western Melanesia*, London: Routledge and Kegan Paul.

Malkki, L. H. (1995) *Purity and Exile: Violence, Memory, and National Cosmology among Hutu Refugees in Tanzania*, Chicago, IL: University of Chicago Press.

Mangabeira, W. (1995) 'Computer assistance, qualitative analysis and model building', in R. M. Lee (ed.) *Information Technology for the Social Scientist*, London: UCL Press.

Marcus, G. (1983) 'One man's Mead', *New York Times Book Review:* March 27: 2–3, 22–3.

Marcus, G. E. and Cushman, D. (1982) 'Ethnographies as texts', *Annual Review of Anthropology* 11: 25–69.

Marcus, G. E. and Fischer, M. M. J. (1986) *Anthropology as Cultural Critique: An Experimental Moment in the Human Sciences*, Chicago, IL: University of Chicago Press.

Marsh, C. (1982) *The Survey Method: The Contribution of Surveys to Sociological Explanation*, London: Allen and Unwin.

Martin, E. (1994) *Flexible Bodies: Tracking Immunity in American Culture – From the Days of Polio to the Age of AIDS*, Boston, MA: Beacon Press.

—— (1997) 'Anthropology and the cultural study of science: from citadels to string figures', in A. Gupta and J. Ferguson (eds) *Anthropological Locations: Boundaries and Grounds of a Field Science*, Berkeley, CA: University of California Press.

Martinez, W. (1992) 'Who constructs anthropological knowledge? Toward a theory of ethnographic film spectatorship', in P. I. Crawford and D. Turton (eds) *Film as Ethnography*, Manchester: Manchester University Press.

Mascarenhas-Keyes, S. (1987) 'The native anthropologist: constraints and strategies in research', in A. Jackson (ed.) *Anthropology at Home*, London: Tavistock.

Mascia-Lees, F. E., Sharpe, P. and Cohen, C. B. (1989) 'The postmodernist turn in anthropology: cautions from a feminist perspective', *Signs* 15(1): 7–33.

Mathews, G. (2000) *Global Culture/Individual Identity: Searching for Home in the Cultural Supermarket*, London: Routledge.

May, T. (1997) *Social Research: Issues, Methods and Process* (2nd edn), Buckingham: Open University Press.

Mead, G. H. (1934) *Mind, Self, and Society*, Chicago, IL: University of Chicago Press.

Mead, M. (1939) 'Native languages as field-work tools', *American Anthropologist* 41: 189–205.

—— (1943 [1928]) *Coming of Age in Samoa*, Harmondsworth: Penguin.

—— (1969) 'Research with human beings: a model derived from anthropological field practice', *Daedalus* 98: 361–86.

—— (1972) *Blackberry Winter*, New York: Morrow.

—— (1995 [1974]) 'Visual anthropology in a discipline of words', in P. Hockings (ed.) *Principles of Visual Anthropology* (2nd edn), Berlin: Mouton de Gruyter.

Merton, R. K. (1988) 'Some thoughts on the concept of sociological autobiography', in M. W. Riley (ed.) *Sociological Lives*, Newbury Park, CA: Sage.

Metcalf, P. (2002) *They Lie, We Lie: Getting On With Anthropology*, London: Routledge.

Mies, M. (1993 [1983]) 'Towards a methodology for feminist research', in M. Hammersley (ed.) *Social Research: Philosophy, Politics and Practice*, London: Sage.

Miller, J. and Glassner, B. (1997) 'The "inside" and the "outside": finding realities in interviews', in D. Silverman (ed.) *Qualitative Research: Theory, Method and Practice*, London: Sage.

Mills, C. W. (1959) *The Sociological Imagination*, London: Oxford University Press.
Miner, H. (1956) 'Body ritual among the Nacirema', *American Anthropologist* 58: 503–7.
Mishler, E. G. (1991) 'Representing discourse: the rhetoric of transcription', *Journal of Narrative and Life History* 1(4): 255–80.
Mitchell, J. C. (1966) 'Theoretical orientations in African urban studies', in M. Banton (ed.) *The Social Anthropology of Complex Societies*, London: Tavistock.
—— (1967) 'On quantification in social anthropology', in A. L. Epstein (ed.) *The Craft of Social Anthropology*, London: Tavistock.
—— (1974) 'Social networks', *Annual Review of Anthropology* 3: 279–99.
—— (1984) 'Social network data', in R. F. Ellen (ed.) *Ethnographic Research: A Guide to General Conduct*, London: Academic Press.
Mitchell, R. G., Jr. (1991) 'Secrecy and disclosure in fieldwork', in W. B. Shaffir and R. A. Stebbins (eds) *Experiencing Fieldwork: An Inside View of Qualitative Research*, Newbury Park, CA: Sage.
Moore, H. L. (1988) *Feminism and Anthropology*, Cambridge: Polity Press.
Moore, S. F. (1987) 'Explaining the present: theoretical dilemmas in processual ethnography', *American Ethnologist* 14: 727–36.
Morgan, D. L. (1997) *Focus Groups as Qualitative Research* (2nd edn), Thousand Oaks, CA: Sage.
Morgan, D. L. and Krueger, R. A. (1993) 'When to use focus groups and why', in D. L. Morgan (ed.) *Successful Focus Groups: Advancing the State of the Art*, Newbury Park, CA: Sage.
Morphy, H. and Banks, M. (1997) 'Introduction: rethinking visual anthropology', in M. Banks and H. Morphy (eds) *Rethinking Visual Anthropology*, New Haven, CT: Yale University Press.
Motzafi-Haller, P. (1997) 'Writing birthright: on native anthropologists and the politics of representation', in D. E. Reed-Danahay (ed.) *Auto/Ethnography: Rewriting the Self and the Social*, Oxford: Berg.
Murphy, R. F. (1987) *The Body Silent*, New York: Norton.
Myerhoff, B. (1978) *Number Our Days*, New York: Simon and Schuster.
Myers, F. R. (1988) 'From ethnography to metaphor: recent films from David and Judith MacDougall', *Cultural Anthropology* 3(2): 205–20.
Nader, L. (1969) 'Up the anthropologist – perspectives gained from studying up', in D. Hymes (ed.) *Reinventing Anthropology*, New York: Random House.
Narayan, K. (1993) 'How native is a "native" anthropologist?', *American Anthropologist* 95(3): 671–86.
Noble, M. (1973) 'Social network: its use as a conceptual framework in family analysis', in J. Boissevain and J. C. Mitchell (eds) *Network Analysis: Studies in Human Interaction*, The Hague: Mouton.

Oakley, A. (1974) *Housewife*, London: Allen Lane.
—— (1981) 'Interviewing women: a contradiction in terms', in H. Roberts (ed.) *Doing Feminist Research*, London: Routledge.
Ochs, E. (1979) 'Transcription as theory', in E. Ochs and B. B. Schieffelin (eds) *Developmental Pragmatics*, New York: Academic Press.
Okely, J. (1983) *The Traveller-Gypsies*, Cambridge: Cambridge University Press.
—— (1987) 'Fieldwork up the M1: policy and political aspects', in A. Jackson (ed.) *Anthropology at Home*, London: Tavistock.
—— (1992) 'Anthropology and autobiography: participatory experience and embodied knowledge', in J. Okely and H. Callaway (eds) *Anthropology and Autobiography*, London: Routledge.
—— (1994) 'Thinking through fieldwork', in A. Bryman and R. G. Burgess (eds) *Analyzing Qualitative Data*, London: Routledge.
—— (1996a) 'Introduction', in J. Okely, *Own or Other Culture*, London: Routledge.
—— (1996b [1975]) 'The self and scientism', in J. Okely, *Own or Other Culture*, London: Routledge.
Oliver, M. (1992) 'Changing the social relations of research production?', *Disability, Handicap and Society* 7(2): 101–14.
Outhwaite, W. (1987) *New Philosophies of Social Science: Realism, Hermeneutics and Critical Theory*, Basingstoke: Macmillan.
Overing, J. (1987) 'Translation as a creative process: the power of the name', in L. Holy (ed.) *Comparative Anthropology*, Oxford: Basil Blackwell.
Panourgia, N. (1995) *Fragments of Death, Fables of Identity: An Athenian Anthropography*, Madison, WI: University of Wisconsin Press.
Papadakis, E. (1989) 'Interventions in new social movements', in J. F. Gubrium and D. Silverman (eds) *The Politics of Field Research: Sociology Beyond Enlightenment*, London: Sage.
Parker, J. (2000) *Structuration*, Buckingham: Open University Press.
Parman, S. (1990) *Scottish Crofters: A Historical Ethnography of a Celtic Village*, Fort Worth, TX: Holt, Rinehart and Winston.
Passaro, J. (1996) *The Unequal Homeless: Men on the Streets, Women in Their Place*, New York: Routledge.
—— (1997) '"You can't take the subway to the field!": "village" epistemologies in the global village', in A. Gupta and J. Ferguson (eds) *Anthropological Locations: Boundaries and Grounds of a Field Science*, Berkeley, CA: University of California Press.
Pfaffenberger, B. (1988) *Microcomputer Applications in Qualitative Research*, Newbury Park, CA: Sage.
Phillips, R. and Sanders, S. (2000) 'Contemporary education policy in Wales: theory, discourse and research', in R. Daugherty, R. Phillips and G. Rees (eds) *Education Policy-making in Wales: Explorations in Devolved Governance*, Cardiff: University of Wales Press.

Pinch, T. and Pinch, T. (1988) 'Reservations about reflexivity and new literary forms or why let the devil have all the good tunes?', in S. Woolgar (ed.) *Knowledge and Reflexivity*, London: Sage.

Pink, S. (2001) *Doing Visual Ethnography*, London: Sage.

Platt, J. (1981a) 'Evidence and proof in documentary research: 1. Some specific problems of documentary research', *Sociological Review* 29(1): 29–52.

—— (1981b) 'Evidence and proof in documentary research: 2. Some shared problems of documentary research', *Sociological Review* 29(1): 53–66.

Plummer, K. (1983) *Documents of Life: An Introduction to the Problems and Literature of a Humanistic Method*, London: George Allen and Unwin.

Popper, K. R. (1963) *Conjectures and Refutations: The Growth of Scientific Knowledge*, London: Routledge and Kegan Paul.

Porter, D. (1997) 'Introduction', in D. Porter (ed.) *Internet Culture*, New York: Routledge.

Porter, S. (1993) 'Critical realist ethnography: the case of racism and professionalism in a medical setting', *Sociology* 27(4): 591–609.

Powdermaker, H. (1966) *Stranger and Friend: The Way of an Anthropologist*, New York: W. W. Norton.

Pratt, M. L. (1986) 'Fieldwork in common places', in J. Clifford and G. E. Marcus (eds) *Writing Culture: The Poetics and Politics of Ethnography*, Berkeley, CA: University of California Press.

Price, L. (1987) 'Ecuadorian illness stories: cultural knowledge in natural discourse', in D. Holland and N. Quinn (eds) *Cultural Models in Language and Thought*, Cambridge: Cambridge University Press.

Prior, L. (1985) 'Making sense of mortality', *Sociology of Health and Illness* 7(2): 167–90.

Pugh, A. (1990) 'My statistics and feminism – a true story', in L. Stanley (ed.) *Feminist Praxis: Research, Theory and Epistemology in Feminist Sociology*, London: Routledge.

Punch, M. (1986) *The Politics and Ethics of Fieldwork*, Newbury Park, CA: Sage.

Quinn, N. and Holland, D. (1987) 'Culture and cognition', in D. Holland and N. Quinn (eds) *Cultural Models in Language and Thought*, Cambridge: Cambridge University Press.

Rabinow, P. (1977) *Reflections on Fieldwork in Morocco*, Berkeley, CA: University of California Press.

—— (1986) 'Representations are social facts: modernity and post-modernity in anthropology', in J. Clifford and G. E. Marcus (eds) *Writing Culture: The Poetics and Politics of Ethnography*, Berkeley, CA: University of California Press.

Rappaport, R. A. (1980) 'Concluding comments on ritual and reflexivity', *Semiotica* 30 (1–2): 181–93.

Redfield, R. (1930) *Tepoztlan – a Mexican Village*, Chicago, IL: University of Chicago Press.

Reed-Danahay, D. E. (1997) 'Introduction', in D. E. Reed-Danahay (ed.) *Auto/Ethnography: Rewriting the Self and the Social*, Oxford: Berg.

Reinharz, S. (1992) *Feminist Methods in Social Research*, New York: Oxford University Press.

Rheingold, H. (1993) *Virtual Communities*, Reading, MA: Addison-Wesley.

Richards, L. and Richards, T. (1991) 'The transformation of qualitative method: computational paradigms and research processes', in N. G. Fielding and R. M. Lee (eds) *Using Computers in Qualitative Research*, London: Routledge.

Riessman, C. K. (1987) 'When gender is not enough: women interviewing women', *Gender and Society* 1(2): 172–207.

Rivers, W. H. R. (1914) *The History of Melanesian Society*, Cambridge: Cambridge University Press.

Roberts, B. (2002) *Biographical Research*, Buckingham: Open University Press.

Roberts, H. (1981) 'Women and their doctors: power and powerlessness in the research process', in H. Roberts (ed.) *Doing Feminist Research*, London: Routledge.

Roberts, J. M. and Sanders, T. (2005) 'Before, during and after: realism, reflexivity and ethnography', *Sociological Review* 53(2): 294–313.

Robins, K. and Webster, F. (1999) *Times of the Technoculture: From the Information Society to the Virtual Life*, London: Routledge.

Robson, C. (1993) *Real World Research: A Resource for Social Scientists and Practitioner-Researchers*, Oxford: Blackwell.

Rosaldo, M. Z. (1989 [1983]) 'Moral/analytic dilemmas posed by the intersection of feminism and social science', in P. Rabinow and W. M. Sullivan (eds) *Interpretive Social Science: A Second Look*, Berkeley, CA: University of California Press.

Rosaldo, R. (1993 [1989]) *Culture and Truth: The Remaking of Social Analysis*, London: Routledge.

Rubin, H. J. and Rubin, I. S. (1995) *Qualitative Interviewing: The Art of Hearing Data*, Thousand Oaks, CA: Sage.

Ruby, J. (1980) 'Exposing yourself: reflexivity, anthropology, and film', *Semiotica* 30 (1–2): 153–79.

—— (1982) 'Ethnography as trompe l'oeil: film and anthropology', in J. Ruby (ed.) *A Crack in the Mirror: Reflexive Perspectives in Anthropology*, Philadelphia, PA: University of Pennsylvania Press.

Sacks, H. (1984) 'Notes on Methodology', in J. M. Atkinson and J. Heritage (eds) *Structures of Social Action*, Cambridge: Cambridge University Press.

Said, E. (1978) *Orientalism*, London: Routledge and Kegan Paul.

Salemink, O. (1991) '*Mois* and *maquis*: the invention and appropriation of Vietnam's Montagnards from Sabatier to the CIA', in G. W. Stocking, Jr. (ed.) *Colonial Situations: Essays on the Contextualization of Ethnographic Knowledge*, Madison, WI: University of Wisconsin Press.
Sangren, P. S. (1988) 'Rhetoric and the authority of ethnography: "post-modernism" and the social reproduction of texts', *Current Anthropology* 29: 405–35.
Sanjek, R. (1990) 'On ethnographic validity', in R. Sanjek (ed.) *Fieldnotes: The Makings of Anthropology*, Ithaca, NY: Cornell University Press.
—— (1991) 'The ethnographic present', *Man* 26: 609–28.
Sayer, A. (2000) *Realism and Social Science*, London: Sage.
Scherer, J. C. (1990) 'Historical photographs as anthropological documents: a retrospect', *Visual Anthropology* 3: 131–55.
Schneider, J. C. and Schneider, P. T. (1996) *Festival of the Poor: Fertility Decline and the Ideology of Class in Sicily, 1860–1980*, Tucson, AZ: University of Arizona Press.
Scholte, B. (1969) 'Toward a reflexive and critical anthropology', in D. Hymes (ed.) *Reinventing Anthropology*, New York: Random House.
Schutz, A. (1967) *The Phenomenology of the Social World*, trans. G. Walsh and F. Lehnert , Evanston, IL: Northwestern University Press.
Scott, J. (1990) *A Matter of Record: Documentary Sources in Social Research*, Cambridge: Polity Press.
Scott, S. (1984) 'The personable and the powerful: gender and status in sociological research', in C. Bell and H. Roberts (eds) *Social Researching: Politics, Problems, Practice*, London: Routledge and Kegan Paul.
Scudder, T. and Colson, E. (1979) 'Long-term research in Gwembe Valley, Zambia', in G. M. Foster, T. Scudder, E. Colson and R. V. Kemper (eds) *Long-term Field Research in Social Anthropology*, New York: Academic Press.
Seidel, J. (1991) 'Method and madness in the application of computer technology to qualitative data analysis', in N. G. Fielding and R. M. Lee (eds) *Using Computers in Qualitative Research*, London: Routledge.
Seymour-Smith, C. (1986) *Macmillan Dictionary of Anthropology*, London: Macmillan.
Shaffir, W. B. and Stebbins, R. A. (eds) (1991) *Experiencing Fieldwork: An Inside View of Qualitative Research*, Newbury Park, CA: Sage.
Sharf, B. F. (1999) 'Beyond netiquette: the ethics of doing naturalistic discourse research on the internet', in S. Jones (ed.) *Doing Internet Research: Critical Issues and Methods for Examining the Net*, Thousand Oaks, CA: Sage.
Shaw, C. (1930) *The Jack-Roller*, Chicago, IL: University of Chicago Press.
Shore, C. (2000) *Building Europe: The Cultural Politics of European Integration*, London: Routledge.
Shore, C. and Wright, S. (1997) 'Colonial gaze to critique of policy: British anthropology in policy and practice', in M. L. Baba and C. E. Hill (eds)

The Global Practice of Anthropology, Williamsburg, VA: Department of Anthropology, College of William and Mary.

Shostak, M. (1990 [1981]) *Nisa: The Life and Words of a !Kung Woman*, London: Earthscan.

Sieber, J. E. (1992) *Planning Ethically Responsible Research: A Guide for Students and Internal Review Boards*, Newbury Park, CA: Sage.

Sillitoe, P. (2007) 'Anthropologists only need apply: challenges of applied anthropology', *Journal of the Royal Anthropological Institute* 13(1): 147–65.

Silverman, D. (1981) 'The child as a social object: Down's Syndrome children in a paediatric cardiology clinic', *Sociology of Health and Illness* 3(3): 254–74.

—— (1985) *Qualitative Methodology and Sociology: Describing the Social World*, Aldershot: Gower.

Skultans, V. (1998) *The Testimony of Lives: Narrative and Memory in Post-Soviet Latvia*, London: Routledge.

Smith, D. E. (1987) 'Women's perspective as a radical critique of sociology', in S. Harding (ed.) *Feminism and Methodology: Social Science Issues,* Bloomington, IN: Indiana University Press.

—— (1988) *The Everyday World as Problematic: A Feminist Sociology*, Milton Keynes: Open University Press.

Smith, M. G. (1962) 'History and social anthropology', *Journal of the Royal Anthropological Institute* 92: 73–85.

Sontag, S. (1966) 'The anthropologist as hero', in E. N. Hayes and T. Hayes (eds) *Claude Lévi-Strauss: The Anthropologist as Hero*, Cambridge: Cambridge University Press.

Speckmann, J. D. (1967) 'Social surveys in non-western areas', in D. G. Jongmans and P. C. W. Gutkind, *Anthropologists in the Field*, Assen, Netherlands: Van Gorcum.

Spradley, J. P. (1969) *Guests Never Leave Hungry: The Autobiography of James Sewid, A Kwakiutl Indian*, London: Yale University Press.

—— (1970) *You Owe Yourself a Drunk: An Ethnography of Urban Nomads*, Boston: Little, Brown.

—— (1979) *The Ethnographic Interview*, New York: Holt, Rinehart and Winston.

Stacey, J. (1988) 'Can there be a feminist ethnography?', *Women's Studies International Forum* 11(1): 21–7.

Stack, C. B. (1974) *All Our Kin: Strategies for Survival in a Black Community*, New York: Harper and Row.

Stanley, L. (1992) *The Auto/biographical I: The Theory and Practice of Feminist Auto/biography*, Manchester: Manchester University Press.

—— (1993) 'On auto/biography in sociology', *Sociology* 27(1): 41–52.

Stasz, C. (1979) 'The early history of visual sociology', in J. Wagner (ed.) *Images of Information: Still Photography in the Social Sciences*, Beverley Hills, CA: Sage.

Steier, F. (1991a) 'Introduction: research as self-reflexivity, self-reflexivity as social process', in F. Steier (ed.) *Research and Reflexivity*, London: Sage.

—— (1991b) 'Reflexivity and methodology: an ecological constructionism', in F. Steier (ed.) *Research and Reflexivity*, London: Sage.

—— (ed.) (1991c) *Research and Reflexivity*, London: Sage.

Stewart, D. W. and Shamdasani, P. N. (1990) *Focus Groups: Theory and Practice*, Newbury Park, CA: Sage.

Stewart, K. and Williams, M. (2005) 'Researching online populations: the use of online focus groups for social research', *Qualitative Research* 5(4): 395–416.

Stocking, G. W., Jr. (1983a) 'The ethnographer's magic: fieldwork in British anthropology from Tylor to Malinowski', in G. W. Stocking, Jr. (ed.) *Observers Observed: Essays on Ethnographic Fieldwork*, Madison, WI: University of Wisconsin Press.

—— (1983b) 'History of anthropology: whence/whither', in G. W. Stocking, Jr. (ed.) *Observers Observed: Essays on Ethnographic Fieldwork*, Madison, WI: University of Wisconsin Press.

Stones, R. (1996) *Sociological Reasoning: Towards a Past-modern Sociology*, Basingstoke: Macmillan.

Strathern, A. and Strathern, M. (1971) *Self-decoration in Mount Hagen*, London: Duckworth.

Strathern, M. (1987a) 'An awkward relationship: the case of feminism and anthropology', *Signs* 12(2): 276–92.

—— (1987b) 'The limits of auto-anthropology', in A. Jackson (ed.) *Anthropology at Home*, London: Tavistock.

Strauss, A. (1988) *Qualitative Analysis for Social Scientists*, Cambridge: Cambridge University Press.

Strauss, A. L. and Glaser, B. G. (1970) *Anguish: A Case History of a Dying Trajectory*, Mill Valley, CA: Sociology Press.

Sudnow, D. (1967) *Passing On: The Social Organization of Dying*, Englewood Cliffs, NJ: Prentice-Hall.

Sutherland, E. H. (1937) *The Professional Thief by a Professional Thief*, Chicago, IL: University of Chicago Press.

Tapper, R. (2001) 'Anthropology and (the) crisis', *Anthropology Today* 17(6): 13–16.

Temple, B. (1997) 'Watch your tongue: issues in translation and cross-cultural research', *Sociology* 31(3): 607–18.

Thrasher, F. M. (1963 [1927]) *The Gang: A Study of 1,313 Gangs in Chicago* (abridged edn), Chicago, IL: University of Chicago Press.

Tobin, J. J., Wu, D. Y. H. and Davidson, D. H. (1989) *Preschool in Three Cultures: Japan, China, and the United States*, New Haven, CT: Yale University Press.

Tonkin, E. (1984) 'Language learning', in R. F. Ellen (ed.) *Ethnographic Research: A Guide to General Conduct*, London: Academic Press.

Tönnies, F. (1955 [1887]) *Community and Association*, London: Routledge and Kegan Paul.
Turnbull, C. (1961) *The Forest People*, London: Jonathan Cape.
—— (1983) 'Trouble in paradise', *New Republic* 188(12): 32–4.
Turner, T. (1991) 'Representing, resisting, rethinking: historical transformations of Kayapo culture and anthropological consciousness', in G. W. Stocking, Jr. (ed.) *Colonial Situations: Essays on the Contextualization of Ethnographic Knowledge*, Madison, WI: University of Wisconsin Press.
Turner, V. (1981) 'Social dramas and stories about them', in W. J. T. Mitchell (ed.) *On Narrative*, Chicago, IL: University of Chicago Press.
Tyler, S. A. (1969) 'Introduction', in S. A. Tyler (ed.) *Cognitive Anthropology*, New York: Holt, Rinehart and Winston.
—— (1986) 'Post-modern ethnography: from document of the occult to occult document', in J. Clifford and G. E. Marcus (eds) *Writing Culture: The Poetics and Politics of Ethnography*, Berkeley, CA: University of California Press.
Urry, J. (1984) 'A history of field methods', in R. F. Ellen (ed.) *Ethnographic Research: A Guide to General Conduct*, London: Academic Press.
Valentine, C. A. (1968) *Culture and Poverty: Critique and Counter Proposals*, Chicago, IL: University of Chicago Press.
Van Maanen, J. (1988) *Tales of the Field: On Writing Ethnography*, Chicago, IL: University of Chicago Press.
Vogt, E. Z. (1979) 'The Harvard Chiapas Project: 1957–1975', in G. M. Foster, T. Scudder, E. Colson and R. V. Kemper (eds) *Long-term Field Research in Social Anthropology*, New York: Academic Press.
Wallman, S. and Dhooge, Y. (1984) 'Survey premises and procedures', in R. F. Ellen (ed.) *Ethnographic Research: A Guide to General Conduct*, London: Academic Press.
Watson, G. (1987) 'Make me reflexive – but not yet: strategies for managing essential reflexivity in ethnographic discourse', *Journal of Anthropological Research* 43(1): 29–42.
Wax, R. (1971) *Doing Fieldwork: Warnings and Advice*, Chicago, IL: University of Chicago Press.
Weiner, A. B. (1976) *Women of Value, Men of Renown: New Perspectives in Trobriand Exchange*, Austin, Texas: University of Texas Press.
—— (1988) *The Trobrianders of Papua New Guinea*, New York: Holt, Rinehart and Winston.
Wellman, B. and Gulia, M. (1999) 'Virtual communities as communities: net surfers don't ride alone', in M. A. Smith and P. Kollock (eds) *Communities in Cyberspace*, London: Routledge.
Wellman, B., Salaff, J., Dimitrova, D., Garton, L., Gulia, M. and Haythornthwaite, C. (1996) 'Computer networks as social networks: virtual community, computer-supported cooperative work and telework', *Annual Review of Sociology* 22: 213–38.

Wellman, B. and Wortley, S. (1990) 'Different strokes from different folks: community ties and social support', *American Journal of Sociology* 96: 558–88.

Wenger, G. C. (1991) 'A network typology: from theory to practice', *Journal of Ageing Studies* 5(2): 147–62.

Whittemore, R. D., Langness, L. L. and Koegel, P. (1986) 'The life history approach to mental retardation', in L. L. Langness and H. G. Levine (eds) *Culture and Retardation*, Dordrecht: Reidel.

Whyte, W. F. (1955) *Street Corner Society: The Social Structure of an Italian Slum*, Chicago, IL: University of Chicago Press.

Wight, D. (1994) 'Boys' thoughts and talk about sex in a working class locality of Glasgow', *Sociological Review* 42: 702–37.

Williams, M. (2007) 'Avatar watching: participant observation in graphical online environments', *Qualitative Research* 7(1): 5–24.

Willis, W. S., Jr. (1969) 'Skeletons in the anthropological closet', in D. Hymes (ed.) *Reinventing Anthropology*, New York: Random House.

Wolcott, H. F. (1994) *Transforming Qualitative Data: Description, Analysis, and Interpretation*, Thousand Oaks, CA: Sage.

Wolf, E. R. (1969) 'American anthropologists and American society', in D. Hymes (ed.) *Reinventing Anthropology*, New York: Random House.

—— (1982) *Europe and the People without History*, Berkeley, CA: University of California Press.

Wolf, M. (1972) *Women and the Family in Rural Taiwan*, Stanford, CA: Stanford University Press.

—— (1992) *A Thrice-Told Tale: Feminism, Postmodernism and Ethnographic Responsibility*, Stanford, CA: Stanford University Press.

Woolgar, S. (ed.) (1988a) *Knowledge and Reflexivity*, London: Sage.

—— (1988b) 'Reflexivity is the ethnographer of the text', in S. Woolgar (ed.) *Knowledge and Reflexivity*, London: Sage.

Woolgar, S. and Ashmore, M. (1988) 'The next step: an introduction to the reflexive project', in S. Woolgar (ed.) *Knowledge and Reflexivity*, London: Sage.

Worth, S. and Adair, J. (1972) *Through Navajo Eyes: An Exploration in Film Communication and Anthropology*, Bloomington, IN: Indiana University Press.

Wright, S. (1995) 'Anthropology: still the uncomfortable discipline?', in A. S. Ahmed and C. N. Shore (eds) *The Future of Anthropology*, London: Athlone.

Yoneyama, L. (1999) *Hiroshima Traces: Time, Space, and the Dialectics of Memory*, Berkeley and Los Angeles, CA: University of California Press.

Name index

Subject index